THE
FUTURE
OF THE
CITY

THE FUTURE OF THE CITY

New Directions in Urban Planning

by Peter Wolf

THIS PUBLICATION WAS MADE POSSIBLE
BY A GRANT FROM THE FORD FOUNDATION

WHITNEY LIBRARY OF DESIGN an imprint of
WATSON-GUPTILL PUBLICATIONS , NEW YORK
FOR THE AMERICAN FEDERATION OF ARTS

To Alexis and Phelan

Copyright © 1974 by Peter Wolf

First published in the United States 1974 by Whitney Library of Design
an imprint of Watson-Guptill Publications,
a division of Billboard Publications, Inc.,
One Astor Plaza, New York, N.Y. 10036

Manufactured in U.S.A.

Library of Congress Cataloging in Publication Data
Wolf, Peter M
  The future of the city.
  (Whitney library of design)
  1. Cities and towns—Planning—United States.
I. American Federation of Arts. II. Title.
HT167.W64   309.2′62′0973   74-941
ISBN 0-8230-7182-0

First Printing, 1974

Contents

Illustrations

Foreword

It is expected that this book will provide citizens and professionals with perspective about the present state and future direction of urbanization in America. The great number of social, legal, political, economic, and design issues that affect the future of the city are often difficult to assimilate. These same issues must be the basis of crucial decisions taken in the public and private sectors that will affect our cities for years to come. It is our conviction that a clear discussion of many of these issues will be of value.

Initially, the present, recent past, and future trends in urbanism discussed in this book were investigated to provide a background to large-scale urban design projects sponsored by The Ford Foundation undertaken by Ulrich Franzen and Paul Rudolph. As it developed, this book became a coherent entity in itself and thus is published as such.

The projects designed by Mr. Franzen and Mr. Rudolph will be displayed in a separate publication and in films.

W. McNeil Lowry
THE FORD FOUNDATION

Preface

This book grows out of concern and interest: concern about the future of our cities and interest in understanding their likely *place* (where they will occur), *shape* (how they will look, how they will be organized), and *attributes* (what they will be like, and the quality of life in them) in years to come.

My experience in recent years convinces me that more and more people are in fact suddenly thinking about cities. Some wonder whether to continue living in town or move to the suburbs. Others consider a move back to the city or one still further out. Many need to decide where to locate a store, a distribution center. Where should major investments be made? Public administrators, candidates for public office, elected officials all seek access to new ideas and innovative proposals germane to their areas. Across the country citizens are increasingly in a position to make fundamental decisions about urbanism as members of local planning boards, as voters in a bond referendum, as advocates or protestors. Faced with options to determine the place, shape, and quality of life for years to come, they seek a basis for decision. This book, it is hoped, will provide some background so that the decisions made by each of us can have as informed a basis as possible.

Why, suddenly, are citizens around the country becoming involved in urbanism, a process once completely dominated by government, business, developers, and big trade lobbies? For one thing, change is occurring faster than ever. More decisions have to be made more frequently. For another, new political awareness has spread across America since 1960. Stimulated by the vibrant lives and shocking deaths of national leaders such as John Kennedy, Martin Luther King, and Robert Kennedy, a wider range of the population than ever before now demands control of

its destiny and of its own environment. A wide variety of "liberation" movements based on groupings of sex, race, and age has begun a shift of profound importance and deep consequence in the foundations of representation, power, and patronage within institutions, business, and government. Interrelated and ultimately unpopular large-scale military, social, economic, and political adventures of no less consequence have been experienced in this country by an increasingly aroused populace. And a new awareness has spread across the country that links, for the first time, questions of our basic resources to the patterns in which we live, and will live, in years to come. For urban planning, particular aspects of these developments are more important than others. New focuses, new methods of building, technological advances in communications, evolving changes in social structure, changing population balances between urban centers and suburban regions, shifting national policies and priorities, and economic trends have a most direct influence on the practice and product of urbanism.

A number of these tendencies are strong elements for positive change with promise of continuing influence, such as a growing demand for a voice in the decision-making process and new respect for resource conservation and for the physical environment. Yet certain continuing influences threaten to remain unchanged inhibitors to substantive progress. Among these the most obvious are the struggle for privilege and profit through the political and planning processes and the use of physical planning as a means of countering social and economic priorities necessary for the health and welfare of the country.

This book does not attempt a global scope, a wide historical span, or an emphasis on architecture. It is, on the other

hand, very much concerned with urban design—what happens at or near ground level as people encounter buildings and transportation. It also limits its considerations, to the extent possible, to the social, political, and economic watershed beginning at approximately 1960. It deals with the city as it is; not especially with New Towns and not especially with utopic redevelopment potentials.

This book focuses primarily on the intermediate scale of spaces, matrixes, and structures. It is somewhere between the limited concern of a single building and the unlimited concerns of an entire city that fruitful intervention in existing cities is possible and meaningful. It is only this scale which is manageable from a project and development point of view; and it is indeed only this scale which is really experienced by the individual in the city. If the evolutionary redevelopment of our cities is to proceed in a vital and progressive way, I believe, it must proceed at the intermediate scale.

Transportation has always influenced city location, city form, in fact the destiny of cities. The impact of the wagon, the barge, the ship, even the railroad are minor compared to the complex, multifaceted influence of the automobile on the evolution and development of cities. In the beginning of this century, when the car was introduced to city streets, it was seen as a dramatic and joyful toy celebrated by most advanced thinkers as a step forward, one that would make the city all the more delightful and available. We now know, after a brief but bewildering experience, that the automobile is able to severely diminish the experience of the individual in the city and to create a pattern of cityless, region-wide habitation never before experienced in the history of man.

Around 1960 (coincidentally coupled with new political and social forces) a greater appreciation of the automobile's impact on cities began to emerge. Since the car has provoked a radical reorganization of urban life, and since mobility remains essential in some form, this book must necessarily devote considerable attention to the issue of movement. Hopefully, understanding transportation's impact *on* our cities will enable a transition towards a more humane environment *in* our cities. In addition, it would be comforting—but perhaps naive—to think that other communities around the world will benefit from our experience.

Since 1960, new awarenesses of fundamental importance have emerged in many aspects of national life and urban planning. Some of these are discussed in the following chapters. But in recent years the gap between awareness and achievement has remained large. Administrative temerity, fiscal penuriousness, foreign preoccupation, legal strictures, and social conflict continue to limit severely the effective development of most promising, innovative urbanistic proposals. If significant progress is to be made in the 1970's and beyond, available progressive planning concepts must be matched by imaginative and workable devices for implementation.

While the organization of this book may appear arbitrary, each chapter centers on an issue or trend that I believe to be of central importance to the understanding of American urbanism in the recent past and the near future. I have tried to include my perceptions of where these trends may be heading. In addition, my intention is to point out directions that appear to me disadvantageous as well as those that seem especially promising, worthy of intensive effort, interest, and support.

There is also a larger, more elliptical organization. Chapter 1, "Downtown," reviews a, perhaps *the,* central issue of our day: Should the older cities survive? Will the older cities survive? If so, how and why? This chapter suggests that the major cities will survive and thrive, perhaps in new ways, in the next several decades. The next eight chapters consider this thesis—and ultimately support it. Chapters 2 through 9 are concerned with a wide range of ideas and trends central to urbanization which are changing and have been changing since about 1960. Many of these have long worked against the survival of the city. In important ways, in my judgment, many of these may now be working to preserve and revitalize cities in America. Thus the focus is not on the future of the suburb, of the region, of the shopping center as satellite city, though surely each of these is of interest and each has its own potential evolutionary pattern. Rather, the focus is on those events and new ideas which are influencing the future of older cities in these times of general pessimism about the future of cities in general.

I believe that cities will survive; indeed that their destiny is now quite positive. But not all cities. Only those with regional prominence: and only those in which aware public and private decisions are made in the near future. Good management, good planning, and awareness of opportunities and of the far-reaching impacts of basic present decisions will determine which cities do in fact thrive in years to come.

PETER WOLF
November 1973
New York City

"Whatever space and time mean, place and occasion mean more, for space in the image of man is place, and time in the image of man is occasion."

Aldo van Eyck
Place and Occasion

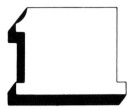

Downtown

For the first time in history, it is conceivable that cities are obsolete. Cities, that is, as special places of intense government, business, commercial, and cultural activity. Civilizations have always been distinguished by the cities they build and by the content of those central places where people live, work, worship, trade, and are protected. In America in recent years, this long history has been challenged.

It has been so severely challenged that retailers, corporations, insurance companies, real estate principals, investors, and families are thinking about the situation and taking action based on their decisions. There is much movement by families and by vested interests away from the cities, and much hesitancy by most people to invest in cities as heavily as they once did.

The 1970 Census underscores the situation in terms of population shifts, which have been dramatic in the past decade. During that time 13 of the 25 largest cities lost population, yet 24 of the 25 largest metropolitan areas gained. It was, indeed, the decade in which the suburbs became a new force in America. In 1970, the nation's suburbs, with more than 71 million residents, contained the largest sector of the population. This is an event of the largest social and political significance, which will surely be reflected in state legislatures and the composition of the Congress. The rural grip on state governments has been loosening since the end of World War II. But it is the suburbs, not the cities, which have wrested the power from traditional political channels. Today, as is known pragmatically by nearly every large-city mayor in the country, "suburbanites are as hostile to the city as the farmers ever were."[1] In state after state, it was found in a recent *New York Times* survey, "rising suburban strength has meant rising opposition to legislation benefiting cities."[2]

In addition, the population which continues to reside in the city is increasingly disadvantaged, elderly, relatively low on the income scale, and very often, in dominant numbers, part of one of several national racial minorities. It is rarely recognized that elected black mayors now govern 92 cities and towns, the largest being Los Angeles and Atlanta. The public school population of many of the largest cities in the United States is now predominantly black.

Rising crime, the infestation of drugs, unbearable welfare costs, high taxes, shoddy services, and poor schools are all increasingly associated with the central cities of the nation. In many instances they are also the current reality. What are the issues? What is likely to occur? How did all this come about?

Slowly, hardly perceived, the initial purpose for downtown has disappeared. City ports have lost their dominance to suburban airports; in-town rail terminals are no longer focal points for transportation and freight. The perfected automobile, enlarged trucks, and a national network of bridges, highways, and new roads have opened up the countryside, causing new residential, industrial, and commercial centers to proliferate at the edges of cities and beyond. The shopping center, the satellite office park, the residential subdivision, regional government, and suburban schools have replaced earlier counterparts which once comprised downtown. Urban organization over the years since World War II has given way to a national profile of spread, sprawl, and distance. And political influence follows centers of population.

Simultaneously, as has always been the case, immigrants from other countries have continued to settle in the cities, there to get a start, a first chance in America. But quite unlike most periods in our short national history, as agriculture declined and small-scale farmers found it impossible to make an independent living, there was also substantial in-migration to the cities by the white and black poor who once lived in the rural countryside. Also, from the 1930's to the present, migration shifts in black population occurred in heavy volume from smaller cities with less opportunity, especially in the South, to larger cities in the Midwest and Northeast which seemed to offer greater possibilities for jobs and public assistance programs.

Thus, as need and purpose are drained from downtown, and as investors and corporations, the mobile, the young, the influential, and the middle class, among others, move from the congestion and tension of the cities to newer accommodations and larger spaces in the suburbs, the older city centers of the nation cease to be resources. They become, rather, residues of inflexible commercial endeavors, of outdated utility systems, and of older and disadvantaged people unwilling or unable to adapt to the spaced-out formation that American life has assumed. Today, cities, and particularly their downtowns, are at a critical point in time. Some will be renewed and revitalized, especially if wise policies and sound decisions are made by public administrators and private interests in the very near future. Many, on the other hand, will probably dissolve before newer patterns of development. There is, I believe, a choice.

Among American city planners there are now contrary views about the importance of old-style cities and their downtown districts. Many urbanists, accustomed to traditional city organization based on European types, feel that dissolution of the center city implies a loss to the region. Without the center, they argue, the profile of a community, is diminished.

Their adversaries respond that the linear sprawl along highway networks found in Houston and Los Angeles is the up-to-date form of late 20th-century American cities. A tight center is inconvenient and irrelevant, they argue, when movement has escalated from pedestrian to automotive rates; when communication is as effective by electric and electronic connection as by face-to-face contact.

These contradictory viewpoints and patterns of urban life visible in America today have a discernible background in a number of dominant attitudes that pervade the American spirit as well as the American flair for dissipation of resources. It has been observed by many, including the historian Frederick Jackson Turner and the architectural historian Vincent Scully, that a restlessness of spirit coupled with a constant quest for new frontiers are fundamental American qualities. The will to move, the need to "progress," the desire for change are all expressed in our frontier history, in our embrace of open trails and roads, and in our automotive society. It is expressed in a vernacular architecture of lightweight impermanent materials, most recently in "mobile" housing. It is expressed in our willingness to build cities in one generation and abandon them in the next. It is expressed in our willingness to ignore the realities of limited resources, limited means, and limitations on space across which people can maintain effective contact, regardless of the quality of electronic communication, mass transportation, or the superhighway system. Our quest for a life that continually exploits resources and is not rooted by identification to the permanence of solid structures and hallowed spaces is revealed in the highways of our country, which weave through the land spawning their progeny, a bland, unchanging similitude of offices, shopping centers, and residential subdivisions calculated to last one, maybe two, generations. Even most airports, hubs of the transportation system, which could define place and region with stunning individuality, reflect a quest for points of transit exchange and interchange no more arresting

than a long stretch of outposts for refreshing the man and exchanging the mount.

These inherent qualities of spirit were expressed in planning proposals of America's most distinguished native 20th-century architect, Frank Lloyd Wright. His urban ideal, Broadacre City, was widely dispersed on the ground plain and lacked strong focus. In America, this attitude, coupled with a spiritual predilection to restlessness and movement, found a sympathetic response and reflection in many of our cities, which first grew along railways and trolley lines, and later along motorways, often without developing an intensive center.

The spatially dispersed vision of the American cities has, from time to time in recent years, been elevated to urban planning theory. Melvin Webber set a lucid framework for such an argument as early as 1964:

"Metropolitan planners [must] free themselves from the obsession with place-ness and . . . come to view urban communities as spatially extensive, processural systems in which urbanites interact with other urbanites wherever they may be. For it is interaction, not place, that is the essence of the city and of city life."[3]

Within the last five years, certain groups of architects and planners have accepted these tendencies in the developmental history of America and converted them into a contemporary cult of urbanism. One such group is centered around the urbane, controversial, historically and socially responsible Philadelphia architects Robert Venturi and Denise Scott Brown. As architects and as individuals, they have a deep-seated appreciation of European urban centers. But they argue—at least implicitly—that dense urban centers of the sort modeled on European prototypes are no longer appropriate to contemporary American life. They believe, and they have gained a considerable number of adherents, that automotive requirements dictate the formation of cities of greater dispersion such as Las Vegas and Los

Angeles. They claim that mass communications media and technological devices of many sorts have the ability to replace the necessity for continual, intense human contact and enforce the possibility of an agreeably dispersed urban form. Indeed, they reason that natural events visible in Los Angeles and Houston are harbingers of new settlement patterns that must be accepted and used effectively. (The Director of Planning for Houston, where there is no zoning of any sort, clearly shares this vision of the up-to-date American city. He describes his job as "watching Houston do its own thing.") It is a viewpoint that accepts highways as an organizing element, even for cities themselves. Thoroughfares become spines for commercial activities. Customers are plucked off the highway into parking lots as they "amble" through town in their cars.

These assumptions suggest a train of thought considered by other planners to be a cynical and short-sighted misreading of the present. It is also an attitude that discounts notions of the city as a complex and varied assembly of well-arranged and carefully organized buildings closely related to adequate parks and varied public spaces. More traditional planners insist that even in America a long heritage of extensive collective human experience underlies a sensed need for identifiable city centers. This well-developed viewpoint, at its most extreme, favors a city with absolutely defined limits and no tentacular suburbs, one whose center is tight, varied, individuated, and irregular. This is the city recalled by Jane Jacobs in the early 1960's, a city the French urban historian Françoise Choay calls the "culturalist model." As Choay correctly points out, "The culturalist model cannot be considered as reactionary, nor even as conservative. . . . For behind it lay the hope of developing an unalienated man who would no more be the simple rational being of the progressivists but a complete person."[4]

In contemporary America, in an odd way, two things are happening at once. The highways have opened up a vast outmigration to the suburbs. The poorer, older, and in increasing numbers the non-white remaining residential population in most cities, has formed a sociological and economic barrier to linkage with the growing suburbs. So, in a sense, the medieval walls of Oxford or Paris have been replaced by the barriers of race and class. Inside the barricade a strangely composed culturalist city is developing, one which serves the region's central banking, centralized business, cultural and institutional needs, limited high-cost housing, and extensive low-cost slum areas. Outside the older center a new and perhaps impermanent urban format has emerged in which highways are the common thread connecting predominantly white middle-class housing subdivisions, office parks, and shopping centers. Will decay seize these suburbs? Will social change modify them? Will the older city centers rejuvenate themselves, or is the economic, social, and population stasis of today relatively permanent? Is the land beyond the suburbs, the farms which people left so recently, now to be exploited? No simple answer, even for any one place, is possible. But the new directions in planning reviewed throughout this book point toward expected but as yet unrealized benefits to the city.

It is clear that continuation of the culturalist model, in a practical sense, has been fundamentally threatened by numerous trends, especially by demands of the automobile. Quite clearly, the disintegration or survival of the traditional urban center will depend in part on whether our near future is composed of a continuation of automotive dominance or a massive reversal in priorities and attitudes. In addition, there are other questions of a highly pragmatic sort whose answers will determine the future growth or dissolution of urban centers. Will habitable housing for all economic groups once again be built in cities? If not, almost surely, commercial and business activities will falter. Will modern utility services remain economically feasible and technically adequate at acceptable standards in older urban

places? Will public places in the city be maintained adequately so that streets and public spaces are usable? Will a realistic form of metropolitan government emerge to deal with transportation, environmental, and even social-welfare issues on the scale at which they actually occur? These very real questions are being asked throughout the country with increasing urgency. The answers to these, and to economic issues of personal and property taxation and investment inducements, will control future settlement patterns in America and the future of its cities.

It is comforting to be able to escape to the suburbs or dream of New Towns and satellite cities, places of presumed promise that offer a way to forget the stubborn complexities that haunt and corrode existing cities. But established suburbs and towns are filling up and are destined to become old places someday. New Towns are built very slowly. The cities are here; many of them have available unused and underused buildings and districts. Unless we learn to deal with this present situation, it is unlikely that we will be any more adept at handling the future, which is, after all, now plus an instant.

What then is the future of most downtowns, those older business districts surrounded by various grades of mixed commercial and residential buildings? The answer involves, in part, the relating of economic realities to social policy.

The economic reality, in most places, is that the infrastructure of older cities—utility lines, water systems, and roads—are old, often overloaded, and in need of extensive repair. They generally serve, even today, more people than they were designed to, and thus serve them inadequately. Yet the ethos of continual growth which has seized all aspects of American life demands that cities continually increase in wealth and population to support the expectations of land speculation and sustain construction booms, and to win an even larger slice of the political and patronage pie. Urban politicians, businessmen, bankers, and merchants of every sort have an immense vested interest

in the continuing *growth* of cities—even if this growth brings crowded housing conditions, poor services, unreasonable land prices, claustrophobic congestion, and other consistent manifestations of an economically healthy city.

On the social side, it has been the presumption for some years in programs such as Model Cities and Urban Renewal that the disadvantaged poor want to stay in the city, indeed even within the ghetto in many cases. How close are these policies to the actual desires of the people they are supposed to serve? And to what extent are these and other similar policies actually devised to prevent lower-income blacks and whites from gaining access to the suburbs? These and other prevailing policies, in large measure, keep a captive urban population within some of the least desirable parts of cities. They remove them farther and farther from better schools, open space, good air, and most important, from the industrial, manufacturing, and construction jobs that were once the reason to leave smaller places with dwindling opportunities.

Now most industrial and manufacturing jobs have left the city. Cheaper land, better access to the national highway network, opportunities for modernized plants —together these have lured many employers away from the city center. But most of the people who depend on these jobs have been forced to stay behind. City redevelopment programs mixed with restrictive suburban zoning now work by chance, if not by unspoken social policy, to once again separate many workers from their source of livelihood. As a result, the cities continue to be burdened with demands for social services and medical support, a physical and institutional infrastructure the city cannot possibly satisfy.

If seen in these contexts, stability or even decline in urban population must be recognized as necessary in the cities if they are to survive. These adjustments are now taking place even without the help of reasonable social and economic policies. When the gates of the ghetto are opened by socially reasonable legislative action and the urban poor are allowed to live and work in *both* the suburban job centers and the cities of this country, then city populations will probably decline even further and more rapidly than in the past decade. Urban places will once again be able to function in a more reasonable and more realistic fashion with the physical and institutional resources available.

In addition, very basic changes are underway in national attitudes and in urban planning programs that will directly affect the street, the urban highway, public transportation, housing, the urban environment, land use regulation, historic preservation, and conservation. These all support a new direction in planning, one which will make it possible, within a decade or so, to recognize renewed vigor in the cities. Principal cities within each region will emerge as regional focal points and will have the resources to increase political, educational, cultural, entertainment, commercial, and economic institutions of regional character. This is the positive future role of major cities. And this is the role that visible pressures now developing will permit these cities to play in the next several decades.

Physical signs of this new activity will appear in a realization that riverfronts, lakefronts, and canals, all so long ignored within the city, represent an opportunity for stunning rehabilitation. It will occur as older districts composed of exceptional but now deteriorating buildings are rediscovered as places capable of sustaining an environment increasingly sought by people. It will first appear, I suspect, in coordinated replanning of major streets.

New Directions

Plan for people, not cars.

Forget growth as a goal; concentrate on the quality of life.

Build and renovate urban housing for all income groups in locations served by transit.

Maintain public spaces and services.

Urban clusters should be tight, integrated with transit, and designed for pedestrians and should contain a variety of spaces and activities.

The available capacity downtown—older buildings, districts, waterfronts, streets, empty spaces, and transit—will be renewed.

Make downtown the regional center where cultural, educational, medical, financial and other institutions, businesses, and government are tightly clustered.

Downtown will increasingly attract residents and investment.

1. New York City, Broadway near Cortlandt Street and Maiden Lane
Lithograph by J. J. Fogerty, 1880

The urban street was chaotic even before the advent of the automobile. It was seldom paved, was not governed by traffic rules until 1910–1915, and was foul-smelling and often congested. But the street was *the* public meeting place, market place, gathering place throughout the history of cities—until the automobile made it dangerous and inaccessible. Today, this major public open space of the city is in large part, more often than not, a parking lot.

The Street

Consider this: the American middle ages, two centuries of thriving rural settlements, a powerful agrarian economy, and strong religious fundamentalism are over. Today, over 75 per cent of the people in this country are clustered together on less than 1.5 per cent of the land. And every day more people are on the move out of the countryside.

Today people cluster in or near the cities, generally dissatisfied with their surroundings, dismayed at the complexity of their existence, and disturbed by urbanization.

How has this happened? It is pertinent to ask what we as a people may be up to, what kind of an urban life we may be settling for. These questions are asked more and more often by more and more of us: What is the promise of our cities? What has gone wrong? What do we want?

It is not easy to begin to answer any of these questions, not easy for most individuals to know what they really want. And yet the issues must be confronted if more can reasonably be expected than has appeared; if a better urban life can be sought after. One way to start is to remember how we got here.

The urban street is a starting place (Figure 1). It has been a large physical and social part of all cities throughout history. The use of this single component is a sensitive gauge by which changes of attitude, evolution of power, and transition of emphasis in urban cultures may be measured. In nearly all cities at all times the street has been conceived of as communal space, as everyman's turf; as the market, the place of assembly, the first place of business to be used by all of the people. Simultaneously, it is the pulsating, often fluctuating border between the private, public, and administrative domains of which all cities have always been composed.

A retrospective glance, focused on the street, to the early years of this century when migration to the cities began, reveals shifts in attitude and changes in emphasis that allow us to begin to see what may have gone wrong and how things may be changing. It also allows us to recognize how decisions made years ago by urbanists, architects, and public officials continue to exert the most fundamental and often most unanticipated impact on the function of cities, on the organization of regions, and on the quality of urban life.

As early as 1910 and for nearly half a century thereafter, the motor car was embraced by progressive urbanists everywhere as a remarkable invention, which it was, with great promise for improving urban life, which it wasn't. Yet throughout much of the city, streets remained dedicated to various public uses such as meetings, markets, and mingling. By the beginning of this century, horses and carriages, which functioned without any rules of the road, already produced traffic jams that are legendary. City streets were often unpaved and obviously unsavory.

Starting around 1910, the introduction of the automobile into the chaotic street *mélange* of people, produce, and horse-drawn conveyances brought consequences which were—for quite some time—far from obvious. The motorcar brought the inherent opportunity for ever-increasing speed of travel. Danger to the pedestrian became implicit, and separation of pedestrian travel and auto routes became essential. And auto routes slowly and unwittingly become fume- and noise-laden corridors, consuming 35 to 40 per cent of all city land.

Because of the motorcar, which for the first time provided both speed and transportation that could move at random (so long as a road existed), cities spread, and locations of living and working became disassociated from one another and from the existing public transportation links—the effective suburban railroads and trolley lines. Accessibility came to be measured in *time* on the road, not *distance*. The impact of these events triggered by the automobile was almost entirely unforeseen and remained generally unrecognized until quite recently.

By 1970, the motorcar had made travel of all kinds on some urban streets almost impossible; had vastly affected the arrangement of cities; had produced and entirely organized the suburban countryside. A changed viewpoint, which emerged in the 1950's, gained strength in the 1960's, and is now a central planning theme, seeks urban transport without the motorcar as we know it. This too has the widest imaginable implications for urban design and urban life in years to come.

In the long interval between 1900 and the 1950's, many progressive architects and city planners presumed that accommodation of the car to the city was possible, necessary, and an interesting challenge. During those years a number of bold and imaginative suggestions, some of which have had lasting influence, were made for the integration of travel by car with the existing urban arrangement.

For instance, Eugène Hénard, architect for the City of Paris and until recently a scarcely known pioneer of modern urban design, recognized as early as 1910 that multi-level arrangement of city streets offered a potential universal solution for accommodating cars in cities. The multi-level street, he argued, provides a realistic means to contain the motorcar in reserved channels and to provide other levels for public transportation, power, and utility service, and even movement of goods (Figures 2, 3). He also designed the first traffic overpass (Figure 4) and recom-

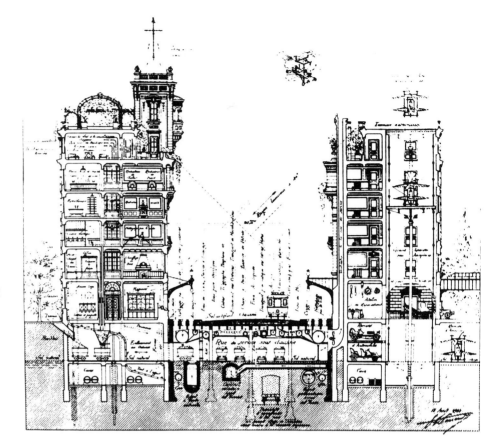

2. Street of the Future, 1910
Eugène Hénard

Hénard proposes a double-decked, multi-level street on which public trolleys, carriages, automobiles, and bicycles circulate in the open air. Below the deck a service street links directly into abutting buildings, while utility conduits and rapid transit channels run along the lowest level. Hénard envisioned helicopter service to rooftop landing pads before the helicopter was invented. Wall conduits suck pollutants such as dirt, smoke, and furnace exhaust into the below-grade trash removal system, then into bins to be carted away by rail-guided service carts below the street. Automobiles are stored within each dwelling so that the street, the public space of the city, remains open for public use.

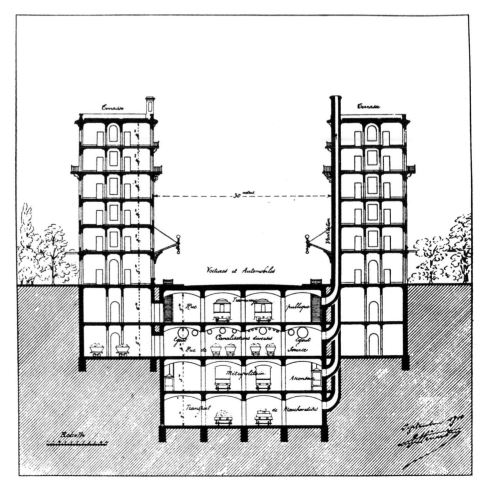

3. Multi-Level Street of the Future, 1910
Eugène Hénard

A five-tiered principal street. The top level is reserved for carriages and automobiles. Just below the deck are public walkways and trams. This level is accessible directly from within adjacent buildings, as is the next lower service level. Linked to the surface by elevators is a public rapid transit deck which surmounts a channel at the lowest level for merchandise delivery and trash removal.

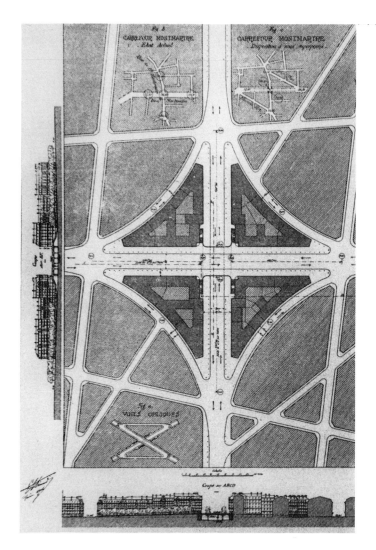

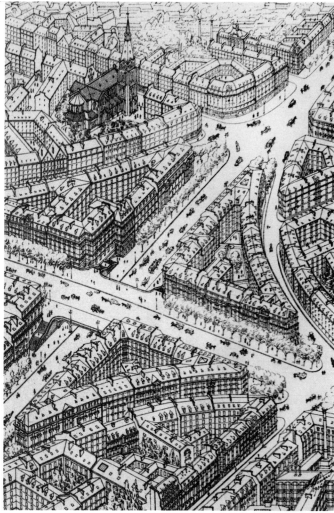

mended the development of subsurface pedestrian shopping arcades beneath major intersections linked to subsurface pedestrian shopping arcades beneath major intersections linked to subsurface pedestrian walkways (Figures 5, 6, 7).

Hénard's comprehension of the city as a volume rather than as a surface is only now being appreciated. It leads directly to contemporary consideration of tiers and levels for the separation of activities with special predetermined points at which linkage by elevator and escalator is available for intensive activity and interchange. In this way the urban street is not asked to perform all functions for all people in one limited space. Its users are separated; its functions are permitted to operate concurrently, as at Rockefeller Center, an avant-garde realization of the 1930's (See Figures 82, 83.) There, pedestrians stroll along sidewalks or through buildings while vehicles circulate and goods are delivered, all at different levels or in separated channels.

It is seldom recognized that the image of the modern city, the city of tomorrow, the city of the future that possessed the

imagination of progressive architects and urbanists for the first half of the 20th century, was dominated by an impulse to redesign the urban street to accommodate automobiles. Yet such a conclusion is unavoidable.

In Italy, in 1914, Antonio Sant' Elia, the flamboyant and enigmatic Futurist architect, proposed a new city composed of immense isolated structures linked by broad, tiered channels for automobiles and other transportation devices (Figure 8). Futurism itself was an influential esthetic movement infused with social and technological optimism inspired by speed, change, and the automobile itself.

In France, Le Corbusier's hypothetical Contemporary City for Three Million People, Voisin Plan for Paris of the 1920's, and subsequent urban scale projects, such as his proposed redevelopment of Algiers, are preoccupied with wide roadways for fast automotive travel (Figures 9, 10). The Algiers project, which proposes to hang buildings beneath auto routes, is one of the first instances in which engineered geometric road contours begin to affect the shape, scale, and location of buildings

4–5. Overpass Intersection, 1906
Plan (left); Perspective drawing (above)
Eugène Hénard

This intersection design anticipates increased traffic requirements, although most vehicles here are still horse-drawn. Stairways are provided so that pedestrians can cross streets or change direction without encountering the danger and obstacle of traffic. Hénard's overpass intersection is not controlled by grade level—the lower road dips below grade and the upper road is suspended on an iron bridge, so that the structure is less disruptive visually and less difficult to ascend, physically. A refined version of Hénard's overpass intersection is the well-known cloverleaf overpass, which solves the left turn problem unanswered in Hénard's design.

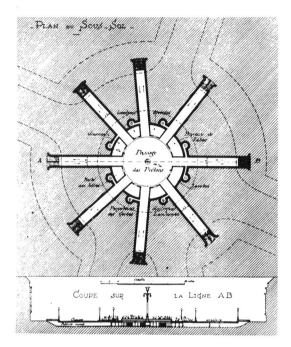

6-7. Carrefour à Giration, 1906. Perspective drawing (above); Subsurface pedestrian passages, plan (top). Eugène Hénard

Hénard isolated the intersection as the critical point in the surface web of the city circulation system. Before his investigation, vehicles were allowed to traverse *étoile* or multiple-branch circular intersections in any direction desired—left, right, or diagonally. Hénard proved that single-direction circulation would greatly speed movement and reduce accidents. Soon after these investigations, traffic regulations were promulgated enforcing Hénard's discovery. This proposal illustrates the benefit of eliminating the center of any major intersection to reduce accidents. In its place an open light court is proposed. At the street surface this court is ringed with fountains and plants. Below grade it becomes the center of an attractive shopping area at the confluence of pedestrian underpassages. Architectural relationships are conceived by Hénard to enforce the multiple concurrent interlocking circles that define the space of the intersection and simultaneously support its multilevel functional requirements. Variants of this plan now appear in a progressive subway station design in Mexico City and are often suggested for complex urban intersections. However, contrary to Hénard's scheme, pedestrians ideally should be accommodated at grade with vehicles dipping down a level to produce grade-separated urban street crossings.

8. La Città Nuova, 1914
Antonio Sant' Elia

This Futurist city design separates levels and types of motion. The architecture of circulation— the road, the sidewalk, the rail line, the bridge —moves toward the architecture of enclosure. Sant' Elia attempts to fuse architectural elements —circulation and structure—into a new city form with dispersed destinations strung along highly engineered channels for rapid travel of all sorts.

9. Une Ville Contemporaine: La Cité, 1922
(above). Le Corbusier

A roadway of countless lanes bisects the city center. Jazzy vehicles and high speed dominate the imagination. The city center becomes a stop along the autoroute. Even Le Corbusier's later schemes, such as the *Plan Voisin de Paris* of 1925, which reveal an increasing awareness of possible channelization for the automobile exposes the continuing impact which the Futurist embrace of speed and movement had on Corbusier's urbanistic schemes during the 1920's. Corbusier's highly sophisticated and sympathetic consideration of people's needs within dwellings is subordinated at the urban scale to his fascination with technology and movement.

10. Algiers Urbanization Plan, 1930
Le Corbusier

This proposed redevelopment of Algiers suspends dwellings below a long, sinuous water-edge autoroute. Buildings in the city center are curved and contoured in response to highway geometry. The scheme clearly reveals the power of the motorcar as a problem to be encountered in urban design. Yet the influence of the motorcar and its attendant engineering here inform a fluid redevelopment scheme of only the slightest relevance for a North African coastal town. The misdirection of such a scheme is now appreciated. Elevated urban highways which ignore their surroundings and sever the city from its own waterfront are now discouraged. On the other hand, Corbusier's post-Futurist recognition that large-scale engineering projects contain formative potential for architecture and urban-scale design is increasingly relevant.

within a city. Le Corbusier also recognized, by the 1920's, the need to control the motorcar and the potential of grade-separated highways to free much of the city surface for pedestrians. However, clearly infatuated with automotive technological promise, the poetic manifestos of Futurism, and the design possibilities explored by Hénard and others, Le Corbusier willingly focused on the street as a place for cars and on the high-speed motorway as the central spine of the city.

Throughout the 1920's and into the 1930's, the mainstream investigation intensified into new ways to fit the ever-growing automotive traffic into the pitifully inadequate older urban streets. By 1931, when the First Regional Plan of New York and Its Environs was issued under the uncompromisingly optimistic and self-assured title, *The Building of the City,* there was no question in the minds of those who prepared it that "we have to recognize as guiding assumptions that the street capacity of Manhattan should be increased to the fullest extent that is practical . . ."[5] A large measure of the plan is devoted to illustrating suggestions by concerned and talented architects and planners of the day who were asked to submit proposals to accomplish this goal.

Solutions that dominate the First Regional Plan for New York include taking over part of the first two floors of all buildings for new traffic lanes, creating second-level pedestrian concourses throughout intensively used parts of the city, and even developing so-called "superstreets," double-decked traffic ways for as many vehicle lanes as possible in the public right-of-way (Figures 11–13).

By the end of the 1930's, the ever-more increasing demands of the public surface space of the center city asserted by automobile traffic compelled Hugh Ferriss to compose a future city of gigantic vertical structures with stepped levels to serve as highways called Metropolis of Tomorrow (Figure 14). In 1939, Norman Bel Geddes, one of the most progressive designers of his day, created the City of 1960 for a Shell Oil Company advertising

campaign, and Futurama, a huge model prepared for the General Motors Exhibit at the 1939 New York World's Fair (Figures 15, 16). In both, he anticipates cities that are shaped principally by superhighways.

This notion is not distant from a concept regaining currency today among those such as Reyner Banham, Robert Venturi, and Denise Scott Brown who suggest that conventional concepts of "downtown" as a place dominated by pedestrian activity and public space are nostalgic reminiscences no longer relevant to contemporary American city life. This articulate band of urbanists and intellectuals accepts the spatial expansiveness and visual clutter of ordinary highway cities such as Las Vegas, Los Angeles, and Houston, arguing that the old-style concrete-strip urban freeway is doing its own thing quite nicely, and has been since the big roads began to cut up major cities throughout the country. This acceptance of the existing situation implies support of an urban organization which is based, actually, on the patterns of life initially produced by speculative land operators working in harmony with unfettered engineering expediency. Followers of this movement, however, seldom bother to consider the implications of defending this particular status quo, and seldom possess the command of urban history that its leaders use with such wit to manipulate visual information and to present cross-cultural urban historical analogies in a glossy, and often engaging, view of cities. So while the sophisticated original proponents of Internal Combustion City no doubt realize, and perhaps simultaneously regret, the unpleasant limitations of the urban future they accept, their considerably less sophisticated architect and planner disciples are headed off on an urban design adventure that leads back to the old American infatuation with the town as a clump of temporary buildings along the side of the road.

Yet the embrace of the automobile as a structuring mechanism for cities reveals a misguided infatuation with a device of the late industrial revolution, whose real

utility for people is non-urban travel. This has not yet been fully understood. Brilliantly promoted by industry and by government programs, and possessing universal allure, the inherent anti-urban qualities of the automobile are still not generally recognized. In America and around the world, planners systematically repeat the drastic mistake of building and rebuilding urban areas for automobiles rather than for people.

Among progressive urbanists in the early 1950's, a new awareness of possible direction began to appear. Decisions were made by individuals to review the use of urban streets in terms of levels of differentiation (Louis Kahn), in terms of the social, sociological, and anthropological context of urban arrangement (Alison and Peter Smithson), and in terms of man's privilege to use public space in the city center (Shadrach Woods). Recent proposals from a number of progressive sources seek to replace private automobiles on selected streets by pedestrian amenities and public transportation.

Contained in this shift is an emerging emphasis on man's experience of the city as a participant in it. This focus, which appeared in the 1950's, vies with a former mainstream preoccupation inherited most immediately from the Beaux-Arts post-industrial-revolution view of the city as a large-scale functional tool to be manipulated by the urbanist.

The architect Louis I. Kahn, an important early proponent of fresh attitudes toward architecture and urban design throughout the 1950's, exposed "serving" devices that had hitherto been concealed —such as light fixture sockets, utility conduits, stairwells, and reinforcing braces—and distinguished these from "served" spaces. This approach was first used in his design for the Yale University Art Gallery, 1951–53.

This same instinct to seek out and express functional differentiation is revealed in Kahn's most important early urbanistic work, his influential graphic study of 1953, "Toward a Plan for Mid-Town Philadelphia." In it Kahn displays, with some presumed awareness of Edmund

PRESENT CONDITION—1 MOVING LANE   ELEVATED SIDEWALKS—3 MOVING LANES   ARCADES FOR STANDING VEHICLES—6 MOVING LANES

SECTION   TYPICAL CROSS SECTION & PERSPECTIVE

STATE OF NEW YORK
TRANSIT COMMISSION

SUPERSTREETS

BETWEEN 2ND & 3RD AVES ON EAST SIDE
FROM HOUSTON ST TO HARLEM RIVER
AND
BETWEEN 9TH & 10TH AVES ON WEST SIDE
FROM 14TH ST TO 68TH ST & BROADWAY
PROPOSED IN CONNECTION WITH THE
METROPOLITAN TRANSIT SYSTEM
MARCH 26TH 1926.

CONSULTING ENGINEERS

DEEPER ARCADES IN BUILDINGS—8 MOVING LANES

**11–12. Process to Increase
Street Capacity, c. 1929**
Cross-sections (top)
Perspective sketches (above)
Harvey Wiley Corbett

The three-stage process, proposed in the First Regional Plan of New York City, would transform New York City into a place where the automobile is given full use of ground level with greatly expanded streets. This plan, it was announced with exuberance, would increase "effective street capacity . . . 700 per cent." People are eventually channeled into second-level pedestrian arcades which penetrate existing buildings and cross streets on new bridges. This evolutionary process would certainly require public control of private space which, however desirable, is not likely to be easily gained. Nor is it likely that complete accommodation of parked trucks, parked cars, and moving private vehicles on the streets of large cities could ever produce positive achievements for a more vital city center or a better city life.

13. Superstreet, 1924 (left)
First Regional Plan of New York City, 1929
Cross-section and perspective
Daniel L. Turner

A new avenue type, the "superstreet," is proposed for New York City. The grade-level right-of-way continues to be used for trucks and cars. A decked upper roadway is also devoted to as many vehicle traffic lanes as possible. Although the suggestion is made in conjunction with consideration of the metropolitan transit system, the focus is quite plainly on providing more and more of the public space of the city for the automobile.

14. The Metropolis of Tomorrow. Overhead Traffic-Ways, 1939. Hugh Ferriss

Ferriss, a skyscraper designer and imaginative urbanist, postulates a future urban world of cavernous, mysterious depths whose stepped-back skyscraper façades are "aligned and made into automobile highways at the fifth, tenth, fifteenth, and twentieth story." Autoroutes across the façades of buildings 60 feet to 240 feet above the ground are unlikely and hardly desirable. But Ferriss expresses the great attraction of the car as a manageable, challenging, and even romantic component of the city in this charcoal drawing.

15. Metropolis City of 1960
Conceived in 1936
Norman Bel Geddes

The city is seen as a network of high-speed superhighways edged by immense skyscrapers and parks. This vision, derived from Corbusier's proposals of the 1920's, was fulfilled in the 1950's and 1960's in some cities and particularly in the suburbs, where highway intersections attract commercial enterprises. The spread of commercial and office clusters into the countryside away from concentrations of housing has replaced the concept of distance by driving time. The nearly complete polarization of living place from working and shopping places has led to a new non-urban life style which is entirely dependent on the automobile. Geddes' vision, rather than portraying a functioning metropolis city, outlines the motorized suburban highway cluster format that is successfully competing with and destroying many older urban centers. On the other hand it can be persuasively argued that these, and their attached enclosed retail shopping malls, are indeed the new, permanent, and proper centers of urban activity.

16. Mall of General Motors Building
New York World's Fair, 1939
Norman Bel Geddes

General Motors commissioned Geddes to prepare its exhibit for the 1939 World's Fair. The Highways and Horizons exhibit he produced was a mammoth scale model which could be toured by spectators in moving chairs. Its theme was "highway progress," and it displayed a conception of "possible superhighways and traffic control methods of the future." Road architecture, with noise and noxious fumes rising to overhanging balconies, as unwittingly recommended in this model, leaves something to be desired. However, the integral handling of the traffic throughways, as a separate system from the principal pedestrian concourse which bridges service roads in all directions, is one of the few positive ways that new urban centers may simultaneously produce an acceptable city life for the individual and accommodate motorized traffic.

Bacon's work in the 1947 Better Philadelphia Exhibition, the possibility of isolating certain locations within large cities as "islands in a sea of traffic" (Figures 17, 18).[6] Served areas are emphasized as places of pedestrian convenience where the delights of intensive, varied activity may be experienced in a busy city center. These are places devoted to pedestrian activities, to shopping and walking and gathering to participate in the life of the city and to observe the people within it. The motorcar, separated from these identified spots, is assigned to particular corridors reserved for high-volume, fast travel; alternately, it is permitted to filter through the central city on selected roadways. In a later formulation of a Philadelphia plan, Kahn considers a more precise differentiation of vehicle- and man-centered space. The center city is surrounded by parking docks, the "harbor for cars" as he calls it, the gateway for man to the city (Figures 19, 20). Especially with his more pragmatic, earlier graphic notation of proposed movement patterns for urban places, in this case Philadelphia, Kahn's special combination of soft mystical insight mingled with hard analytic incisiveness forms a basis of important proposals. His suggestion is not dependent on costly multi-level urban organization, but on sufficient differentiation of existing places and streets so that conflicting spatial demands of traffic and pedestrian circulation are met at grade in a practical manner.

Kahn's comprehensive and imaginative diagrammatic presentation of concepts in the early 1950's, somewhat dependent on Bacon's earlier Greenway System, and his eloquent and poetic explanation of these concepts in his accompanying text, made a major impact on the thinking of advanced professionals. Ironically, in this case as in many others throughout the history of ideas, it is not necessarily the originator who makes an idea widely accepted but rather the successful publicist of the idea. In urbanism and architecture this often means that credit goes to an individual who can draw well, think well, *and* develop an understandable verbal polemic

to accompany ideas and drawings.

At about the same time as Kahn was developing his urbanistic proposals for Philadelphia, leadership in Western urbanistic thought and practice evolved from the generation of Europeans active during the late 1920's in establishing the *Congrès Internationaux d'Architecture Moderne* (CIAM)[7] to a younger international group born in the late 1920's and 1930's. Perhaps the clearest evidence of this shift was the formation of Team 10 in 1953.[8] The English architects Alison and Peter Smithson, together with Candilis and Woods, working in France, all founding members of Team 10, took early roles in analytic determinations that subsequently led to new attitudes toward the urban street which were closer to Kahn than to Le Corbusier.

The Smithsons work from the context of the individual family and its needs for places to relate to larger groups, for a replacement of the traditional street within the city (Figure 21). They attempt to formulate a new theory of city organization which rejects traffic circulation as an initial determinant, much as the little-known but progressive French theorist Henri-Jules Borie had, as early as 1865 (Figure 22). But their efforts have not as yet led to radically new decisions by most planners about the placement and accommodation of the motorcar in the city. They have, however, succeeded in directing other urbanists to new analytic criteria for urban planning which are extracted from the social sciences.

Shadrach Woods, on the other hand, worked simultaneously to achieve an acceptable social environment and to discover dynamic principles of urban organization. He concluded that traffic and people must be separated, by design, at points of intensive activity. Costly and hypothetical solutions dependent on multi-level organization in the built-up city were rejected by him in favor of a simple pedestrian mall, which he called "Stem" to connote its extensibility through time and space (Figures 23, 24). As developed in the early 1960's, "Stem" is a proposed organizing principle of urban centers grow-

ing out of Bacon's and Kahn's earlier Greenway concept. Housing and commercial activities are integrally related; pedestrians and automobiles are rigorously segregated. The principles proposed by Woods are demonstrated today partially and temporarily in experimental closing of commercial streets to create pedestrian malls, in a few well-organized, multi-use shopping centers, and in the occasional city enclave. But these are generally accomplished today without regard to scale, daily activity cycles, servicing requirements, or fundamental urban growth and organizing principles.

One of the earliest and certainly one of the most complete recent excursions into permanent change in the use of older urban streets in the United States has been in Minneapolis. In the late 1960's, commercial desperation, civic pride, and strong local leadership culminated in the conversion of Nicollet Avenue, a faltering downtown shopping thoroughfare, into Nicollet Mall, an eight-block-long pedestrian way shared only by pedestrians and public buses (Figures 25, 26). As a result, commercial activity is increasing and downtown is again becoming a regional focal point. The Minneapolis experiment is gaining attention from a wide variety of planners and civic leaders. No change in building form was necessary; no change in urban organization was attempted. Only the street's use and design were modified.

In addition, in Minneapolis, as suggested long ago for New York and other congested centers (Figure 27), a network of pedestrian overpasses is being built above busy commercial streets (Figures 28, 29, 30). Older buildings are being linked to one another; the volume of the city, not just its surface, is being utilized; and manifest priority is being given to the individual rather than to his automobile.

By the early 1970's, an increasing number of competent proposals existed for the redevelopment of major urban streets around the country. These generally forbid entry of the conventional automobile for routine purposes. The prevailing theme is now: "streets for the people." The commercial disaster

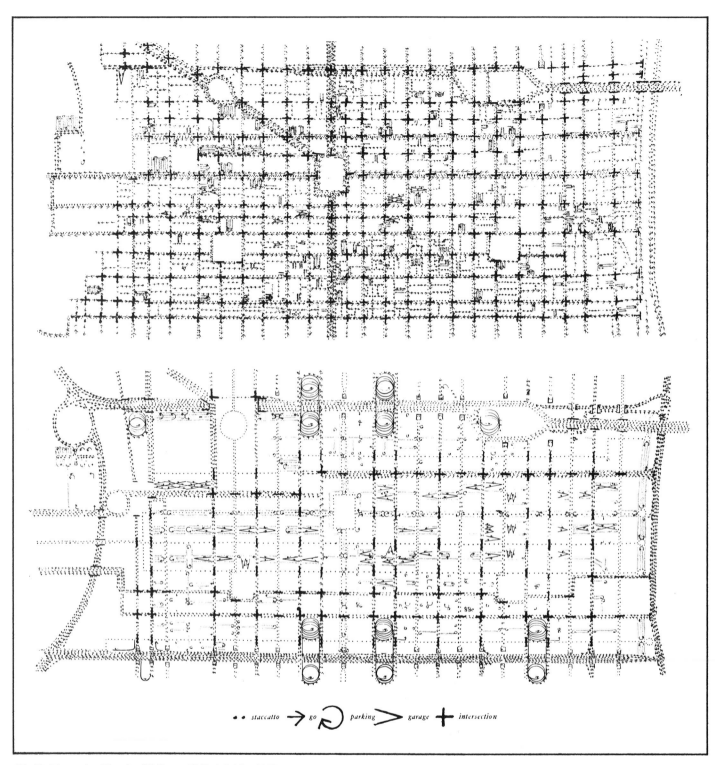

. . *staccatto* →⟶ *go* 🗘 *parking* ❯ *garage* ✛ *intersection*

17–18. Toward a Plan for Midtown Philadelphia, 1953
Existing Movement Pattern (top); Proposed Movement Pattern (above). Louis I. Kahn

The existing pattern of traffic on downtown Phila-delphia streets is analyzed and illustrated in pattern language, developed by Kahn for this purpose (Figure 17, top). The pattern language analysis reveals that all streets are used the same way in the present city for trolleys, buses, trucks, cars, and pedestrians with varying speed and movement characteristics. The proposed plan collects, organizes, and rationalizes the available street system with emphasis on peri-pheral parking docks and reserved pedestrian areas (Figure 18, above). Collecting related types of travel movements, reserving other parts of the city grid for predominantly pedestrian activity and still allowing vehicle access for municipal services and essential travel are all expressed diagramatically in this simple and implementable structuring device.

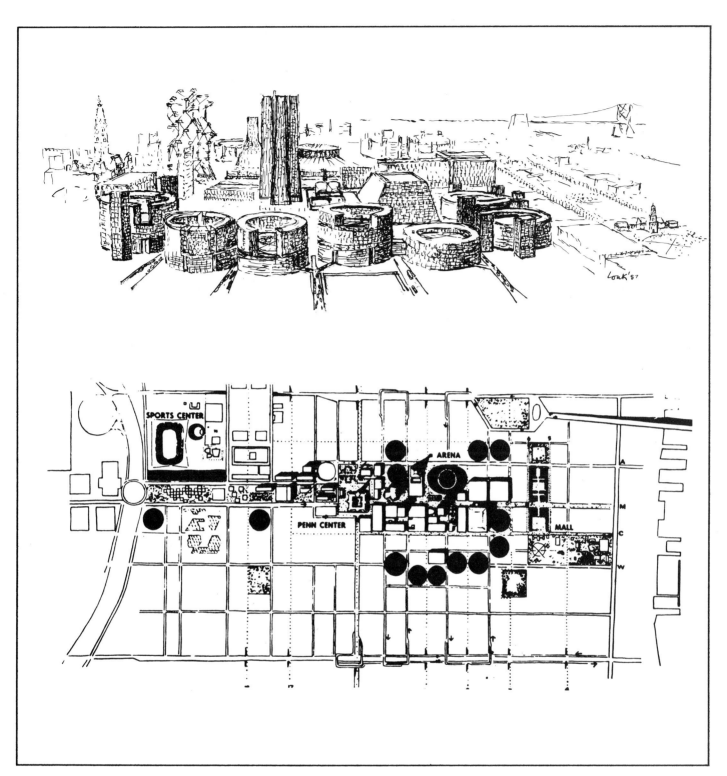

19–20. Proposal for Center City, Philadelphia, 1956
Perspective drawing (top)
Plan, 1956–57 (above). Louis I. Kahn

In the manner of a medieval walled city, Philadelphia is surrounded by protective parking docks to house all non-essential incoming vehicles. On entry for work or for shopping, the rural marauder is forced to pass through the sentinel gate, the parking dock or garage, and there deposit his anti-city weapon, the car.

21. Golden Lane Project, 1952
Street, perspective drawing
and photomontage (above)
Alison and Peter Smithson

22. Aérodômes, Paris 1865 (right)
Henri-Jules Borie

The English architects and Team 10 members
Alison and Peter Smithson propose an exclusively pedestrian street through large residential complexes. Streets are stacked at intervals
in vertical layers (Figure 21, above). The street-
deck in the air is given life by provision of communal access to many dwelling units. Its width
can accomodate enough people for it to become
a social entity. According to the Smithsons,
"Decks would be places, not corridors or balconies: thoroughfares where there are shops,
post boxes, telephone kiosks. . . . The flat block
disappears and vertical living becomes a
reality. . . . The refuse chute takes the place of
the village pump." Such an idea has respectable
though perhaps unrealized sources in the fas-
cinating work of Henri-Jules Borie, whose 1865
Aérodômes possess wide perimeter pedestrian
walks, rooftop schools, and interior public markets for clusters of tall residential buildings which
must be called the first domestic skyscrapers
(Figure 22, right). Wide pedestrian deck streets
at various levels are proposed on the circum-
ference of each residential block; pedestrian
overpasses cross existing streets and linked
buildings and roofs are developed as streets in
the air for promenade and play, long before Le
Corbusier's remarkable *Unité d'Habitation* of
1948. The Smithson work is becoming well

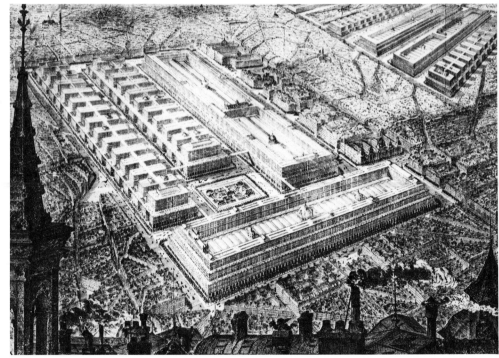

known, and their desire to find an urban street
substitute is important. However, it is increasingly important to ask, why should people be
forced off the ground level of the city? It is increasingly evident from elevated pedestrian concourse experiments in England, America, and
elsewhere that commercial enterprises, pedestrian activity, and urban vitality are best mingled
at grade.

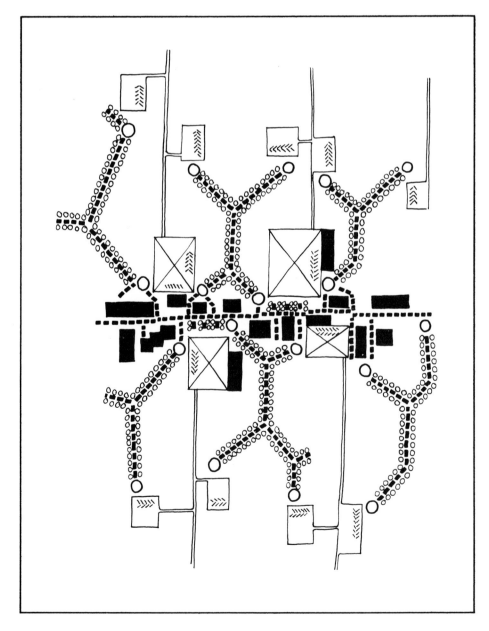

23–24. Stem, 1961
Perspective drawing, 1966 (left)
Diagram (lower left)
Shadrach Woods

A schematic organizing principle, *Stem,* is a pedestrian way lined with public and commercial buildings (Figure 23, left). Long, low apartment dwellings extend to either side, with secondary pedestrian ways running through and/or under them. Low parking-garage roofs become playgrounds. Motorized and pedestrian traffic meet only as, and where, planned, at the entrances of apartment buildings or parking lots. Cars must be parked in open lots at the edge of the community or in underground garages along the Stem. Open at both ends, a Stem makes possible the inclusion of a fourth dimension—time —in urban planning. Stem can be extended or its direction changed; new types of buildings can grow up along it. As its metaphorical name implies, the Stem is meant to generate growth by accommodating a successful and pleasant community life. The fanciful sketch by Shadrach Woods shows life along a Stem (Figure 24, left). High buildings are raised on stilts, giving an open, eye-level view to the strolling citizen who, unhampered by automobile traffic, moves along this low-scale, active urban domain at the supremely human pace of 2 m.p.h.

pedestrian walkways

commercial and public buildings

apartment buildings

underground parking lots

surface parking lots

automobile roads

25–26. Nicollet Mall
Minneapolis, Minnesota, 1961–65
Plan of a two-block area (right)
Aerial view (lower right)
Lawrence Halprin & Associates, Inc.
(Landscape and Urban Design)
and Barton-Aschman Associates, Inc.
(Urban Planning and Engineering)

At the heart of downtown Minneapolis, a major shopping street is permanently closed to conventional traffic for eight blocks (Figure 25, right). The right-of-way is shared by wide pedestrian walks and a narrow transitway for buses and taxis. More than just a pedestrian travel corridor, the walking area is planted and supplied with benches, fountains, and street sculpture to convert the once sterile and ordinary street into a pleasant meeting and lingering place for people (Figure 26, below). The result has been renewed commercial vigor along Nicollet Mall and a considerable amount of pedestrian activity drawn to the street because of its pleasant quality and active surroundings. The possibility of closing commercial streets to automobile traffic has gained considerable attention in a number of cities recently. There is increasing evidence that such measures do indeed increase shopping activity and are thus beneficial to commerce. And there is overwhelming agreement among pedestrians who have experienced the freedom of walking on wide, quiet roadways closed to ordinary traffic that the sensation is liberating and returns to urban man a sense of presence and dignity in his all-too-often dehumanizing street environment.

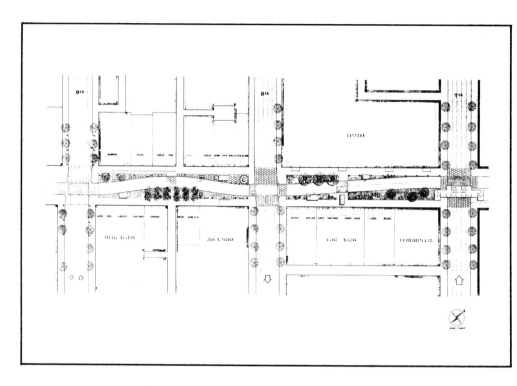

wrought on the central city by the automobile is being recognized; the environmental disaster wrought on the central city inhabitant has been revealed.

Thus Roosevelt Island (formerly Welfare Island) is planned as an island-city, a New Town-within-a-town from which all automobiles except service vehicles will be excluded. Planned by Philip Johnson and John Burgee in the mid-1960's, it reflects this new emphasis for urban areas (Figures 31, 32, 33). Unfortunately, as development proceeds, many of the important planning concepts are being sacrificed. But still, because it is an idea whose time has come, because it is a small, isolated area, and because it can be served by transit to its metropolitan surroundings, it may very well be a new island city without the automobile; it may be the first New Town almost completely dependent on public transit.

A scheme of the late 1960's by Mary Hommann, a New York urban planner, is more representative of the current trend as it is limited to a single, popular midtown commercial street (Figure 34). Space on the street (Madison Avenue) is redistributed so that the 80 per cent of the public right-of-way that is currently the domain of cars, is reserved for people and for electric transit. Outdoor recreation places, quiet "caravans," and pedestrians thereby share the reorganized street on one level.

In a recent Ford Foundation supported urban design scheme by Ulrich Franzen, perhaps the most extensive and complex automobile limiting suggestion to date has been proposed (Figures 35, 36).[9] Franzen suggests barring all conventional cars from the East Side of Manhattan between 57th and 96th Streets and in their place operating rental electric personal transit vehicles and a variety of improved public transit. Except for public service lanes, the interior of the street—the old automobile right-of-way—becomes available as parks, playgrounds, a central location for neighborhood facilities such as daycare and preschool centers, and as new-found public land for district service facilities such as police stations, firehouses, schools, and city administrative offices.

27. Broadway Looking North From Exchange Place
Drawing by Harry M. Pettit, from *King's Views of New York 1908–1909* by Moses King

A complex multi-level vision of the city from the bold first decade of this century. The heady optimism of a strong urban center, a booming real estate market, a proliferation of money-making skyscrapers are all captured. Long, decked pedestrian and transit galleries parallel the façades of buildings. The central street is a busy transit way above which light, airy bridges provide a network of pedestrian passages. Many routes are populated with people, pavilions, and general activities. This romantic and optimistic view of the city captures poten- tials still not realized, especially in alternatives to the conventional urban street and the creative use of roofs, which are both being investigated by research groups today. Together, the roof and the street account for almost 100 per cent of the land area of the city. And yet they are still largely ignored. It is encouraging to note that the National Endowment for the Arts Division of Architecture is supporting renewed investigation of urban roof areas as a part of its 1973 City Edges program.

28–30. Minneapolis Skyway System
Photograph, 1970 (right)
Existing Skyways, plan, 1973 (far right, top)
Proposed Skyways, plan, 1973 (far right; bottom)
Minneapolis Planning and Development Department

A total of 64 skyways, of which 11 are existing or programmed for construction, are expected to connect 54 blocks of downtown Minneapolis by 1985 (Figure 30, far right, bottom). Primary skyways form a north-south principal axis (black). Feeder lines are intended to serve the rest of the area (grey). Underground concourses and fringe parking areas are linked directly to the skyways. The skyway system is also designed for extension and growth. Entrepreneur developers are encouraged to link their own buildings into it. Consideration is being given to providing the primary lines with mechanical people-movers which might be used for night-time freight distribution. The possibility of enclosing Nicollet Mall along its three principal shopping blocks is also under consideration (grey dash). Downtowns are desperate to keep their commercial vitality. This vitality has been challenged for over a decade by the shopping center and later the enclosed shopping mall near suburban residential areas. In Minneapolis, a capable Department of Planning and Development has joined forces with energetic business groups to make downtown more cohesive and more comfortable. In a place where winter weather is brutal, enclosed elevated pedestrian passages have been planned and quite a few have already been completed (Figures 28, right, and 29, far right, top). As in most downtowns, Minneapolis sidewalks are crowded; street crossing is hazardous and waiting for cars irritating. Automobile exhaust is spewed on the pedestrian, diesel odors from bus exhaust surround him, and the noise of incessant street repairs, construction, and traffic make walking through the downtowns of America a thoroughly disagreeable experience. These environmental realities are countered by elevating the pedestrian passageways to bridges which link to existing buildings at mid-block, creating a concourse level in the city. Therefore, the Minneapolis plan is especially notable because it deals with an existing city in an evolutionary way. It is not a product of utopic planning for a new place. Were it such, pedestrians would be accorded prime consideration on the grade level. But in Minneapolis, as in most older cities, this is a possible but difficult alternative to work out. Consequently much time and energy has been wisely devoted to working out and negotiating questions of how the bridges are financed, who is responsible for their maintenance, what is public space, and what is private space within the concourse levels of older existing buildings linked by these bridges. As welcome as these climate-controlled linkages are in a city which is cold about half of the year, a comprehensive system of clear graphics to direct those unfamiliar with the network is lacking nor was the design of the bridge juncture with existing buildings given proper consideration.

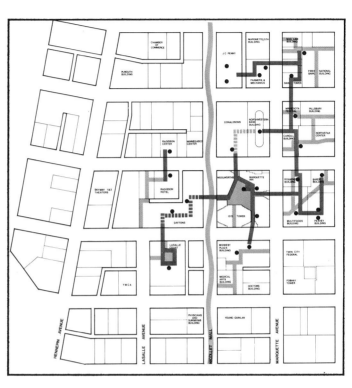

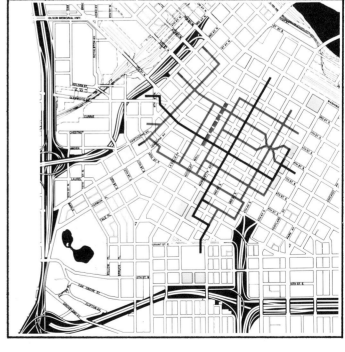

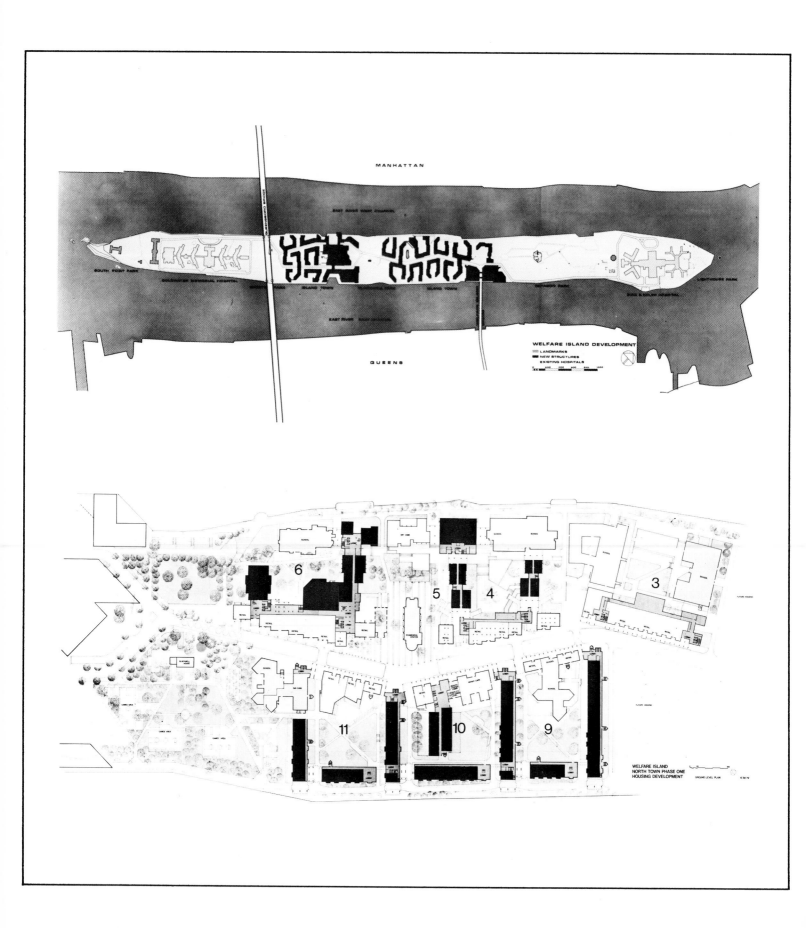

31–33. Roosevelt Island Redevelopment Plan, 1969
Plan (top left); North Town, Phase One, 1972, plan (left)
Street scene, perspective drawing (above)
Philip Johnson and John Burgee

A new planned island community between Manhattan and Queens is being built. The initial scheme omitted all private automobiles and combined mixed-income housing, institutional, commercial, and limited retail space with expansive promenades, large park areas, and older hospital structures (Figures 31, top left, and 33, above). As phased development advances under the direction of the Urban Development Corporation, some of the initial planning details are being compromised, but the overriding principle of a car-free island has held —so far. Bridge connection to Queens terminates in a massive parking structure. Louis

Kahn's medieval gates of the 1950's are being built past which only delivery and service vehicles will be allowed. Within the island, electric jitney shuttle buses are planned to circulate throughout the community. External transit to New York and the region is eventually to be via subway from a new island station and perhaps initially by aerial tram from Manhattan. What effect this rigid elimination of the car will have on life on Roosevelt Island is still uncertain. But what is clear is that in a far-from-perfect translation from plan to reality the principle of no automobiles has survived—and survived only because it is an idea whose time has come

because of the destruction of urban public space and of the urban environment produced by the automobile itself. It is regrettable that the initially planned mixture of dense housing clusters sited in relation to the water, green spaces, and well conceived and coordinated pedestrian ways has not survived quite so well (Figure 32, left). The boldness of the entire enterprise and the comprehensive redevelopment of a new-town-in-town on a difficult, challenging, and potentially spectacular site signals the need for leadership by a public agency in large-scale urban development.

34. Caravan Plan for Midtown Manhattan, 1965–69
Mary Hommann

This proposal, among others aimed at liberating the 35 to 40 per cent of the city pre-empted by streets, suggests a means to convert existing city streets for greater use by people and for more effective public transit. The street right-of-way remains but its space is reallocated: conventional cars are eliminated with only a service corridor reserved for taxi and emergency vehicles. Pedestrian space is assembled principally on one side, where a wide, extended plaza of over half the total street width is available for strolling, sitting in cafés, and observing. Silent, low, electric transit "caravan" vehicles glide through a fixed central zone and sidewalks are retained along all buildings for window shopping and goods delivery. This redistribution of the street surface recognizes implicitly the owner-ship base of the street itself as public property. And yet this property has for years been delegated almost exclusively to a narrow range of uses by a narrow range of users, predominantly car and truck owners. Redistribution of the street so that it becomes available to local residents and pedestrians would enhance life in the city and return a substantial amount of land to residents of the city. In addition, in a street now freed of most air pollutants by electric transit, Hommann proposes the use of cross-avenue buildings to create physical continuity in the city and a visual sense of enclosure. If properly scaled, this could contribute to an improved sense of "place" in many cities now dominated by long avenue vistas.

35–36. An Avenue, Manhattan
Photograph c. 1970 (top right)
Proposed Redevelopment, 1971–73 (right)
Ulrich Franzen

The old multi-lane traffic artery gives way to a place now designed for people. The streets once again become the active public space which may be used for community facilities, parks, or even temporary theaters. Small electric rental transit pods take people on limited rights-of-way and are then abandoned, to be picked up by the next user. This illustration is a fragment of a much larger, quite complex scheme worked out by Franzen during the last three years, which contains a number of important prototypical suggestions for redevelopment of transportation and public space in cities.

Currently, of course, this vast area of valuable public land is deeded in principle, if not in fact, to the private and limited use of people in automobiles.

The differentiation of street use within urban areas, still only in a germinal stage, is likely to become increasingly responsible for actual experiments within cities and in some cases subsequent transformation of the street's use. In 1970, New York City experimented with closing major avenues to traffic on specified days on the strength of recommendations initiated by the innovative Urban Design Group within the City Planning Commission and then further refined by the Mayor's Office of Midtown Planning and Development.[10] Pedestrians came out of hiding to walk fearlessly and joyfully along quieter, cleaner Fifth and Madison Avenues.

New pedestrian malls in older city centers are gaining acceptance and popularity around the world. A record of successful tests, and in many cases subsequent permanent closing of major commercial streets to automobiles, in the last several years exists in many places from Oxford Street, London, to State Street, New London. Yet in New York, even as plans are underway to convert some of Fulton Street in Brooklyn and nine blocks of Nassau Street in lower Manhattan into permanent commercial pedestrian malls, a recalcitrant uptown merchant group combined with a regressive and powerful automobile lobby, known as the taxi industry, have prevented even an adequate long-term test of the idea on Madison Avenue. The concept is correct. In all cases people have found new satisfaction in recapturing the open public space of the city—the street. The experience of the city without fumes, noise, traffic, or sidewalk congestion is exhilarating. With this good feeling, people enjoy shopping and the potential emerges for new commercial and public amenities such as enclosed or outdoor cafés, seating areas, and shopping pavilions.

Also, a number of streets in selected residential areas around the country have recently been closed to traffic and successfully transformed into urban playgrounds, not on a temporary schooltime play-street basis, which is common in the city, but permanently (Figure 37).

Many other urban residents, in their own neighborhoods, are becoming increasingly aware of the options available to them. The hundreds of block associations in New York City, for instance, now generally give street festivals in spring or summer. City authorities close the street; people, sales booths, dancing platforms, live bands, carnival rides, fortunetellers, rummage sales, sidewalk cafés, and outdoor beer gardens take over.

In the near future it is to be hoped that certain streets in each neighborhood will be closed permanently except for service lanes (fire, ambulance, and so on) and "developed" as neighborhood resource centers: parks, playgrounds, outdoor recreation areas, cafés, public gardens. And what about swimming pools? Tennis courts? There is no end to the possibilities.

Total closure of the street is not essential for very real progress to be evident. It has been discovered that even the systematic reduction of traffic on residential streets promotes increased resident socialization, a sense of greater well-being and a feeling of community in the city, as well as an opportunity for neighborhood children to play safely with one another near their homes (Figure 38).

In general, new implementative techniques, administrative determinations, and public demand for more complex use of the auto-congested public space in the city will be seen during the 1970's as a long-delayed reaction to the uncontrolled freedom of the motorcar in urban centers. As a consequence of these developments, urban form would once again be conceived in relation to transportation needs, rather than as a function of them. Considerations such as the positioning of buildings, the location of public spaces, and most of all the quality of urban life which have been

obscured for so long by preoccupation with the vexing demands of the motorcar should again begin to affect the design of cities.

In many respects, of course, cities are not actually designed any longer by the master hand of a designated representative backed by the vast authority once held by kings and popes. Instead, incremental change takes place, project by project, sometimes in the context of a master plan, often without one. These cumulative changes, in existing cities, produce the context in which we live. Each is of fundamental importance. Each signals where we may be going. Each is where we are.

In the near future, evolution of older urban areas will pivot around decisions made regarding the urban street. Streets can be imaginatively and actively integrated into urban redevelopment schemes if public access to the street space is reinforced rather than restricted. However, there is a danger that much new building will take place in, over, and even under city streets. Due to relocation requirements and patterns of fragmented ownership, there is little other easily accessible land in our cities. The streets are controlled under single (city) ownership; the streets are where the space is. At the same time, the cities desperately need capital and increased taxable real estate. The temptation will be to "sell" the streets, which is in effect what happens in air-rights transactions and when "superblocks" are created. Each of these may bring revenue to the city while transferring more of the space from the public into the private or semi-private domain. At the same time, of course, each confiscates even further the individual's access to the public space of the city. This temptation must be watched and resisted.

Alternatives do exist. One of them is to be certain that streets become more rather than less available and attractive to people. The urban street is where action is needed, and where it will take place. The quality of that action is going to determine the quality of urban life for years to come.

37. Bedford-Stuyvesant Superblock, New York, 1969
I. M. Pei & Partners and M. Paul Friedberg & Associates

Recognition of the street as a core element capable of all ranges of public use could transform man's experience in urban centers. Consciousness of potential for the street and dedication to its realization is increasingly apparent. Here the street, precious public property which has been a long-neglected space reservoir at the heart of all urban residential districts, is converted to needed passive and active recreation turf. Different functions at different intervals of the day are also a possibility.

38. Social Interaction as a Function of Traffic, 1972. Donald Appleyard and Mark Lintell

This diagram illustrates the impact of traffic on neighborhood social interaction from the resident's viewpoint based on interesting recent studies. Interviewed neighborhood residents declared decisively that as traffic increased, there was a specific decrease in neighborhood friendliness, socializing and playing on the street, and safety in the neighborhood. Though results of such a study are always difficult to evaluate, the conclusions are logical. Increased fumes and noise, danger of moving cars, and cars parked in the street are all deterrents to voluntary pedestrian use of the sidewalk-street right-of-way for casual, leisure-time purposes. The physical and emotional relief and sense of well-being experienced when walking in a safe, attractive, quiet urban street are rarely known by city residents and visitors. But the experience is, one hopes, to become increasingly available in the coming decade as differentiation of street uses grows within cities; as more streets and more of the street becomes available to more people more of the time; as urban transportation alternatives are provided, however slowly and painfully. The alternative is, I expect, continued alienation of people from the cities and gradual decline of the cities themselves.

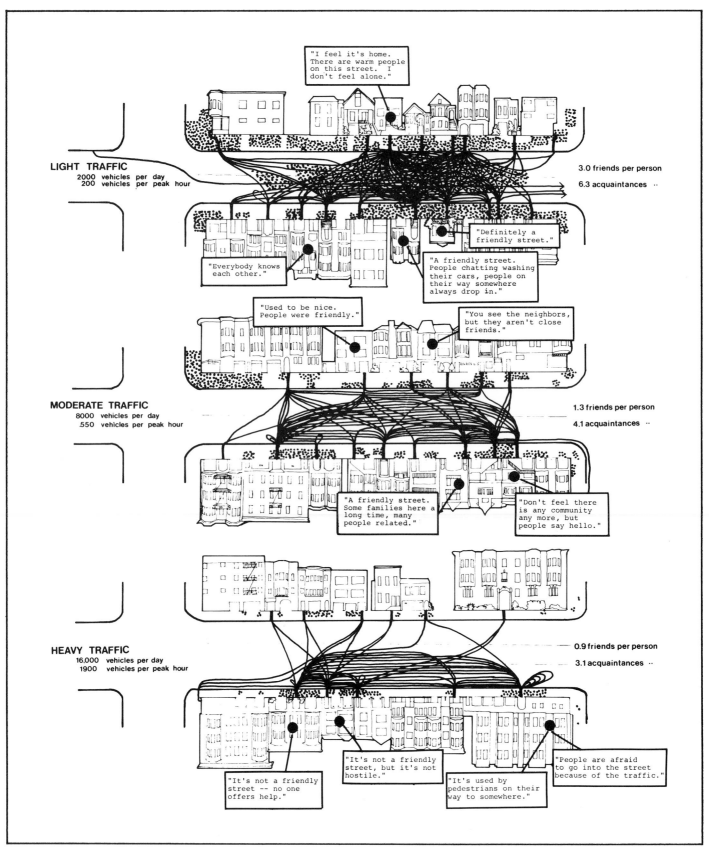

New Directions

The street is the major public space of the city and should be predominantly for pedestrians and public transit.

People prefer to be at grade, not forced to walk up onto platforms or down into corridors.

Streets should be used in a variety of ways.

Separate pedestrians from traffic and link their accessways to structures.

Integrate streets into development and redevelopment schemes. Make them part of the planning and development parcel so that three-dimensional consideration of the street is built into the process.

Take the control of street use away from highway departments and give it to planning agencies.

39. Aerial Freeway Views

In America, during the explosive freeway building period from the late 1940's through the mid-1960's, little distinction was made between urban and rural highway design. Like the railroad era which preceded it, the era of the great roads was dominated by land speculation, unfettered engineering, and little regard for financial or social costs. The program was financed by federal funds earned from tax on fuel and for the most part benefited land developers, trucking interests, and automobile companies. These engineering patterns of grace and beauty, of a type never before created by man, were built in massive concrete interchanges. In the countryside they created new crossroads, new nodes for development, entirely new settlement patterns—suburban America. In the cities, wide interchanges with access ramps and 6-, 8-, and even 10-lane roadways rammed through the older towns, creating dislocation and disassociation within the impact area, and in many instances dissolution of the city's residential, retail, and business vitality.

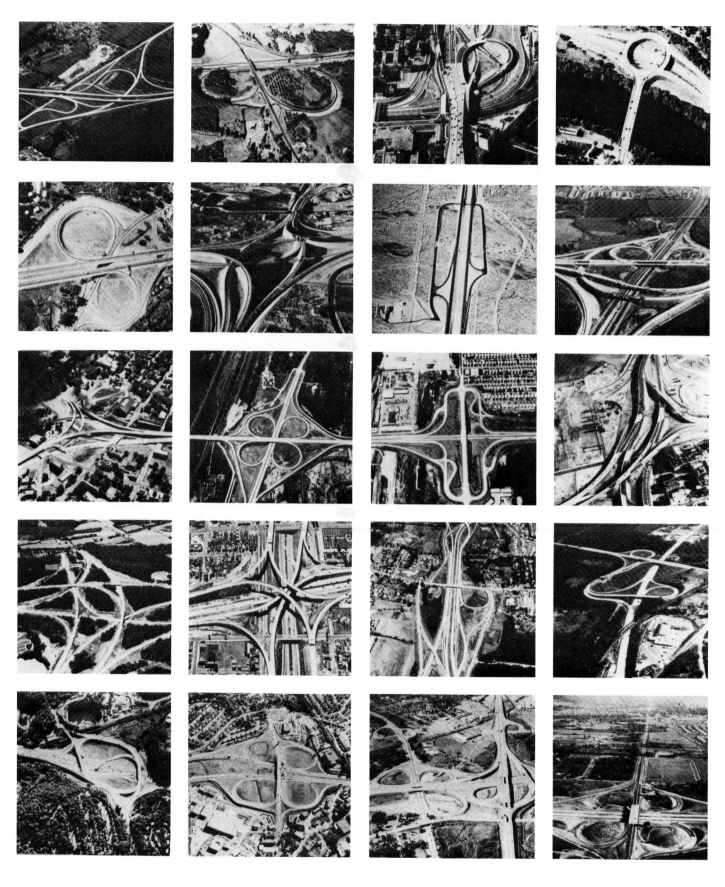

The Urban Highway

High-speed travel by car in urban centers is the Futurist dream that became an American nightmare. To make it all possible highways were built from city to city during the 1930's and 1940's. To make it inevitable, wide and often elevated superexpressways were carved into the cities during the late 1950's and 1960's. It is almost as if the American highway engineer and his enthusiastic political and administration supporters of the 1950's and early 1960's saw no difference between building a railroad or power line across open, unpopulated countryside and building a highway through a densely-populated urban area (Figures 39, 40, 41). Then during the 1960's, public attitudes and social pressure stopped the urban freeways. In San Francisco, New Orleans, Baltimore, New York, and elsewhere the big-city highways were halted.

How did the present situation begin? And what is its importance? Before 1956, most highways were built by the state from local funds. Then the Highway Trust Fund was set up to channel the federal gasoline tax directly and exclusively into nationwide highway construction. The massive amount of funds generated was spent to build the most road possible for the money available, taking into consideration nothing more than engineering criteria, minimal highway safety standards, and ease of highway corridor acquisition. Dislocation of people, disruption of communities, and disservice to large portions of the population were ignored. The federal government made available 90 per cent of the money to do the job. The states got the jobs, the contracts, and the total "economic benefit" by putting up only 10 per cent of the money. Local politicians around the country couldn't resist the temptation. Each tried to get as many freeways as possible.

Besides the considerable social costs of

this program, which has embittered people throughout the country, the capital costs of the Interstate Highway System are now estimated to be $63 billion. And the result has been to link American cities by penetrating them with large swaths of concrete, often with perilous consequence to the cities themselves. Local barriers, urban blight, and suburban sprawl are all related to the direct and indirect effects of the urban highway program, as many people began to realize in the late 1960's.

Today the urban freeway is recognized as a physically divisive element able to shred urban context into meaningless fragments—fragments of dislocated communities and severed patterns of human association.

In the mid-1960's, a number of crucial things began to happen which signaled a new direction in national attitudes on many and often interrelated levels. Opposition to the federal highway program surfaced. Local residents expressed their alarm at the visual and aural blight that accompanies the insertion of a highway into neighborhoods. People resisted being thrown out of their houses by a massive road project, and replacement housing was demanded when dislocation was inevitable. Locally organized resistance, a sort of urban dweller's revolution, proved effective. It curtailed or stopped highway construction in a number of cities. As a consequence, many urban highway projects planned in the 1950's and early 1960's were halted, rerouted, or redesigned. Today, the conventional, wide, open-cut freeway cannot slash into cities merely to facilitate through traffic and the daily ebb of the suburbanite's journey to and from work.

The recent history of the Lower Manhattan Expressway, intended to link Manhattan's West Side Highway to the Holland Tunnel and the East Side

bridges, first proposed by Robert Moses in the heady freeway days of the 1930's, is a case in point.

After the route was finally designated to run across lower Manhattan, the future freeway corridor became, as it always did in such cases, doomed urban terrain. Condemnation was imminent for years. No one would move into the area and owners couldn't sell and move out. Gradually blight, neglect, and despair became the principal physical and social characteristics of the designated corridor. All the time, land and building values were decreasing. While the highway department *could* wait, the people *had* to wait. This happened along New York's Broome Street, and around the country wherever major urban highways were planned.

In the case of the Lower Manhattan Expressway, as a result of growing public consciousness of the national urban highway problem—and their potential power to influence the building of highways—and as a result of the sensitive attitude to these issues within the Lindsay Administration, Shadrach Woods was commissioned in 1968 to prepare a preliminary urban design study of the highway and its immediate impact area. This brought Woods back to America—permanently —after 20 years of professional practice in France. And it brought information to the problem. It also gave the opponents of the highway time, during crucial years in the evolution of America's attitude to the urban highway, to develop their case and to marshal support. They were successful. The route has been officially "de-mapped." It is no longer a part of the New York regional transportation planning program. But traffic, and particularly persistent trucking requirements through and around Manhattan assure that the issue will linger for years to come. For the moment, however, de-mapping has oc-

40. Across the Continent, 1868 (right)
Currier and Ives Lithograph

**41. Power Transmission Lines,
Arizona** (lower right)

The railroad was the lifeline of a community in
most places before the highway building era
(Figure 40, right). The location of the railroad
often determined the location of a town and all
of the major activities within it. The transcontinental railroads, when built, struck out across
the American countryside on rights-of-way
often provided by the government itself.
Throughout much of the 19th century, large
pieces of terrain abutting the railroads were
held for speculation by the railroad companies
and quite a bit is still retained by them today.
In this century, massive power-line rights-of-way
have been spread across the land (Figure 41,
below right). The mid-20th century highway
building era represents another wave—and
probably the last—when the land will be used
so recklessly. In America, land is still very abun-
dant. Most of it remains uninhabited. Across the
country, and especially in the cities and their
surrounding regions, a new reverence for the
environment exists for the first time. Public
interest in land as a resource rather than as a
commodity is growing. This new trend will have
profound implications in years to come on all
aspects of planning, land settlement patterns,
and especially on the once easily obtained
privilege of undertaking massive projects which
use the land recklessly or for the private benefit
of special-interest groups.

curred to assuage political protest and to avoid dealing with a most complex urban design problem. The situation, at the moment, as Shadrach Woods said not long ago, recalls Marcel Duchamp's apt remark: *"Il n'y a pas de solution. Donc, il n'y a pas de problème."*

Each highway built and not built around the country has its own story. Some are more celebrated cases than others. New Haven's Oak Street Connector is a famous late 1950's example of what, until very recently, the highway program could do to a city (Figure 42). It is a rough, open-cut, massive highway that was shoved through the city by powerful political and economic forces. It is a highway that precedes a transition of power and awareness in this country, at least at the citizen level, away from the urban freeway. It is a highway that assisted in producing conventional regional sprawl, massive urban dislocation, diminution of public transportation, fragmentation of the city, and a self-feeding requirement of linkage to other, equally massive highways (Figure 43). The slum replaced by the Oak Street Connector, like the slums many highways around the country have replaced as part of their rarely stated "urban renewal" function, is now a highrise, high-cost residential and commercial strip development. But is the slum gone? No. It only moved. Indeed, it expanded as privileged, mobile urban people moved down the freeway to outlying open land.

In other notable cases, the highway did not go through. The first time this happened, with major national consequences, was in Baltimore in the late 1960's (Figure 44). There an entire urban design concept team was hired, a new development in itself, which is discussed in more detail later. The team was expected to represent a balanced viewpoint. It was composed of local highway engineering firms anxious to see the highway built; a traffic and transportation consulting firm, Wilbur Smith and Associates, expected to dispassionately analyze alternate routes, impacts, and implications from the viewpoint of traffic generation; and Skidmore,

Owings & Merrill, the well-known architectural firm whose respect for the environment was premised on previous work and on the views of some of its partners. The study dragged on for over two years. The cost mounted to over $1 million. The methods finally employed by the architects, especially to engage residents' interest and to advise those who would be displaced by the highway, were without precedent at that time. They actually went to the neighborhood, to the people, held meetings, and prepared storefront displays.

As an alternative to the conventional open-cut freeway for certain dense commercial or institutional areas, the architects and planners proposed a complex, multi-level decked highway to cover, visually and physically, the intrusion of the road. New public facilities all along the route were also promised. But the final answer from the people in the city, spoken loudly enough to be heard by local politicians and federal funding authorities, was "No." And the highway through the city, through a massive slum area, across the harbor, and skirting upper-income residential districts, was stopped. That was in 1968. The word was out. And citizens around the country heard it.

Lately they've even heard it in the suburbs. The long proposed Rye-Oyster Bay highway bridge summarizes the situation. Planned and studied since the mid-1950's and supported by the most powerful political forces in New York and Connecticut for nearly 20 years, the 6.5-mile span, estimated to cost over $100 million, has now been dropped even by its most ardent initial supporters, including New York's Governor Rockefeller. Rising local protest centering on environmental and ecological issues resulted in action within the U.S. Department of the Interior and U.S. House of Representatives, which made construction nearly impossible. Senators got the message. The Governor got the message. In the summer of 1973, in a dramatic reversal of his long-held position, Governor Rockefeller instructed the New York State Department

of Transportation and the Metropolitan Transportation Authority to cease planning work on the highway bridge itself as well as its extensive interchange roads and accessways.

After the Baltimore incident of 1967–68, and a number of others in major cities around the country, new directions in thinking about, planning for, and building urban highways in America emerged. The critical years were 1967–69, but the change began around 1965. A group of "urban advisors" appointed by the federal government in 1965 issued, in 1968, *The Freeway in the City,*[11] a report to the Federal Highway Administration. This group of advisors was composed of experienced landscape architects, consulting engineers, urban planners, structural engineers, and architects. Such a combination of disciplines brought together by the Federal Highway Administration indicates recognition in mid-decade that a new basis was necessary for the development of urban and interstate freeways.

In the introduction to this 1968 report, which proved to be the source of a number of new federal policies, the Federal Highway Administrator, Lowell K. Bridwell, revealed the extent to which public protest and local community reaction to the highway program had already affected federal policy. He stated:

"Highway transportation cannot be allowed to function apart from or in conflict with its environment. Inevitably, it directly affects the quality of the environment, for better or worse. Inevitably, it interacts with other personal and community aspirations in such areas as conservation of natural beauty, provision of parks and playgrounds, preservation of historic sites, improved housing and schools and neighborhoods, cleaner air, and general community well-being. And inevitably, the potential for conflict between the highway and these other values is greatest in America's densely populated urban areas."[12]

Major recommendations ensued, including design alternatives for depressed,

**42. Oak Street Connector,
New Haven, Connecticut**
Aerial view (right)

**43. Projection of Proposed Throughway,
Connectors, and Enlarged Streets,
New Haven, Connecticut**
Plan (bottom right)
New Haven Redevelopment Authority

The Oak Street Connector in New Haven is a
typical American urban highway of the freeway
building era (Figure 42, right). The city is severed. Its edge becomes a long ribbon unravel-
ing into the countryside along the freeway. Parking
becomes a city problem and a principal com-
petitor for land. Housing for lower-income families is lost forever, or at best for decades. The
daily ebb and flow of commuting produces massive lines of traffic, long time and space separation of work from residence, and a downtown
deprived of maximum potential commercial, retail, and entertainment vitality. If New Haven did
not have Yale University downtown, a massive
employer and generator of funds and activity,
then it, like so many smaller and medium-sized
cities around the country, could have been
sapped fatally by the puncturing gash of the
highway. Compared to the growing life of cities,
the necrosis process is short. An urban freeway
takes about a decade from the decision to build
to the opening of the road. In this case, the decision occurred in 1951, the highway was financed
in 1955, engineered in 1956, constructed in
1957–58, and opened in 1959. Within another
decade this road, like others around the country,
had induced major peripheral development
within New Haven and extensive concomitant
secondary and tertiary land development beyond the city in a wide area. The urban highway
is never an isolated incident (Figure 43, bottom
right). It must be linked to other highways. Heavy
traffic is not dissipated, as originally intended
by the urban freeway; rather, more is generated.
Therefore a network plan is required when a
highway is considered. The network becomes
not only a dominant control over the city, but
also a self-fulfilling prophecy of greater need
for more concrete to contain more traffic.

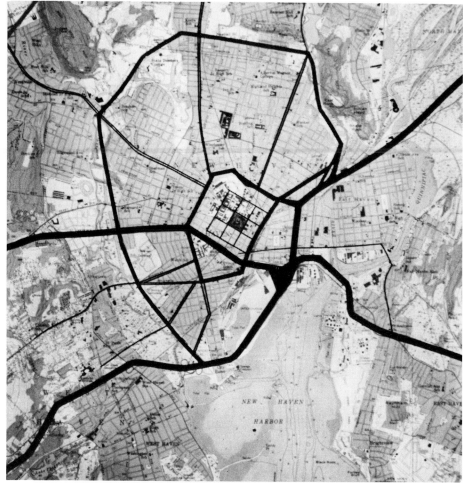

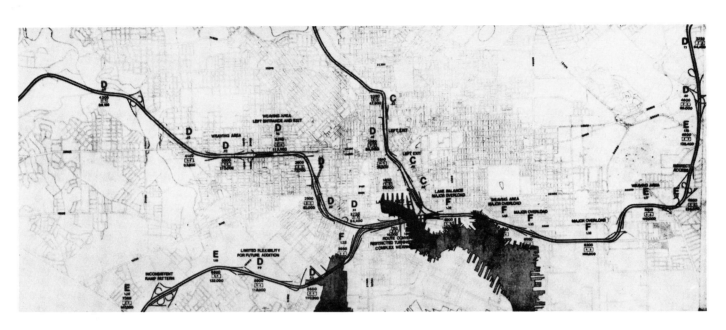

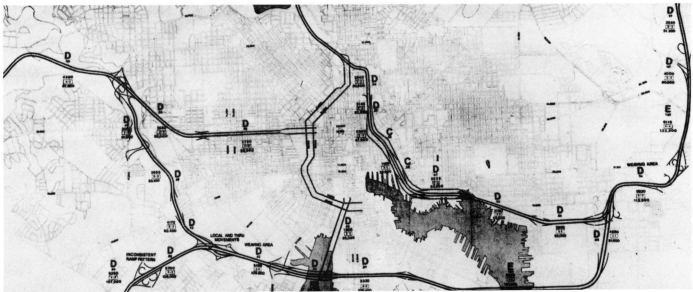

44. Alternative Proposed Urban Highway Networks through the City of Baltimore, 1968. Traffic engineers' diagrams

When traffic engineers deal with roads, they think and calculate and project in terms of "volumes" and "capacities." What is meant by "volume" is traffic (existing and expected); what is meant by "capacity" is the ability of the highway to handle the traffic and keep it moving adequately. Each link in the highway network is evaluated in terms of volume/capacity ratios expressed in letters (like school grades) from "A" to "F." "A" means the traffic flows without restrictions at desired speed; "F" means slow speeds, the highway acting as storage area. The near-New York City parts of the Long Island Expressway, known as "the world's longest parking

lot" is a perfect "F" segment. Mobility desires, when analyzed, show the expected: they show through-traffic needs, especially for commercial vehicles; and they show that by the mid-1960's many people wanted to get to the city from the suburbs to make a living; and to get out again at night in the neatest, straightest line possible. The amazing aspect of traffic engineering during much of the highway building era is that these desires were given absolute preference over desires, say, for people to keep their homes, for urban stores to keep their trade, for people to use their parks. What these diagrams, used in the massive, heavily funded Baltimore high-

way study illustrate, is how remote traffic engineering (even under the relatively enlightened circumstances of the Baltimore Urban Design Concept Team Study) is from the urban context with which it is dealing. The abstraction, required partially by the complex evaluation task the traffic engineer must complete, was rarely complemented until recently by an offsetting evaluation and awareness of the impact a highway causes on people and places. The expedient use of large-scale, two-dimensional aerial maps, which is common practice among traffic engineers, is itself partially responsible for the dissolution of people, streets, and structures.

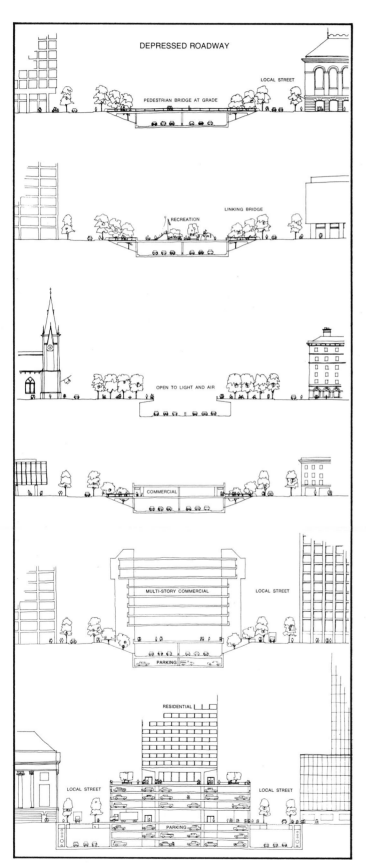

DEPRESSED ROADWAY

LOCAL STREET
PEDESTRIAN BRIDGE AT GRADE

RECREATION
LINKING BRIDGE

OPEN TO LIGHT AND AIR

COMMERCIAL

MULTI-STORY COMMERCIAL
LOCAL STREET
PARKING

RESIDENTIAL
LOCAL STREET
LOCAL STREET
PARKING

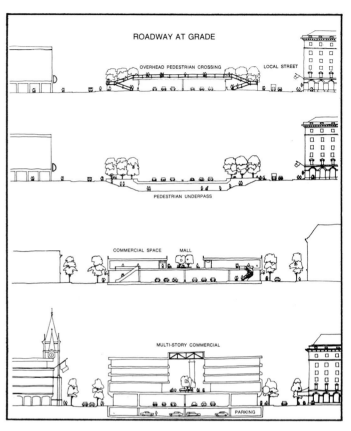

ROADWAY AT GRADE

OVERHEAD PEDESTRIAN CROSSING
LOCAL STREET

PEDESTRIAN UNDERPASS

COMMERCIAL SPACE   MALL

MULTI-STORY COMMERCIAL
PARKING

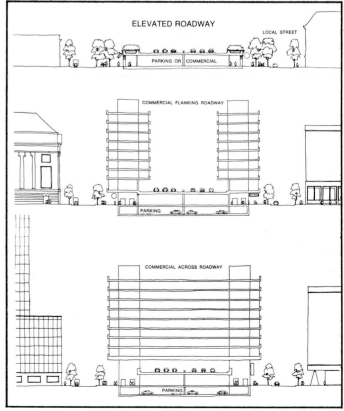

ELEVATED ROADWAY

LOCAL STREET
PARKING OR COMMERCIAL

COMMERCIAL FLANKING ROADWAY
PARKING

COMMERCIAL ACROSS ROADWAY
PARKING

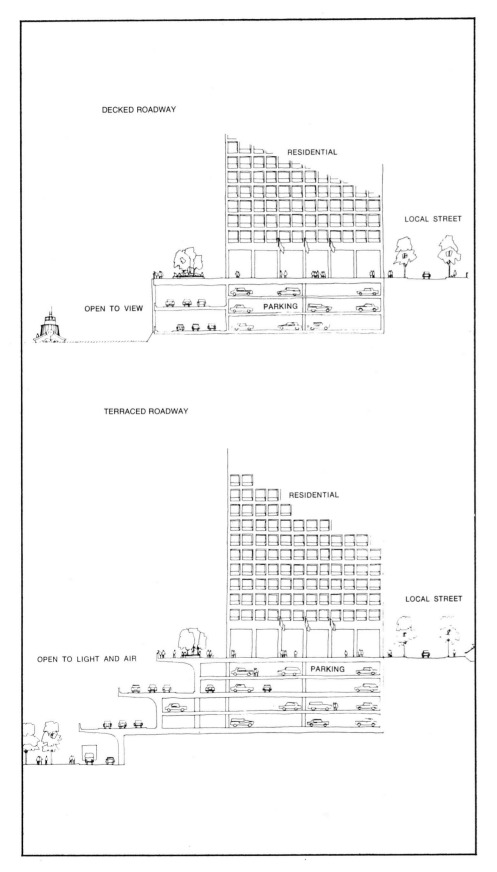

DECKED ROADWAY

RESIDENTIAL

LOCAL STREET

OPEN TO VIEW

PARKING

TERRACED ROADWAY

RESIDENTIAL

LOCAL STREET

OPEN TO LIGHT AND AIR

PARKING

45–49. Alternative Possibilities of Roadway Placement Within the Multi-Use Corridor, 1968
The Urban Advisors to
the Federal Highway Administrator

By 1968, the first handbooks of design possibilities for multiple use of urban freeway corridors began to appear. Situations, opportunities, costs, community attitudes, and road sponsorship for the first time were seen as germane to the built configuration. Alternatives to the naked, wide, fenced concrete runway are presented in "how-to" diagrams. This and other subsequent handbooks for urban multi-use highway corridors which proliferated after 1968 recall the flurry of "how-to" general urban planning books which were compiled in Europe during and just after World War I. Perhaps very thorough destruction is required before the conditions for change exist. Today, these diagrams for multi-use urban freeway corridors continue to be an influential source of design ideas and still cover most of the potential alternatives.

elevated, and at-grade highways (Figures 45–49). In each case the design potential was based on multiple-use possibilities for the corridor itself. For the first time in America it was proposed that the federal government consider highway planning not as an isolated engineering procedure, but in the context of social, political, economic, and physical ramifications. It was suggested that federal authorities "coordinate freeway considerations with the comprehensive planning of every community affected."[13]

Other recommendations developed in the 1968 report, like those cited above, are now the substance of new federal policy. The official Instructional Memoranda issued in 1969 was the crucial directive to:

". . . encourage the multiple utilization of urban freeway rights-of-way. Urban freeway corridors must be more efficiently used to provide urgently needed space for such other purposes as housing, commerce, industry and recreation. This concept envisions the highway as but one occupant of the right-of-way land and the space above or below it. Its planning, if related to renewal, can help structure the city in a more efficient and orderly way. The use of the space beside, below, or above the freeway should be planned and designed at the same time as the freeway itself.

"It is urged that the Department of Housing and Urban Development join with the Department of Transportation in the initiation of a series of major projects demonstrating the possibilities of the imaginative multiple use of freeway corridors. Such projects could become an instrument of developing new procedures, financial aid programs, and enabling legislation."[14]

This recommendation became government policy in 1969. Now, limited federal highway funds are available for feasibility studies, for liaison with local agencies and community groups, and to build mini-parks, recreational facilities, and most significantly, to finance (under certain cir-cumstances) costly platforms over highway rights-of-way to "promote and encourage desirable public and/or private uses of land areas beneath, over and adjacent to the highway."[15]

These first signs of crucial assistance to the planning and implementation of urban freeway areas for the benefit of local residents were coupled with other significant new policy decisions in 1968. Most importantly, after years of unconscionable neglect, it became mandatory to provide adequate and comparable replacement housing to anyone evicted by eminent domain for a highway. In addition, more reasonable if not completely fair financial settlements with individuals dispossessed by a highway right-of-way became customary. These changes, however late, became long-needed new directions in national highway planning by the end of the 1960's.

Recognition by planners and architects that highways in urban areas could be very much better is lamentably late. On the other hand, urban designers, sociologists, and planners with recognized humanistic attitudes were generally kept out of highway route planning, engineering, and design until quite recently— until the traditional highway building groups found they were blocked, in most cases, at the edge of the city.

In recent years, a number of studies have been undertaken by architects working alone or within "urban design concept teams" to determine how highway corridors might better be used, how they might incorporate needed non-highway use through urban places and still solve transportation problems. Many proposals have been put forward in recent years for existing and proposed highways. The Cross-Brooklyn Expressway Plan, a proposal for a "linear city" of schools, housing, and community facilities suspended above a highway to be built over rail tracks, is a characteristic example (Figure 50). The newly developed corridor concept for community facilities between previously separated neighborhoods was announced with great optimism by Mayor Lindsay of New York in 1967 as the "first . . . major new highway being planned as an integral part of an overall community development proposal." But nothing was built; the project was scrapped.

During the same year, the Museum of Modern Art sponsored an exhibition, *The New City: Architecture and Urban Renewal*. It included a study design by Jaquelin T. Robertson, Richard Weinstein, Giovanni Pasanella, Jonathan Barnett, and Myles Weintraub that proposed decking 37 blocks of New Haven railroad tracks and Upper Park Avenue north of 97th Street to the Harlem River to provide a traffic-free pedestrian spine for schools, shops, restaurants, and theaters connected to new mixed-income housing on either side. In the late 1960's, the notion of decking over urban rights-of-way was still new and experimental enough to warrant public display and support by a major cultural institution.

There had, of course, already been some limited development, during the early 1960's and even before, within air rights above highways. Boston's Prudential Center was built over the Massachusetts Turnpike; high-rise apartments in New York straddled the George Washington Bridge aproaches; and there was similar development in Chicago and elsewhere. But these remained single-point enterprises where special circumstances made multi-level air-rights development feasible at one particular place.

The possibility of using an urban highway corridor as a development opportunity, however, was not seriously considered until the mid-1960's. One of the most complete investigations of this kind is clearly Paul Rudolph's Ford Foundation-supported urban design proposal for the Lower Manhattan Expressway and its surrounding area. Rudolph became interested in the problem about 1967, when it still appeared possible that the highway would be built (Figure 51).[16] That Rudolph would use a major public grant to consider the seminal question of the freeway in the city and that The Ford

50. Proposed Linear City above the Cross-Brooklyn Expressway, Brooklyn, New York, 1967

Perspective section. McMillan, Griffis & Mileto (Corde Corporation, Conceptual Development)

This proposal recognizes the use of urban expressway corridors, if properly decked, as newly found urban land. On a deck over the road, public facilities are proposed along a pedestrian mall. The thoroughfare afforded by depressed rail lines and roadways eliminates barriers to community cohesiveness and development.

Changes forced on the national highway construction program through public pressure in the mid-1960's have made federal assistance available for the planning and construction of many urban amenities including places to live, places to learn, and places to enjoy urban life as part of a highway program. In the years ahead,

the substantial funds available for the highway program must be used for more balanced urban transportation programs, including public transit, and for the planning and development of more socially oriented amenities within the cities as a part of urban transportation corridors.

51. Lower Manhattan Expressway Urban Design Proposal, 1973

Perspective section. Paul Rudolph

Rudolph's study of the proposed Lower Manhattan Expressway Corridor is perhaps the most complete and complex ever undertaken for an urban freeway. The route provides an opportunity for decked-over development of needed housing and other facilities within contiguous neighborhoods. The highway is defined by low-rise buildings situated along most of the route and intensive development at major intersections and at the bridge gateways to the city. Transit lines, park spaces, and various public amenities are integrated into the concept. In many places an A-frame system composed of residential modules is proposed as a structural system for both the residential buildings and the highway covering deck. Many crucial details such as ventilation of the highway route, noise, structural vibration insulation, and economic feasibility remain unresolved. Nevertheless, Rudolph's approach foresees a way to bind together previously isolated city fragments and points out potential ways to insert new freeways into older cities.

Foundation by 1968–69 was interested in the project and interested in its investigation by an established architect with a strong design reputation are both clear signals of the very new attitude—backed by great power—that had made itself felt by the end of the 1960's.

In the beginning of the 1970's, it is inconceivable that a new urban highway, no matter how badly needed, could be proposed without attendant "joint-use" propositions intended to provide public, environmental, social, and civic benefits in the corridor. With this new condition comes discovery of the urban highway corridor as a divisive cut in the urban tissue that may be healed with a massive allocation of resources imaginatively deployed for building sites and badly needed public land.

Why has the opportunity for well-planned use of such urban space generally failed to be realized? The answer does not lie in flawed concepts or weak planning. Rather, the problem occurs in economic and social barriers to implementation. A long-span covering deck over a highway is costly. Only rarely are adequate federal and/or local funds available to offset the increased cost. Intricate questions related to neighborhood demands and local disagreement over goals for the highway corridor have been damaging in a number of cases. In others, the complexity of working out shared ownership of air space, unresolved financing, and disagreement concerning maintenance responsibilities among federal, state, municipal, and private interests has stymied implementation. In addition, the proper ventilation of enclosed or decked highway tunnels remains a technical question without an adequate, financially feasible solution.

In the coming decade, new potentials for existing, older urban highways may very well be recognized by alert communities as one of the few ways to obtain substantial planning and development funds from the federal government for large-scale urban projects. The highway program does possess a potential means to improve urban transportation and at the same time to gain needed money for corridor-related urban development.

The revised, updated highway program is certainly not a prescription that will instantly solve urban problems. But it is improving as a program. Local citizens can participate in a number of ways, including in the selection and approval of corridors, and 90 per cent financing from the capital-rich Highway Trust Fund is now available for certain kinds of planning and collateral development within an Interstate Highway corridor.

In addition, in 1972, the highway program was broadened even further so that funds formerly restricted to highway construction became more readily available for public transit and for the planning that accompanies it, as discussed in Chapter 4, "Public Transportation."

We are certainly in the midst, at long last, of public and political awareness that appropriate movement channels and design of what should be over, under, and around them is very different in cities than in the countryside. In the city, the economic reality of relatively expensive land and relatively diversified usage should have made this distinction clear long ago. The social disaster of the highway program was ignored as were the adverse social impacts of other urban federal programs of the 1950's and 1960's. This is more understandable when one recalls the predominantly middle-class suburban and rural political power structure of the country, allied during those years against the then still naively reticent and unorganized city population.

Recently, it has become clear that better design, much greater sensitivity to the physical and social environment, and much more sophisticated cost-benefit economic feasibility analysis, which includes social costs and benefits, must be developed if urban freeways are to be acceptable.

The proposed redevelopment of Manhattan's dilapidated West Side Highway exposes the current situation. The New York State Urban Development Corporation, in collaboration with various city, state, and federal agencies, proposes to rebuild the West Side Highway in two stages; initially from the Battery to 42nd Street, and subsequently from 42nd Street to the George Washington Bridge. The initial segment is now included in federal government plans and budgets for redevelopment as an Interstate Highway. The West Side Highway Project, an assembly of professional representatives of city and state planning agencies in close contact with federal agencies, will recommend quite soon, after several years of study and after required public hearings, what they believe should be done with the first-phase segment. The most promising and most expensive of five alternatives now under study, of those which include rebuilding the massive highway, is known as the "outboard alignment" (Figures 52–54). The now-elevated road would be moved "outboard" into the Hudson River and built in a below-grade-level tunnel, out of sight. Such a costly proposal would never have been studied, much less proposed by a highway engineering and design consortium, even five years ago.

Along with the highway, several of the alternatives project the inclusion of a transit line. The potential for transit should be studied with care. Much of the transit right-of-way is already there, along the Penn Central freight tracks. In addition, implementation of the transit line is not inconceivable, even without a redeveloped highway. Through the new and as yet untested, "interstate transfer" provision of the Federal Highway Act of 1973, cities and states may now get a credit for unused interstate highway funds and thereafter apply to use this money for rail facilities and for transit passenger equipment.

Along with the new, possibly depressed highway, planners calculate it would be possible to create over 400 acres of new land along the entire corridor. This landfill area along the edge of the present city could be used for a wide variety of purposes, including housing, recreation, community facilities, and new piers. Who

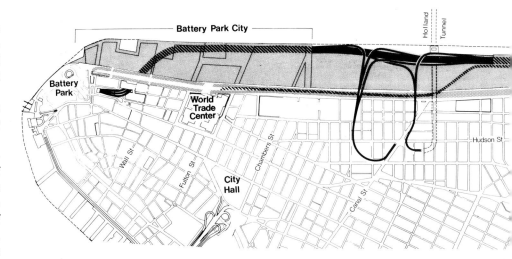

TYPICAL CORRIDOR STREET LOOKING WEST SHOWING EXISTING ELEVATED
WEST SIDE HIGHWAY AND A PIER HEADHOUSE

"Outboard" Proposal, plan (left)
Perspective sketches (lower left)

Highway Uncovered
Highway Covered Depressed
Frontage Road
Landfill
Transit Route

Hudson River

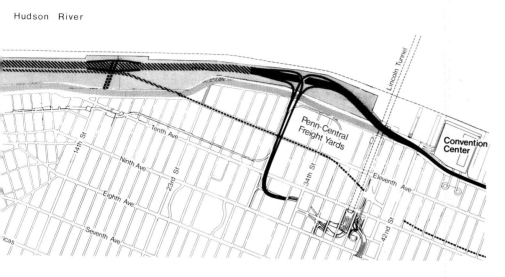

SAME STREET WITH DEPRESSED "OUTBOARD" ALIGNMENT

The West Side Highway along the Hudson River in Manhattan may be entirely rebuilt. Five alternatives are being considered. One of these involves simple maintenance of the existing highway; one involves removing and rebuilding the superstructure alone; one involves removing the superstructure and replacing it with a boulevard at grade. The final two alternatives are to replace the road with an interstate highway, either in the bed of West Street or in a so-called "outboard alignment." Of the massive *Interstate* redevelopment proposals that have received most of the planners' attention, the most promising for the area south of 42nd Street is to move the highway from its present location and sink it below the river in a concrete waterproof box (Figure 52, left). This becomes feasible by first building a cofferdam to contain the river, then sinking the new roadway in and backfilling over the concrete casing. One result, as shown in (Figures 53, 54, lower left) is to open the city and its vistas to the water again. Another, because of the backfilling and decking over the road, is to extend the edge of the city outward from its present edge, West Street. It is estimated that this solution would provide 250–350 acres of new land in Manhattan between Battery Park and 42nd Street. It is also estimated that such an agreeable solution to a structurally dangerous elevated and blighting urban highway would cost around one billion dollars. A major issue which must be resolved, if an outboard plan is ever to be built, is who controls the new land: the city, local planning groups, a special public authority, or private developers to whom it might be leased or even sold. These and others are each possible alone or in combination. Also, what will be permitted to take place on the new land? And what assurance can be made that the publicly paid for and publicly created land will serve basic objectives of the city, as opposed to personal objectives of special vested interests? These issues must be clearly exposed and well resolved if this costly redevelopment scheme is to move forward. The very best alternative may very well be simply to rebuild the highway to accommodate present traffic through 50–50 sharing financial programs available from the federal government. In trade for 90 per cent federal funding offered in the Interstate program, access to truck traffic must be accepted. Some estimate that an interstate highway (unless encased in a tunnel) besides producing greatly increased air and noise pollution would increase the current vehicle load on the road. So the Interstate alternative has some flaws. A number of the highway alternatives contain a new bus or rail transit line. Through the "interstate transfer" provision of the Highway Act of 1973, funds could be made available for a transit line and passenger equipment as an alternative to the Interstate Highway.

would control this land and the ground rules for disposing of it are, of course, matters of crucial importance.

All proposed alignments and configurations thus far remain flawed, however, by inadequate resolution of the visual and aural impact of the proposed project on Frederick Law Olmstead's linear, heavily used Riverside Park and its surrounding residential neighborhoods. It is in all likelihood impossible, because of recent success by citizens in obtaining restraining legislation in Albany, that the highway could be built to Interstate standards through Riverside Park. Indeed, local residents have gained such power in the highway planning process quite recently that the City of New York is now providing funds to neighborhood Community Planning Boards the entire length of Manhattan so that each Board may hire its own consultant to analyze and comment on the redevelopment proposals. Thus the federal government and the State of New York, through the State Department of Transportation, would like to rebuild the large, snake-like urban-edge highway. The city isn't sure. Some interests in the city want the old highway to be improved and expanded. Other interests don't. Residents are all organized, to some extent, through the Community Planning Boards and various independent committees. The outcome is to be watched. If anything is built, it certainly will not be a traditional urban highway independent of myriad "social benefits" to the city's residents. Indeed, the West Side Highway, if rebuilt to new standards, is likely to be exploited more thoroughly for community and public benefit than any roadway in this country has ever been before. Whether these standards will be adequate, whom they will really serve, and other social, economic, and environmental questions remain to be answered.

Whether and where new highways or additional freeways are needed in most urban areas is a different question altogether, one which warrants the most intensive examination. Decisions taken, even in the improved context now prevailing for highway construction, will affect city arrangement, local life style, land development patterns, and the disposition of public transit for years to come.

New Directions

Urban highways dissipate tightly built urban centers.

The movement of people, not vehicles, must become the first priority of urban transportation planning.

Highway planning must be thoroughly integrated with total community development objectives.

Existing urban highway and rail corridors now hold promise for development of public facilities and amenities by conversion to multi-use, multi-level linear districts.

Transportation facilities must be planned by teams of professionals including urban designers, not by engineers alone.

Problems of administration, financing, ventilation, and engineering of multi-level, multi-use transportation corridors should receive priority attention.

55. The Subway, 1950
George Tooker
Egg tempera on composition board, 18½" × 36⅛"

Using most older urban public transit in America
is a choice of last resort. It is generally poorly
located, inconvenient to reach, overcrowded,
environmentally unacceptable in terms of light,
temperature, and sound, and generally depres-
sing, as expressed in this painting by George
Tooker. In addition, the badly repaired, unat-
tractive, dimly lit New York subway stations and
their maze of security gates, iron railings, and
narrow stairways do convey a sense of unpleasant enclosure, even entrapment in a chaotic and
temporary urban jail, involuntarily entered and
gladly left.

Public Transportation

In conjunction with new attitudes toward the city street and the freeway during the 1960's, a shift in urban transportation possibilities emerged. It became clear that the traffic jam, ever growing, would not dissolve with wider and more roads. It was proven by a number of tragically vivisected cities that freeways can only reach downtown if downtown becomes a magnificently engineered, multi-tiered interchange. A solution exists: more, better, and different kinds of public transportation.

Public transportation is not new to America. Numerous forms were common in the 19th and early 20th centuries and did much to shape certain cities. But most transit networks were originally private business speculations, investment boondoggles, and parts of land development schemes. The urban trolleys and elevated rails had similar sources.

With the automobile came a new scenario. The car offered door-to-door convenience and total route flexibility. It got less and less expensive as mass production became more sophisticated. It began to compete with revenues and profitability of public transport lines. Simultaneously, after being used for speculation or land development, public transit lines (which were usually privately owned) were allowed to deteriorate.

During the last decade, transit systems everywhere in America have been languishing under the combined disadvantages of stabilized or declining use and sharply rising operating costs. Between 1956 and 1966, for instance, the number of motor vehicles in the United States increased 24 million, while transit patronage declined by 3 billion riders, or 25 per cent. And the trend continues. So does the deterioration of the service, equipment, and experience on most urban transit systems. Today, most people's experience with urban transit is not far from that depicted by George Tooker in his painting *The Subway* (Figure 55).

Yet in the 1960's, new interest in public transportation appeared, and new studies of transportation policies and transportation economics were given significant priority for the first time. The United States government, through the Department of Housing and Urban Development (HUD) and the Department of Transportation (DOT), investigated methods of transforming transportation in urban areas of the United States. In 1966, amendments to the Urban Mass Transportation Act of 1964 called specifically for the Secretary of the Department of Housing and Urban Development to study and prepare a program of research, development, and demonstration of new systems of urban transportation. The "New Systems Study," involved 18 months of research and analysis under the auspices of HUD during 1967 and 1968, the same years that the highway program was at a watershed, as discussed earlier. Focus was on the most advanced available technologies and materials.[17] These studies do not suggest that an immediate balance in urban transportation is even possible. They do identify innovative devices for urban areas such as moving pedestrian belts, mini-trains, mini-buses, and the like. A large number of "urban mass transportation demonstration projects" devised to discover and test new and better uses of buses, commuter trains, and rail rapid transit have also been pursued in recent years.[18] Not one of these projects was funded before 1960. The great majority have been allocated funds only in the last five years. And many are only now being evaluated.

Studies of transit possibilities, even the development of new hardware through demonstration grants, do not lead quickly to change. No one has yet devised a way to make public transit profitable, and profit is the motivation that in America produces quick action. On the contrary, transit equipment is exceedingly expensive. Transit operations have traditionally (but not necessarily) required a large labor force and with that goes a large price tag. Rights-of-way in urban areas, if not already owned, are almost impossible to obtain. And, most retarding of all, there is a very strong resistance among automobile owners and their agents, who run the streets and highways of the city, to permit any more of the once public right-of-way to be made available to public transit vehicles and devices. Indeed, as astonishing as it may sound, and exceptions do exist on short route segments, commuter transit buses are still not even allowed to use most parkways, highways, and freeways into many cities.

Nevertheless, in recent years the second age of bus and rail public transit in America has begun. For instance, in San Francisco, in spite of some technical difficulties, the first new urban rail system in 60 years in this country recently opened for business. The Bay Area Rapid Transit (BART) network will eventually serve most of the San Francisco metropolitan area. In New York, after 30 years of delay, squandering of funds, and insufficient political and social pressure, a subway is being constructed under Second Avenue to link parts of Queens and the Bronx to Manhattan. The new Lindenwold rail commuter line from Philadelphia to the South New Jersey suburbs began service in 1969 and now carries 42,000 riders daily, 40 per cent of whom are former automobile commuters.

In Washington, work is underway on the Washington Metropolitan Transit Authority's 98-mile subway system that is expected by 1979 to link downtown

Washington with Maryland and Virginia. Miami now has plans for a 59-mile, fully automated, elevated high-speed rail transit system to be constructed in the late 1970's, which is projected to carry 400,000 passengers daily. Boston has recently stopped superhighway construction and completed expansion of its rail transit lines to Quincy. Other transit programs are under study there. In November 1971, residents in Atlanta and surrounding regions accepted a one per cent regional sales tax to raise the local share of funds necessary to improve bus service throughout the region and to inaugurate planning for a regional rail system. In September of 1973, voters approved financing for a $1.56 billion regional public transit system that will operate in six counties in and around Denver, Colorado. Baltimore and Buffalo have new transit systems in advanced planning stages. And in cities throughout the country, experimental use of new bus routes, exclusive bus lanes on highways, and other measures to improve transit and thus induce more riders to use the systems are underway or planned. Moreover, the recent evidence of national and international shortages of gasoline is likely to further accelerate planning and development of transit systems.

By 1972, interest in transit reached sufficient intensity in the United States that the first international conference and exhibition was held on the subject in Washington, D.C. It was called Transpo '72, the First United States International Transportation Exposition, and was sponsored jointly by most public and private agencies, associations, and societies involved with transportation. Besides conferences on many transportation-related subjects during the week-long event, detailed displays were mounted at Dulles International Airport of new transit vehicles, hardware, and equipment. Such a conference and international exposition would not have been held in this country and given major support by the United States Department of Transportation until very recently.

On an administrative level, promising changes have been made in federal and state government. Within HUD, the Urban Transportation Administration was established recently to provoke and promote a renewal of public transportation in urban areas. In 1968, the United States Department of Transportation (DOT) was formed. As a component of DOT the Urban Transportation Administration was transferred from HUD and reconstituted as the Urban Mass Transit Administration (UMTA). Now, for the first time in this country, a federal department is funded explicitly to support and control all transportation. Within it, a major division is charged with the development and extension of transit services in urban areas.

In 1970, the first federally approved mass transit subsidy bill became law. A sum of $3.1 billion spread over five years was designated to revive or build subway and bus systems across the nation. This is a beginning. But the amount is pitifully small in comparison with the magnitude of national need, and the schedule of fund distribution is unsatisfactory. Evidence indicates that an outlay of at least $10 billion over four years is needed to redeem the nation's mass transit systems and make public transit truly attractive and convenient.

In the summer of 1973, another major initial gain for the support of urban transit throughout the country was achieved in the Highway Act of 1973. Through provisions in the Act, a portion of the massive Federal Highway Trust Fund was earmarked for urban transit—for the first time. For almost 20 years this fund, stocked annually by federal taxes on gasoline, tires, and truck tonnage, had been restricted to road-building uses. A major shift in political emphasis and public priorities is at least symbolically displayed in the long, much publicized, and hard-fought penetration of these funds by groups interested in transit.

But the terms of the new three-year, $23 billion highway bill reveal how minimal the gesture is to urban transit. In year one, no funds may be used for transit. In year two, $300 million will become available; in year three, $800 million is to be used for transit. Thus, over three years, only about $1 billion is even potentially available from the Fund in all 50 states for capital spending on buses, rail systems, or subways. And, as in the past, these funds might not actually be released by the federal government. In addition, no funds may be used for maintenance or operating subsidies, both badly needed if older urban transit systems are to improve, or in some cases even survive. An additional $3 billion is allocated in the bill from general revenue funds for mass transit grants to urban areas. Additional funds can, for the first time, be claimed through the "interstate transfer" provision of the Highway Act of 1973. This provision allows states and cities to waive their rights to Interstate Highway money from the federal Highway Trust Fund and to obtain instead general funds from the United States Treasury for transit equipment. The transfer concept is still untested. And the approval process to obtain transfer funds as initially outlined is laborious, time-consuming, and expensive. Also, there is a specific limit to this "contractual obligation of the United States," as detailed in the new act. The total amount available to the transit line cannot exceed the amount that an alternative segment of Interstate Highway would have cost in 1972. This is, of course, a severe limitation. In addition, the federal matching share of the project drops from 90 per cent to 80 per cent.

Even with these various new provisions in the recent Highway Act, about 80 per cent of the funds, or some $19 billion of the $23 billion, remains basically restricted to construction of interstate freeways, urban highways, and rural and secondary roads. Indeed, rural and secondary roads alone, which serve only a small fraction of the number of people who use urban transit, are allocated nearly the same amount of funding support as is national transit. But the precedent is set. The trend is clear. The political power is shifting and the successful invasion of the Highway Trust

Fund after years of negotiating by pro-city transit forces reveals the shift. The next time around, a greater emphasis on transit is predictable.

Even though some progress is evident in obtaining new funds for new transit construction or purchase of new equipment, little progress has been made in gaining federal assistance for transit operating subsidies. Without them, more than 230 local transit systems have collapsed in the past two decades. With them, dramatic increases in patronage have quite recently been proven possible. For instance, after Atlanta reduced transit fares from 40 cents to 15 cents, patronage increased dramatically. When a subsidy allowed San Diego to lower mass transit fares from 40 cents to 25 cents, use of the system shot up an astonishing 72 per cent. But few cities are capable of subsidizing transit in a meaningful way, and it is not likely that their ability to do so will increase in years to come. Meaningful federal and state subsidies geared to sustaining and expanding transit service in the cities should be a national funding priority. Such a program could even serve as an incentive to cities. If subsidies were tied to increased transit patronage, cities might work to improve local planning efforts and realize urban design concepts that connect new and renewed urban development to the transit ways of the city. These badly needed subsidies could also assist urban areas in meeting standards laid down by the Clean Air Act and save enormous amounts of fuel and energy, now wasted by overuse of the private automobile.

Inter-urban rail transportation, too, is being publicly supported for the first time in America. The National Rail Passenger Corporation (Amtrak) was established in 1970 as a quasi-government corporation to take over and run essential intercity passenger trains in areas of high-density travel when the alternative is service abandonment.

This non-profit corporation is a mechanism to assure the continuation of some passenger rail service in critical corridors, to improve selected roadbeds, and to acquire badly needed new rolling stock. Obviously, it is also a way for once monopolistic, now moribund private corporations to be bailed out by the federal government.

Operations began May 1, 1971. But Amtrak, at least so far, has not extended intercity rail service. Indeed, quite the opposite has been the case. When Amtrak was first established and initially funded, over half of the nation's intercity trains were immediately discontinued. The new network continued a trend of sharp contraction of rail passenger service, trimming the national total of passenger trains in daily operation to only 180, serving about 300 cities. As a comparison, over 350 such trains were in service at the beginning of 1970, nearly 500 during 1969 and 20,000 at the peak of rail passenger service in the late 1920's.

Amtrak then is clearly a rescue operation to let private owners out of the unprofitable rail passenger business and to still maintain a network of the most heavily used passenger trains. Success requires stabilization of service, securing of adequate public funds for subsidies, and stimulation of demand for train service through major improvements in performance and quality.

In 1973, there is no evidence that the rescue operation is really working. The federal administration has recently recommended a 14 per cent reduction in the remaining 26,300-mile network, which would leave medium-size cities such as Louisville, Nashville, Columbus, and Dayton without any passenger train service.

Amtrak does not actually run the railroads. It pays their deficits, and additionally, guarantees the railroad companies a 9 per cent profit above operating costs. This national adventure in subsidized intercity rail transit lost only $153 million in its first full year of operations and a $124 million deficit is forecast for 1972–73 operations. The loss is expected to decline to under $100 million next year. Consider this comparison: a three-year loss of roughly $375 million will be experienced by Amtrak at the outset. This deficit is the justification used for continued reduction of service. And yet the new federal highway bill allocates some $19 billion for roads and highways in three years, or roughly *50* times the funds budgeted for intercity railroads. At the same time, because of relatively small losses incurred by Amtrak, demand is persistently made to curtail service, a service that functions as a major alternative to highway use and to new highway building. If significant funding levels were allocated to inter-urban rail transit, enough to permit new, modern, fast, comfortable equipment coupled with frequent schedules, a network of major regional rail systems could be developed, and the costly highway program could be curtailed. The result might very well be better service for more people, better environmental conditions, and better allocation of our national economic and natural resources.

The promise of inter-urban rail, I suggest, is in short and intermediate distance trips—trips of one to six hours, such as the New York–Boston TurboTrain run (Figure 56)—which can service regions extending over 600 miles. The experience of the few recently modernized regional lines such as the Lindenwold in Philadelphia and the Skokie in Chicago suggests that strongly increased patronage can be attracted to transit with good equipment and desirable schedules; concurrent improvement in the economics of operation are also experienced. Only the proper public commitment is needed. And manifest public support for an *alternative* to more traffic lanes, huge cloverleafs, acres of downtown parking, and mindboggling traffic jams can make it possible.

At the state and regional levels, new government agencies were developed during the late 1960's and early 1970's to ensure redevelopment and continuance of urban public transportation, often with an emphasis on region-wide service rather than the traditional limiting and irrelevant strictures of city and town boundaries. The New York Metropolitan Transportation Authority (MTA), an agency of wide

56. TurboTrain
United Aircraft Corporation

The Turbo Train, which now runs between Boston-New York and Montreal-Toronto, is a high-speed intercity passenger train operating on standard tracks. It is powered, not by electricity as conventional intercity and commuter trains are, but by aircraft-type gas turbine engines. The train is designed to be unusually comfortable, to make travel agreeable to the passenger. It is engineered to have fast acceleration, high cruising speeds and a balanced banking system—all to cut travel time between stops. Because it is made of lightweight materials and driven by highly efficient turbine engines, its exhaust effluents are only about one-fourth those of internal combustion engines of equal horsepower. Thus the TurboTrain travels on existing rights-of-way between cities, but it does so at high speed, at reduced pollution levels, and with considerable passenger comfort. Such competitive advances in interurban travel promise to reduce future dependence on cars and on short-haul air travel, which itself still generally requires large amounts of energy consumption and automobile trips to and from airports. The promise of linking regional centers one to another and cities within a region one to another with convenient, desirable, effective transit should be pursued on a far wider scale in years to come. Reduced congestion, reduced interruption of the land, reduced dissolution of settlement patterns, reduced pollution all occur. So does increased convenience for people and a rational network upon which an orderly development pattern may be based within urbanized regions.

power and comprehensive responsibilities for public transportation in the New York City metropolitan area, was established on March 1, 1968. Since then, $2.5 billion has been authorized for public transportation by a statewide bond issue. This, the largest bond issue ever approved by voters, is indicative that public transportation developed by local public agencies is an idea whose time has come. Through formulated policies and MTA-funded studies, the means of extending and improving public transportation in the New York metropolitan area are being explored and implemented for the first time in half a century. And, perhaps even more indicative, in 1971, three years after the initial transit bond issue was passed, a second State Transportation Bond Issue of similar magnitude was defeated in spite of immense support at all levels of government because, in large measure, the public felt that an inadequate proportion of funds was in fact earmarked for transit as opposed to highways.

In 1973, New York State attempted to get another transportation bond issue approved. This time the amount was $3.5 billion. But this time the majority of funds, over $2 billion, was designated for transit. The bond issue was actually defeated, but the shift from less than half for transit in 1971 to more than half for transit in 1973 indicates how the political and social wind is blowing.

In addition, in New York and New Jersey strong pressure is being placed on the Port Authority, for the first time since it was set up in 1921, to actively fund and support mass transit. If 1962 covenants against support of transit contained in Port Authority bonds can be removed, as has been courageously, persistently, and effectively argued by Theodore W. Kheel, then some $1 to $3 billion could be freed for mass transit in the New York metropolitan area. The covenants were slapped on the Authority's bonds as a protective measure by its own conservative administration in 1963. A decade later, opposition to these restrictions is growing and public attitudes are changing. Lately

57. Future Transit Way, 1970
Westinghouse Electric Corporation

These sketches illustrate direct linkage from a high-speed rail movement system into the destination by the use of clean, quiet electric equipment. Possibilities of this sort of service at upper levels through cities are still unfortunately remote. There is still no recognized public right-of-way other than the conventional street. Moreover, power supplies in older places are already overtaxed. It takes over a decade for new communities to generate enough travel demand to support a high-speed rail transit way. So old and new cities continue to grow without the expensive but ultimately desirable ingredient of initially planned public transportation to link the environs to the center city. After all, we are still in an age when it is considered very progressive to reserve medians in highway corridors for possible highway expansion or for future public transportation. These, of course, are not the answer. They enforce patterns of development, just as the highway does—linear sprawl.

even Governor Rockefeller, perhaps sensing a new political trend, has joined in denouncing the segregation of Port Authority funds earned on the region's bridges, tunnels, land and sea transportation, as well as on various privileged real estate holdings, from assistance to the region's public transportation.

New York State is not alone in organizing for transit. Although over 230 local transit *systems* have collapsed in the last two decades, there are more than 140 local transit *authorities* in the United States today. This is twice as many as eight years ago and seven times the number in 1945. The systems previously created, which are traditionally independently operated, are declining. But the number that combine into public authorities is increasing.

New directions in technology and design of transportation systems are also emerging for the first time in decades, in large part as a result of the urban mass transit Research and Demonstration Grants mentioned previously. New systems and hardware ideas cover the whole range of transit demand from transcontinental and intercity travel to the localized need of intracity urban trips and even very specialized requirements satisfied by escalators or horizontal moving pedestrian ways. For instance, a so-called Future Transit Way has been proposed which can enter an apartment or office building to link directly with escalators and elevators (Figure 57). An elevated, three-mile, 10-station modernized transit system circling lower Manhattan has been recommended recently after exhaustive professional study. Moving pedestrian conveyors or "people movers" as they are sometimes called, which function effectively within and outside of buildings, have been updated since their vogue in the late 19th and early 20th centuries. These are in fact finally appearing in some subway stations, large amusement park areas such as Walt Disney World's Tomorrowland, and in carefully planned proposals for dense urban areas (Figures 58, 74). In addition, at heavily used and increasingly dispersed airports, moving horizontal pedestrian conveyors (Denver and elsewhere) as well as trains run on rails and rubber tires (Houston, Tampa, Seattle, Fort Worth, and so on) are operative or planned (Figures 59–61). These closed-area systems at airports may very well provide important testing grounds for the development of similar devices in busy parts of cities within the next several years. The system used in Seattle is already being adapted by Westinghouse for an urban transit line in Pittsburgh.

When totally random movement is a goal for use in existing city streets, a wide variety of devices similar to electric golf carts and small, wheeled electric automobiles are now often proposed and some are actually available.

When systems that cannot move at random (fixed guideway systems) are desirable for use in existing city streets, other types of equipment have been proposed and some of it tested quite recently. One such system, a low-slung enclosed electric surface vehicle known as "caravan," has been studied recently for New York by Mary Hommann (Figure 34). Numerous other types of urban public transit systems which operate on grade level are being designed and evaluated; some are now actively promoted by manufacturers (Figures 62, 63).

Such emphasis on exhaust-free, enjoyable-to-ride, and innovative public transportation is very much a product of the last half of the last decade. Between 1965 and 1970, a number of systems were developed by manufacturers with federal grants; some of these obtained large-scale public exposure at the World's Fairs in Brussels and Montreal as well as at international trade expositions and large amusement parks such as Disney World and Disneyland. For instance, at Expo '67 in Montreal, electric mini-trains delivered grateful passengers directly to their destinations—in some cases to the interiors of buildings (Figures 64, 65). At Disney World, the most exciting New Town in America, a sleek monorail whisks visitors several miles from hotel interior

to exposition grounds.

The completely new city of EPCOT, now in preliminary stages near Disney World in Florida, is to be serviced by radial transit lines which converge and mesh with local transit in a gigantic transportation center that serves as the center of the city (Figure 67). This principle of organization around transit lines was propounded for many of the French 19th-century utopic and futuristic cities. It still makes sense for a new city; and it is still unfortunately nearly impossible for an older one.

World's Fairs of the last century, of course, often displayed innovative public transportation devices, especially moving pedestrian conveyors. Indeed, one proposed as early as 1887 by Eugène Hénard

for use at the 1889 *Exposition Universelle* penetrated World's Fair structures to provide visitors with an effortless overview of the fairgrounds and buildings (Figure 68). Pedestrian conveyors were actually used and praised at the Chicago World Columbian Exposition in 1893; and an elevated moving pedestrian platform route through the 1900 *Exposition Universelle* at Paris was thoroughly enjoyed, heavily used by visitors, and highly praised by critics (Figure 69). Twenty-five years earlier, an inventive proposal to link actual urban areas together with a moving elevated pedestrian belt was made by Harold Speer for lower Broadway in Manhattan (Figure 70).

Throughout the 19th century, bridges

58. Chatelet Métro Station, Paris

This pedestrian conveyor runs approximately 440 feet horizontally below ground to connect two subway lines. On it people are transported effortlessly in a continuous movement system which handles parcels and luggage as easily as it does people. The soft rubber flooring and side walls make the ride comfortable and safe.

Many pedestrian conveyors are now appearing where very heavy demand and luggage or package transport requirements coincide. The latest regional airports and huge suburban shopping centers increasingly include internal moving pedestrian platforms.

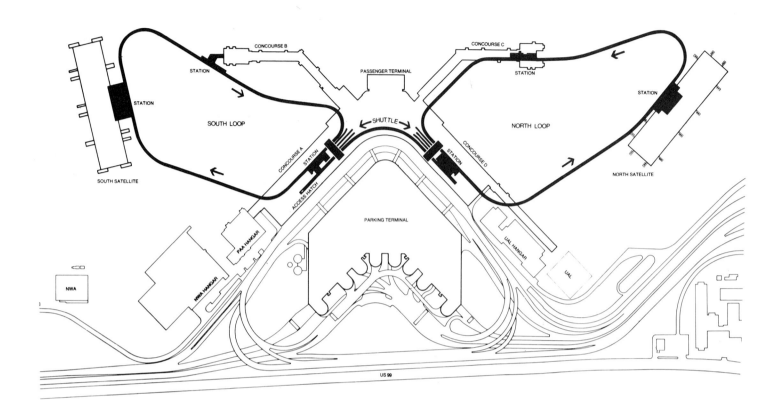

59–60. Transit System for Sea-Tac International Airport, Seattle, 1973
Route plan (above)
Transit car (right)
Westinghouse Electric Corporation

An underground closed transit loop links satellite air terminals to parking areas (Figure 59, above). This fixed route shuttle facilitates short trips with heavy luggage (Figure 60, right). It also makes more rational development of an airport facility possible. Similar technology, now thoroughly tested at airports around the country (at Tampa International Airport a similar device has carried over 25 million passengers since it began operation in 1971) could be adapted for use in urban centers. Indeed, a transit line based on Seattle's equipment is now being planned for Pittsburgh. These small, rubber-tired cars operate in a fixed guideway that could be established in cities on the streets themselves. The technology is ready. The streets are there. Fixed routes could be established and along them intense urban development and redevelopment might be concentrated. The peripheral parking dock, not unlike Kahn's notion of the 1950's (Figure 19) becomes all the more possible. The residential, commercial, retail, entertainment, cultural, and business activities which constitute the city can be conveniently clustered in specific districts if such a transit device is used.

61–63. Rapid Transit Cars
Dashaveyor (left)
The Bendix Corporation
Personal Rapid Transit (center)
Transportation Technology, Inc.
Dual-Mode Airtrans, 1973 (bottom left)
LTV Aerospace Corporation

Small-scale transit modules which operate within a fixed guideway are promising. They can be inserted directly into the existing urban street. No buildings need be lost, no people dislocated, no costly and disruptive tunneling is required. Noise and air pollution drops dramatically and mobility increases for more people. Much of the street could then be liberated from car, truck, bus, and taxi for public purposes, for display, for all sorts of other possible uses. Equipment is already available which could be used. The Bendix Corporation's Dashaveyor is a guideway-controlled vehicle which accommodates 12 seated or 20 standing passengers and obtains a speed of 20 miles per hour (Figure 61, left). Transportation Technology, Inc., has developed a Personal Rapid Transit vehicle which travels on air cushions in a guideway (Figure 62, center). It can travel at ground level, along the side of a building, or even through one. Its objective is to provide passengers safe, convenient, secure, nonstop service directly from origin to destination. For the immense Dallas/Fort Worth Airport the LTV Aerospace Corporation has designed a dual-mode transit system it calls Airtrans (Figure 63, bottom left). One type is restricted to a guideway like the Westinghouse System. But the same cars may be fitted with an operator, steering wheel, and auxiliary power to make them capable of random movement on ordinary streets.

64–65. American Pavilion
at Expo '67, Montreal
Geodesic Dome and Mini-Train (above)
Buckminster Fuller
Interior (right)
Cambridge Seven Associates, Inc.

A huge exhibition space is served by an
elevated, electric mini-train. Spectators ride
through the exhibition to acquire an overview
effortlessly, or use the mini-train as transportation directly into the building (Figure 64, above).
World's Fair schemes have a way of being good
ideas that don't become a part of the lasting
scheme of things. This is as true of buildings as
it is of organization and transportation concepts,
such as this one which implies a desirable relationship between buildings and the means of
getting into them on public transit. The gap is
explained by the fact that large exhibitions are
well financed instant cities, underwritten privately or by government agencies for short-
term publicity. Everything works for a while,
and doesn't have to function for very long. All
things are new together at once, not organically
and incrementally, the way towns and cities are
established, rather, with instant need to dazzle,
move, and feed thousands of people a day. So
the World's Fairs in which such remarkable
physical events occur present a glimpse of what
might be possible if one suspended realities
of time, ordinary growth, and conventional
financing.

66. Monorail and Contemporary Resort Hotel
Walt Disney World, Florida

Today the elevated three-mile circuit monorail at Disney World links parking facilities, recreational areas, hotels, and the Magic Kingdom theme park. The silent electric monorail train stops inside the Contemporary Resort Hotel. People's destination becomes the transit stop. The structure of motion and the structure of enclosure are integrated in this, the most exciting and most carefully planned new town in the world. The monorail system at Walt Disney World makes a 2,500-acre domain conveniently, comfortably, and quickly accessible to people. It also helps to establish, at station points, activity development zones with easy access by people. Other areas can be selectively reserved for open space, land conservation, and less intensive activity of other sorts, by the simple device of omitting a station stop. It is often forgotten that elevated rail lines have been built right into and through commercial warehouses in cities. The remains of such a line still link many of the older warehouse buildings on Manhattan's West Side. Similar imaginative planning for transit as an integral part of enclosed spaces is altogether possible in urban areas. Implementation of the plan, however, though highly desirable, requires a confluence of fortunate circumstances. Buildings and transit ways must be developed simultaneously. Intense use must be assured to warrant high hardware and maintenance costs. Development capital must be found in the public sector to support most transit construction and operating subsidies are also generally necessary. For elevated transit ways, substantial engineering issues, including proper construction of the supporting beams to allow adequate lighting to streets below, must be dealt with. Convenient access is resolved by situating stations within buildings themselves. Then the elevator becomes the means of access to the elevated monorail. And people working, shopping, and living both above and below the right-of-way can use it conveniently.

67. EPCOT, Transportation Lobby, 1966
Walt Disney Productions

Walt Disney, as a part of the total concept of the use of a nearly 28,000-acre holding in central Florida, always intended an experimental new town. His "Experimental Prototype Community of Tomorrow" (EPCOT) is seen as an idea in constant transition. Its initial if somewhat vague concept focuses on a vertical core composed of a sequence of multi-level platforms which contain transportation nodes, shopping and community services. A sense of the city center as the place that integrates serving elements and served spaces is vividly portrayed. Such intense integration and clustering of urban elements, Disney realized, would also assist in preserving a 7,500-acre tract as a nature area.

68. Proposed Train Continu (below)
1889 Exposition Universelle, Paris. Eugène Hénard

A guideway through the World's Fair exhibition grounds is proposed with open and covered seating pavilions for long excursions and standing room for short trips. The entire fair would have been observable from the pedestrian conveyor as it moved through principal exposition buildings, in this case the *Galarie des Machines*.

69. The Moving Sidewalk (bottom)
1900 Exposition Universelle, Paris

This elevated moving pedestrian sidewalk was one of the great successes of the 1900 World's Fair. People enjoyed the large exhibition without exhausting themselves. It is surely time that moving conveyors, now proven for 70 years, become commonplace, providing greater convenience and the potential for much improved urban design wherever people carrying packages move in dense crowds or for distances too long to walk and too short to necessitate fast transit.

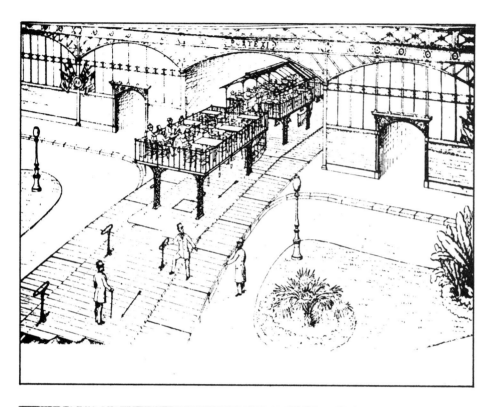

70. Elevated Moving Sidewalk Planned for Lower Broadway, New York, 1874. Harold Speer

One can imagine, as Harold Speer did, a great moving pedestrian belt outfitted with pavilions and observation posts as an exhilarating, quiet, clean way for people to move to their destinations above the clutter and congestion of the street surface. Notice that this suggestion for Broadway includes provision for pedestrian entrances directly into buildings one story above the street. The roadway below is freed for surface delivery, merchandise unloading and through-district travel. Developing and attaching such an elevated movement mechanism in older, densely-developed centers would be difficult but not impossible, given proper legal and planning tools combined with sufficient economic incentives. Whether an elevated transit system suspended above the sidewalk would be desirable, however, is doubtful.

71. The Brooklyn Bridge, 1870–1883
View *c*. 1898, Washington Roebling

The Brooklyn Bridge is one of the most stunning multi-level, multi-modal transportation links ever built. A ramp across the bridge links pedestrian traffic from Brooklyn to New York. That spectacular span across the East River still provides an appealing promenade. In addition, grade-separated channels were provided for railed transit trains and for electric trolleys. Horse-drawn lorries and carriages used the right-of-way now taken over by the automobile.

were designed for multi-level linkage for all types of transit between parts of the city. Of these, the stunning Brooklyn Bridge in New York is clearly the most complete (Figure 71).

In our own era, a fundamental stimulus to returning to these efforts has been the urban transportation disaster of the automobile, national revulsion to air pollution, new awareness of sound stress, and harrowing traffic. At the same time, a number of now unacceptable contradictions emerge. The most evident of these is the specter of the most prosperous post-industrial nation in the world with inadequate resources devoted to development and production of essential public transit systems. Thus today's city-dweller must still accept public transit conditions often little better than those endured at the beginning of this century.

However, today American industries, such as electrical hardware and aircraft manufacturers, preoccupied with armaments throughout the last 30 years of war, are now slowly groping toward the vast transportation hardware market as new trends in public sentiment and public policy concerning transit become evident. They have been assisted in this effort, in many cases, initially by federal mass transit Research and Demonstration Grants. Thus Westinghouse has developed and promotes a variety of systems based on the elevated Transit Expressway; Rohr has a tracked air-cushion vehicle and a Monocab system suspended from guideways; United Aircraft built the Turbo-Train, which runs between New York and Boston; the Ford Motor Company intends to build a rubber-tired ''people mover'' transit system; LTV Aerospace Corporation is producing an intra-airport transit system for the new Dallas-Fort Worth airport; Grumman Corporation is building an air-cushion long-range train-like vehicle (Tracked Air-Cushion Research Vehicle); Bendix Corporation has demonstrated the Dashaveyor guideway controlled people mover; Transportation Technolgy, Inc. has a people mover that runs on air cushions; and there are many others

in varying stages of development and testing.

Many of these devices are being developed under contracts let by the Urban Mass Transportation Administration of the Department of Transportation, as mentioned earlier. Significant public investment is now being made for the first time in America to develop more advanced hardware and transit systems software. In addition, millions of their own dollars are now being spent by various corporations on long- and short-haul public transit for the first time. As a result, it is finally possible that modern, comfortable, efficient urban and interurban transportation will be available and promoted by powerful corporate interests in the not-too-distant future.

But it is not enough to have growing federal and state programs that display a new willingness to finance urban bus and rail transit. It is not enough to have massive corporate enterprises turning their attention to building and marketing transit devices. And it is not enough to become aware that transit ways and pedestrian ways rather than the conventional street could very appropriately become the organizing elements of the city center. Each of these thrusts ignores a central question: *How* should transit be used in the cities, in the overall complex design and redevelopment of cities?

What are some of the alternatives? Transit systems can be planned and built *independently* of everything else that is happening, or could happen, as one was recently, in Toronto. The Yonge Street subway line built in the 1960's was a fine engineering achievement but one accompanied by relatively few urban design considerations. What was accomplished? Faster, more pleasant transportation became available. But the transit line was planned without regard to potential and programmed new buildings, without regard to linkage into new structures, the places people were going. Nor was there any economic strategy to recapture funds for subway maintenance and operations from private development profits stimu-

lated by the publicly financed subway. So land prices skyrocketed as land assemblage took place around the station stops. New buildings were built. Former owners, residents, and businesses were replaced. A process of unplanned replacement renewal took place that was not very different from what happens when a new highway goes through a city or an older suburban area. That is one alternative.

Nearly the same process can currently be seen the length of Second Avenue in Manhattan. There, the new subway line is being anticipated: land assemblage is rampant at stop locations; new buildings are going up or are planned along an avenue which is suddenly desirable because access to it via the subway will be so very much improved. This is the traditional way that real estate developers capitalize on transit. Yet no public recapture of the real estate value created by this massive public expenditure of funds has been planned.

As construction of the new line gets underway, urban design criteria to connect new destinations with the new transit system are just now being considered by the New York City Planning Commission and the Metropolitan Transportation Authority. A mechanism for implementation of design concepts remains to be worked out. It is still possible that crowds will be forced to pour through limited apertures into a street (which is not where they are going, which is hot, cold, dirty, or noisy) and then across wide truck- and car-filled traffic lanes, and finally to their destinations, often a very new building very near the subway platform. A massive opportunity exists for better transport for people mixed with more effective, innovative, pleasant-to-experience urban design along Manhattan's Second Avenue. If the opportunity languishes, unseized in the very near future, the losers are the public, the people of the city. In the long run, if city life and the experience of moving around and through the city aren't very much improved, the losers may very well be the speculator, the investor, the owner-builder who is left with space no one wants

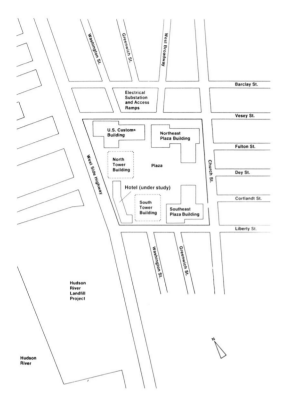

72–73. World Trade Center
New York City
Site plan (above)
Photograph, 1973 (right)
Minoru Yamasaki and Associates

Unfortunately, in spite of ownership by an agency involved in the transportation business, properly-sized accessways from the transit system below to the building above were neglected. Platforms, escalators, and stairways do not properly service the morning and evening peak hour rushes of people. The current low priority given people and linkage between movement systems and urban destinations is unfortunately illustrated by the World Trade Center. The World Trade Center, which competes with privately financed buildings in New York City, is over 10 million square feet in five linked buildings of publicly subsidized office and commercial space built by the Port Authority of New York and New Jersey. The project originally was budgeted at $100 million to $200 million but it has now grown to a mammoth, out-of-scale enterprise costing about $850 million.

to use, with property no one wants to buy. It has already happened in many places. And the loss of a major opportunity with a new transit system is a crucial loss to the long-term health and viability of any urban area.

In some instances, another alternative is visible, the creation of halfhearted, inadequate, and perfunctory transit system links that move people to and through buildings. The recently completed World Trade Center in lower Manhattan, developed and owned by the Port Authority and subject to serious criticism on a number of counts, is unaccountably misplanned in terms of skillfully accommodating the building to transit (Figures 72, 73). The building site straddles a major commuter rail line. It has pedestrian platforms right there within the gigantic 10 million square foot complex which houses 50,000 workers and through which 80,000 people pass daily. Yet the connections to the various buildings in the complex are generally unclear to the traveler; more important, they are too small for the traffic that must pass through them. From the subway interior to the office building interior, people are crowded together in unnecessary masses by an agency whose business is, ironically, transportation.

But there are better alternatives that have not been entirely neglected in recent years. By the early 1970's, renewed emphasis on public transportation in public funding programs and private research and development has led to a number of specific urban design proposals which suggest more promising future potentialities. These generally reveal a long-neglected predilection toward integration of public transportation with structures and city spaces that began in the late 19th century, only to be forgotten for so much of the automobile-dominated 20th century. These new directions look in a positive and creative way toward new transport forms; toward considerations of linkage by transit within and between urban places; toward a more equitable, interesting, and pleasant use of public space; toward concern for the individual's real travel problem—getting

from his front door to his office or shop door.

For instance, a more thoroughly considered alternative was presented in 1966 as a generic proposal by Brian Richards. Richards, an accomplished English urbanist and people-moving systems expert, illustrated a prototypical Central Area Development scheme which deserves more attention than it has received (Figure 74). In it, a continuous pedestrian-moving belt is the organizing central element, roofed over by a glass canopy so that light fills the movement spine. Adjacent to it, with direct linkage, are buildings, lobbies, and transport interchange points.

A rather similar notion for the very high densities required in central areas of New York City, and one which deals with a typical underground subway, was developed in 1968 for the New York Regional Plan Association by a team of architects and urban planners led by Rai Okamoto and Frank Williams (Figure 75). Using the familiar, although often

specious, analogy between urban organization and systems in nature, it is called the "Access Tree." But this clear and influential graphic study does make a fundamental point: escalators and elevators should be positioned, properly sized, and carefully planned to link rail transit "roots" to the horizontal corridors within buildings, the "branches" of the system that distribute people to their actual destinations. The proposal is a demonstration of the possible rational organization of buildings related to horizontal and vertical transportation services. It expresses the potentialities of clustering tall structures where access is convenient. The proposal is an updated, rationalized version of privately financed Grand Central Terminal-Park Avenue, and Rockefeller Center, remarkable early urban planning achievements but ones rarely repeated (Figures 76–83). It is only with recent joint public-private developments such as the large, new Montreal subway-related central city real estate projects, about which more is

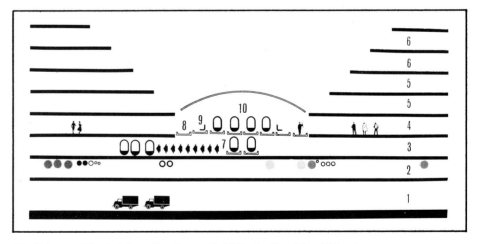

74. Proposed Central Area Development, 1966. Section. Brian Richards

A pedestrian and transit concourse level (4) is established with direct access to continuous horizontal pedestrian conveyor (9) boarded from the conveyor belt station (8). A local-service automated mini-car lane (10) surmounts a by-pass through-route for similar vehicles (7). The transportation concourse level is open to light through the curvilinear glass canopy which assures year-round heat and air conditioning and good light control. Notice that the traveler on public transportation is not shoved underground or out into the street congested with private

vehicles but instead is given the priority of natural light and direct access to the activity level. The entire urban district is organized around clean, quiet, efficient internal transitways. This section through a prototypical, dense urban area deserves careful evaluation and analysis for it is applicable in a wide range of potential redevelopment situations. One possibility is that the pedestrian transit line concourse could be in an existing, conventional, redeveloped urban street.

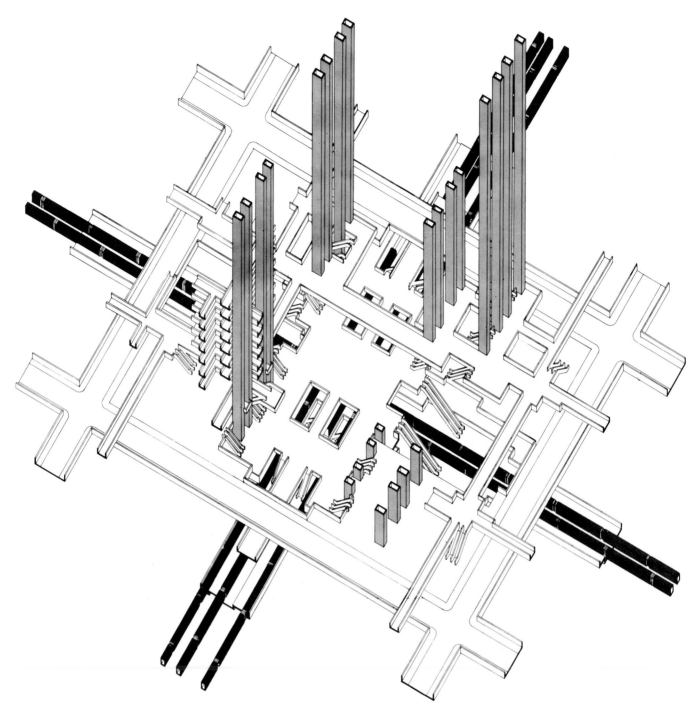

75. The Access Tree, 1968
Frank Williams and Rai Okamoto
(consultants to the New York
Regional Plan Association)

This is a diagram of a basic organizing principal for intensive activity around points of urban circulation. It illustrates the principle that people's destinations should be related to the way people travel if the city is to be convenient and rationally organized. Thus the trip from subway to office door (including rail platform, elevator, building corridors) becomes the basic planned frame upon which commercial buildings are hung, located, and developed. The roots (black tubes) are high-speed commuter trains and subways. The trunks (grey cores) are elevators and escalators which lead to the branches: the office corridors and sidewalks. Construction of offices, this proposal recognizes, should be encouraged at transit points, where links with transportation can be designed into

new buildings as they develop, as occurred initially in Rockefeller Center and around Grand Central Station in New York. The alternative, which prevails in most cities and most of New York, is random spawning of enormous buildings, based solely on speculative site assembly opportunities and marketing decisions. The result is disruption of roads for utility line linkage, inconvenient and dull arrangement of building mass, loss of potential communal open spaces gained by clustering of buildings, and disastrous bottlenecks at every level of the urban circulation network. Most of all, ease of movement and convenience for people is sacrificed through the omission of circulation planning as a determinant of urban structuring.

76. New York Central Railroad Yards over which Grand Central Station Was Built, c. 1900 (below)

77. Grand Central Station, 1903–13. Perspective section (bottom). Reed & Stem and Warren & Wetmore

The rebuilding of Grand Central Station in the early 20th century initiated an immense, well-planned urban redevelopment scheme. The new terminal was linked by pedestrian ramps to all surrounding streets, public transit lines, and suburban rail platforms. In addition, the open rail yards and tracks from 42nd to 96th Streets were decked over in stages. The new upper level became Park Avenue. Today the vitality of midtown Manhattan near Grand Central Station persists. Direct and convenient linkage into the urban and suburban transit lines from shops, restaurants, and commercial services along the connecting links creates one of the most successful and convenient urban nodes anywhere in the world.

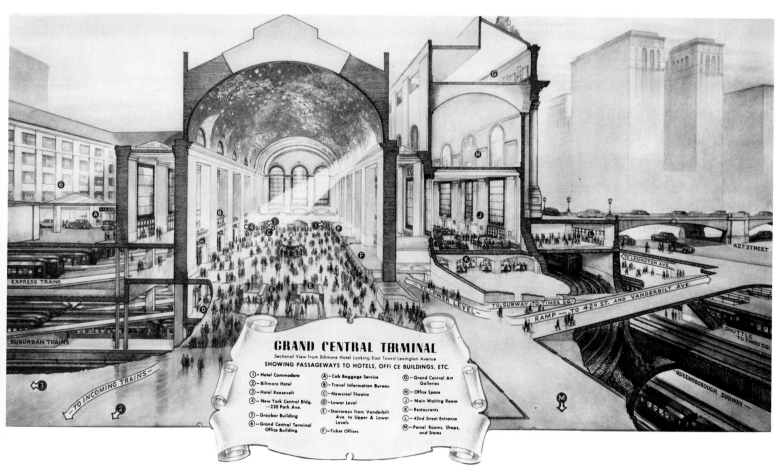

GRAND CENTRAL TERMINAL

Sectional View from Biltmore Hotel Looking East Toward Lexington Avenue

SHOWING PASSAGEWAYS TO HOTELS, OFFICE BUILDINGS, ETC.

1 – Hotel Commodore
2 – Biltmore Hotel
3 – Hotel Roosevelt
4 – New York Central Bldg. —230 Park Ave.
5 – Graybar Building
6 – Grand Central Terminal Office Building
A – Cab Baggage Service
B – Travel Information Bureau
C – Newsreel Theatre
D – Lower Level
E – Stairways from Vanderbilt Ave. to Upper & Lower Levels
F – Ticket Offices
G – Grand Central Art Galleries
H – Office Space
J – Main Waiting Room
K – Restaurants
L – 42nd Street Entrance
M – Parcel Rooms, Shops, and Stores

78. NEW YORK CENTRAL RAILROAD YARDS OVER WHICH PARK AVENUE WAS BUILT, *c.* 1900

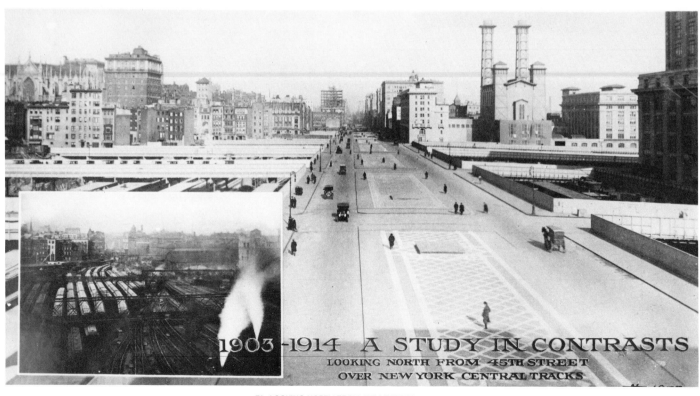

1903–1914 A STUDY IN CONTRASTS
LOOKING NORTH FROM 45TH STREET
OVER NEW YORK CENTRAL TRACKS

79. LOOKING NORTH FROM 45TH STREET, *c.* 1913

80. LOOKING NORTH BETWEEN 50TH AND 51ST STREETS, *c.* 1923

81. LOOKING SOUTH AFTER 1928

78–81. Park Avenue

As a part of the redevelopment of Grand Central Station, the open rail yards which bisected Manhattan were covered between 42nd and 96th Streets (Figure 78). In their place, on an immense steel bridge, present-day Park Avenue came into being (Figure 79). The transition was dramatic. Soot, noise, and blight gave way. The depreciated East Side became a contender for new building and major investment. Park Avenue, by the 1920's, was laid out with a pleasant, meandering pedestrian mall with seating niches down its center (Figure 80). The road right-of-way was restricted to minimal space serving the luxurious new residential buildings. The park malls were destroyed in 1928 when they were squeezed down into traffic islands. The automobile took over. Park Avenue, appropriately named at the outset, became an urban speedway. The brief history of Park Avenue is a vivid illustration of how a multi-level urban transit corridor redevelopment can be gracefully and humanistically completed, only to be subsequently perverted by a misguided emphasis on the automobile.

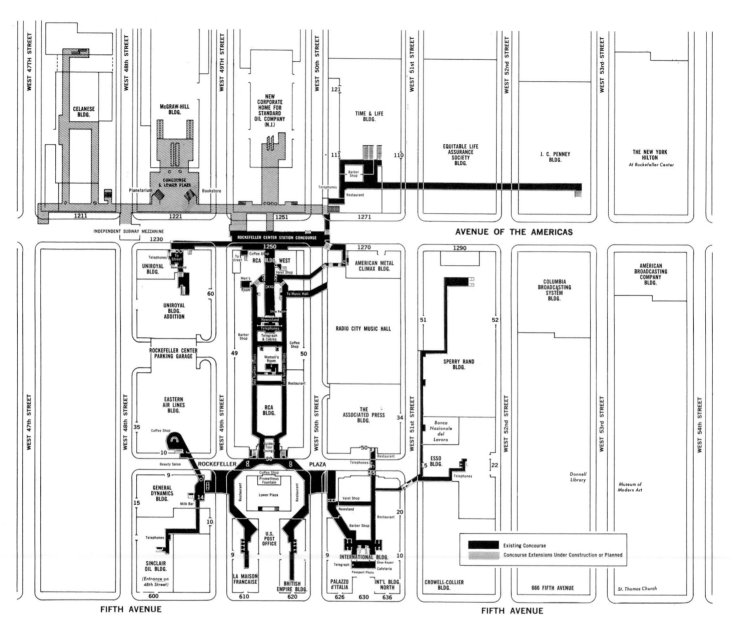

WEST 47TH STREET · WEST 48TH STREET · WEST 49TH STREET · WEST 50TH STREET · WEST 51st STREET · WEST 52nd STREET · WEST 53rd STREET

CELANESE BLDG.

McGRAW-HILL BLDG.

NEW CORPORATE HOME FOR STANDARD OIL COMPANY (N.J.)

TIME & LIFE BLDG.

EQUITABLE LIFE ASSURANCE SOCIETY BLDG.

J. C. PENNEY BLDG.

THE NEW YORK HILTON
At Rockefeller Center

CONCOURSE & LOWER PLAZA

Planetarium   Bookstore

Barber Shop

Telephones

Restaurant

1211   1221   1251   1271

INDEPENDENT SUBWAY MEZZANINE

AVENUE OF THE AMERICAS

1230

ROCKEFELLER CENTER STATION CONCOURSE

1250   1270   1290

UNIROYAL BLDG.

RCA BLDG. WEST

Men's Room

AMERICAN METAL CLIMAX BLDG.

AMERICAN BROADCASTING COMPANY BLDG.

60

UNIROYAL BLDG. ADDITION

Shoe Repair

Newsstand

Telephones

Barber Shop

Telegraph & Cables

Coffee Shop

To Music Hall

RADIO CITY MUSIC HALL

COLUMBIA BROADCASTING SYSTEM BLDG.

51   52

ROCKEFELLER CENTER PARKING GARAGE

49   50

Women's Room

Restaurant

SPERRY RAND BLDG.

EASTERN AIR LINES BLDG.

RCA BLDG.

THE ASSOCIATED PRESS BLDG.

34

Banca Nazionale del Lavoro

35   Coffee Shop

10

Guided Tour Lounge

50

Telephones

Restaurant

Donnell Library

Museum of Modern Art

Beauty Salon

ROCKEFELLER   PLAZA

ESSO BLDG.

5   22

Telephones

9   14   Milk Bar

Coffee Shop

Prometheus Fountain

45

GENERAL DYNAMICS BLDG.

Restaurant   Lower Plaza   Restaurant

20

15   10

Valet Shop   Newsstand

Telephones   U.S. POST OFFICE

Barber Shop   Restaurant

Existing Concourse

Concourse Extensions Under Construction or Planned

9   9

SINCLAIR OIL BLDG.

(Entrance on 48th Street)

Telegraph

INTERNATIONAL BLDG.   10

Shoe Repair   Cafeteria

Passport Photo

600

LA MAISON FRANCAISE   BRITISH EMPIRE BLDG.   PALAZZO d'ITALIA   INT'L BLDG. NORTH

CROWELL-COLLIER BLDG.

666 FIFTH AVENUE

St. Thomas Church

610   620   626   630   636

FIFTH AVENUE   FIFTH AVENUE

WEST 47th STREET · WEST 48th STREET · WEST 49th STREET · WEST 50th STREET · WEST 51st STREET · WEST 52nd STREET · WEST 53rd STREET · WEST 54th STREET

82–83. Rockefeller Center, 1929–39

Underground Concourse plan, 1970 (above); Aerial view (right)
Reinhard & Hofmeister, Corbett & Harrison and Hood & Fouilhoux

The celebrated prototype of dense urban development which successfully integrates transportation networks and pedestrian systems is Rockefeller Center in New York. Off-street parking is provided, as are huge subterranean truck docks and shipping rooms 34 feet below street level for servicing the center without interruption to surrounding street activity. The circumstances of large land assembly under private control, a maverick dedication, and collaboration with architects to create an office center in a relatively unproven part of midtown (New York's offices in the 1930's were generally clustered downtown, and midtown office buildings were farther east or south) combined to produce this remarkable plan. Rockefeller

Center proves that good planning can be good business. It has been more than profitable. Its presence has stimulated growth in midtown, and its own confines have more than doubled in size from the original three-block, 14-building complex. Principles of pedestrian concourse linkage between transit ways and building interiors have generally been maintained in the recent expansion of Rockefeller Center along the Avenue of the Americas. It is unfortunate that little of the original sensitivity to massing, preservation of agreeable, usable coordinated open spaces, and high design standards have been preserved in the recent expanded development of Rockefeller Center.

said below, that the realization of such "nodes" is again becoming a reality.

The "Access Tree" also contains a sense of economy of space and the possibilities of diversity of scale in urban settings. It argues that land should be reserved and lower buildings at lower rent scales planned some distance from the dense cluster. This strategy allows the survival of small shops, reasonably priced restaurants, and services of all sorts which now must struggle to survive and very often fail in successful, high real estate value urban areas. It also proposes that the experience of travel on subways and other systems be made more congenial through introduction of physical and psychic amenities such as sunken plazas open to the street and sky through which one enters the subway station. Montreal, Mexico City, and other cities already have transit stops designed this way. New York does, too, in a very few places and only very recently.

The concept of access tree and node implied by Richards and so vividly illustrated by Okamoto and Williams signifies a new recognition of the significance of the node in urban design. Until very recently, the transit way and its all-important node was thought of, when considered at all by urban planners, much as they thought of the city itself—in terms of physical massing, in terms of conventional design criteria. Thus Kevin Lynch as recently as 1960 in his popular book, *The Image of the City,* tends to distinguish the node for its visual qualities and as a visual decision point on a path through a city rather than as a functional central transportation interchange. Lynch concentrates on the necessity that "the traveler must see how he enters the node, where the break occurs and how he goes onward." Okamoto and Williams are much more concerned about the linkage from a functional viewpoint. They seek a means to link movement systems to one another, to connect the node and the paths leading to it. This change in emphasis from Lynch's work of 1960 to the *Urban Design Manhattan* work of the late 1960's indicates a trend toward a sys-

tems and process approach which is becoming the basis of urban design, as it is of many aspects of contemporary American thought and culture. Older traditions in urbanism emphasize the location of buildings and monumental urban plazas or spaces with little attention to the leftover service elements of the city, such as the transit way and ordinary street. The tendency in the late 1960's, which is increasing today, is to try to examine the way in which the city is *used* by people and thereby to make experience in the city more agreeable to them from the conventional visual viewpoint as well as from the viewpoint of convenience, ease of movement, sensible dissipation of pedestrian and other forms of traffic, and other functional matters that unless solved leave the experience of the city, no matter how beautiful parts of it might be, both disappointing and disagreeable for most of the people most of the time.

A growing number of specific proposals for particular urban areas to integrate public transportation into the activity center and even into buildings have been presented quite recently. These confirm the growing impact of ideas presented in the later 1960's on more recent urban design suggestions. For instance, in 1969 (replacing a banal and much assailed plan of 1965) the firms of Conklin & Rossant, Harrison & Abramovitz, and Philip Johnson & John Burgee proposed a new 100-acre linear town, Battery Park City, at the southwestern edge of Manhattan, to be built predominantly on landfill in the Hudson River (Figures 84, 85). Its enclosed main street, as originally proposed, was to be served by a quiet, electric internal guiderail or monorail which the architects claim could eventually extend to other parts of lower Manhattan. However, actual completion of a new type of linear transit system now seems unlikely.

Indeed, the most recent indications are that actual development will be far from innovative. A lamentable and conventional deterioration of the project from progressive proposal to conservative implementation is all but assured for this

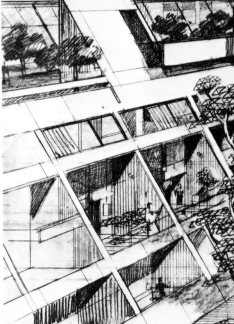

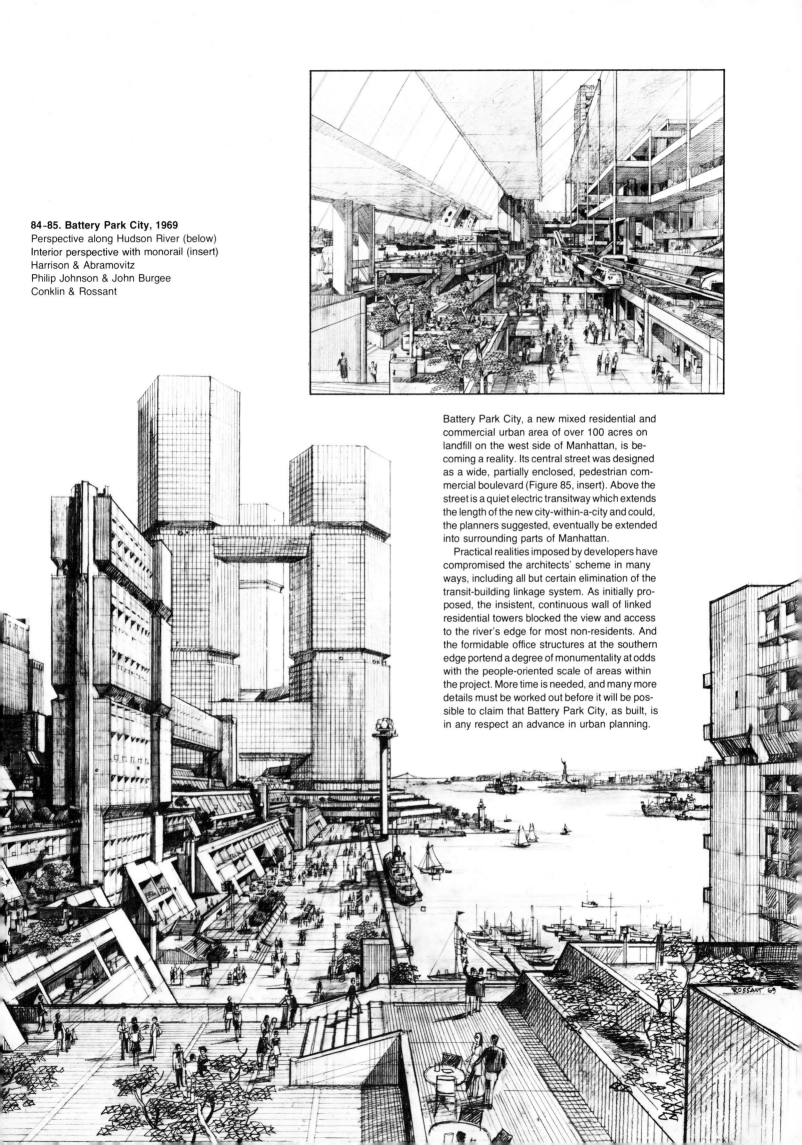

84-85. Battery Park City, 1969
Perspective along Hudson River (below)
Interior perspective with monorail (insert)
Harrison & Abramovitz
Philip Johnson & John Burgee
Conklin & Rossant

Battery Park City, a new mixed residential and commercial urban area of over 100 acres on landfill on the west side of Manhattan, is becoming a reality. Its central street was designed as a wide, partially enclosed, pedestrian commercial boulevard (Figure 85, insert). Above the street is a quiet electric transitway which extends the length of the new city-within-a-city and could, the planners suggested, eventually be extended into surrounding parts of Manhattan.

Practical realities imposed by developers have compromised the architects' scheme in many ways, including all but certain elimination of the transit-building linkage system. As initially proposed, the insistent, continuous wall of linked residential towers blocked the view and access to the river's edge for most non-residents. And the formidable office structures at the southern edge portend a degree of monumentality at odds with the people-oriented scale of areas within the project. More time is needed, and many more details must be worked out before it will be possible to claim that Battery Park City, as built, is in any respect an advance in urban planning.

86–87. Regional Center Redevelopment Proposal, 1973
Perspective section (right)
Plan (bottom right)
Ulrich Franzen

This is a fragment of a comprehensive redevelopment proposal for the east side of Manhattan betweeen 57th and 96th Streets. The principal access to the proposed Regional Center is clustered along newly enclosed Third Avenue between 58th and 63rd Streets (Figure 86, bottom right), where today in the same general area, a retail and commercial center composed of Alexander's, Bloomingdale's, shops, restaurants, movie theaters, and public or semi-public facilities of other sorts already exist.

In the proposal, a key element is the glazing over of Third Avenue. The enclosed public space becomes a multi-level, thoroughly integrated activity spine (Figure 87, right). At the upper level along one side, a monorail carries shoppers through and around the Regional Center. The former street is reserved for electric service vehicles, personal transit pods, and caravan buses. Above the original street a new pedestrian concourse links directly into the second-floor level of all existing and anticipated new stores and shops. Below the original street a well-designed transit station links the existing Lexington Avenue subway to the new Second Avenue and 63rd Street lines now under construction. A series of escalators and elevators connects all levels.

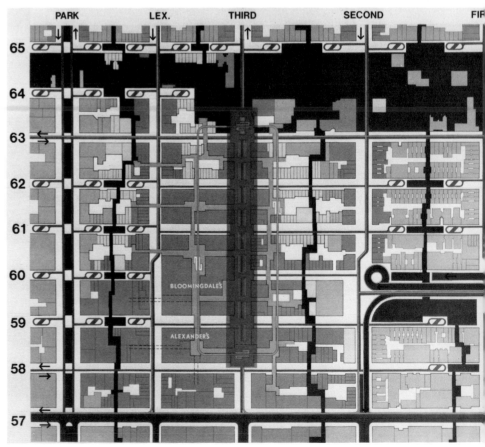

major mixed-income residential, commercial, and retail city-within-a-city of over 14,000 residential units. The service and transportation spine, the very essence of the project, may very well be compromised by an anxious public development authority unwilling or unable to convince the actual developers that imaginative planning makes good long-term economics. The developers are no doubt asking pertinent and unresolved questions such as: How would an interior transit line be financed? Who would operate it? Could it in any conceivable way actually link to the older and entirely different transportation systems in the city? This project points up fundamental issues that inhibit the development of innovative transit systems on a limited basis in older urban areas. Indeed, the entire enterprise calls to question the wisdom and feasibility of considering railed transit systems as organizing devices at any scale less than citywide. And the entire transit system should be developed incrementally over many years with public financing.

A recent urban design proposal by Ulrich Franzen, mentioned previously, goes the whole way. It takes the problem of the street and tries to develop solutions largely dependent on new movement systems on a city-wide basis as a means to salvage the agreeable aspects of urban life and the public space of the city. For example, Franzen considers Manhattan's Bloomingdale's-Alexander's retail complex along Third Avenue between 58th and 63rd Streets susceptible to imaginative new development as a regional center (Figures 86, 87). He proposes to link the new Second Avenue and Queens crosstown subway lines in a well-designed transit node and to integrate them with a moving pedestrian belt which would link the long-haul subway systems to an intimate, through-store excursion at upper levels. The proposal is itself very extensive; the integrated transportation and commercial node at the proposed regional center is only one component. The proposal, supported as it was by a generous Ford Foundation grant, is sufficiently comprehensive to warrant considerable interest and

careful study.[19] Its concern for the integration of multi-level urban spaces and movement systems at nodes of intense activity refers back to progressive suggestions of the 19th century, recalls the most successful large-scale urban development schemes of the 20th century, and looks forward to refined and improved uses of these concepts. Its emphasis on new transit opportunities integrated with the recapture of public street space for new uses without destruction of buildings or relocation of people in residential areas is both practical and very much a proper concern of the most progressive urban design. However, the issue of implementation, especially of new fixed guideway transit devices to serve limited, enclosed spaces remains a defiant problem.

Indeed, the earliest suggestion for linear urban structuring integrated along a transit line, the Crystal Way in London, a bold pre-subway proposal of the 1850's, also languished at the outset because of high-cost technical requirements unmatched by capabilities and inadequate public sponsorship (Figures 88, 89). Today, realization of linear urban transit linked to and integrated with building nodes in existing cities continues to prove immensely difficult even though need is recognized and technical feasibility exists. The exceptions are those rare places in an urban center where strong vision has merged with fortunate economic and physical circumstances such as the Grand Central Terminal and Rockefeller Center areas of New York, and quite recently, the Place Ville Marie district of Montreal. The Grand Central area of New York grew up because of the convergence at a *point* of regional railroads and local transit. The value of this convergence was recognized and later realized by the New York Central Railroad Company, whose bold private real estate venture produced Grand Central Terminal and Park Avenue. The developers of Rockefeller Center capitalized on the purchasing power of an immense fortune applied to low-cost depression wages and materials, long-term land leases to leverage financing, and pre-existing as well as planned transit.

Today Montreal is a notable example of what can still be done in an older city center with sufficient imagination, a solid understanding of long-term goals and objectives, strong and willing ownership patterns in the central city, and an unusual urge to legal, economic, and physical design innovation. There, land ownership by the Canadian National Railway, bold financing, and imaginative physical planning combined with rational judgment exercised by Canadian planner Vincent Ponte have together scored solid gains in redevelopment of an older city center. Montreal's downtown core, languishing a few years ago, is now a vital commercial, entertainment, and retail center of integrated transit, public spaces, and building interiors (Figure 90). And the center continues to grow, continues to strengthen, and continues to emphasize amenities for people. The focus on people—on planning for people rather than for things and for vehicles—has paid off handsomely for everyone, and promises to continue doing so (Figure 91).

Except in the very special cases of Rockefeller Center, Grand Central, downtown Montreal, and a few others such as Philadelphia's Market Street East, implementation of urban development schemes planned with and integrally linked to rail transit has proven very elusive. Questions of long-term ownership structure, legal responsibility, policing costs, and development cost-sharing ratios usually destroy the legal, tax, and financing benefits between public and private sector programs and policies that make such plans appear economically feasible in the first place. The highest priority should be given to developing legal, tax, zoning, and financial mechanisms to permit the effective integration of urban public transit with complex new structures. It is through such integration that coherent and congenial experience at the city center is possible.

In the United States the problem of actually producing a well-articulated and well-designed node must inevitably involve concepts and strategies of joint development; that is, development in which

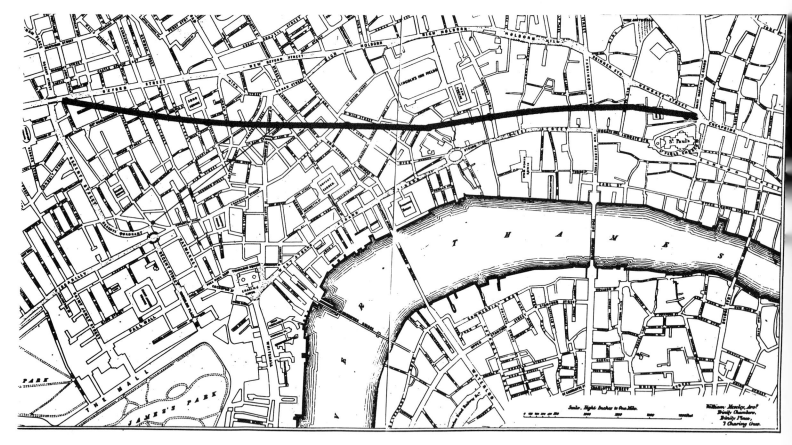

88-89. The Crystal Way, London, 1855. Plan of Route (above)
Perspective section (right)
William Moseley

Designed before any subway had been built to extend several miles through London from Regent's Circus to St. Paul's (Figure 89, right), this generously scaled, double-level linear arcade suggested a new urban organization at a remarkably early date. It is not just an enclosed pedestrian street, nor simply a glass-roofed pedestrian mall suspended over city rail transit. Rather, the circulation channels, separated according to type, are designed as integral parts of the shops, stores, hotels, and houses that border them (Figure 88, above). Access between buildings and the covered mall is provided all along the upper pedestrian level. Below, the sub-basements open onto transit rail lines to facilitate circulation, merchandise delivery, and trash removal. Such sensible continuous enclosed linkage between the circulation channel and the structure for utilities, goods, and people still exists only rarely today, though its possibilities are increasingly recognized. This proposal for an urban renewal scheme through an expanse of inexpensive land in central London was backed up by a financing plan and structural detail which seldom accompanies innovative proposals today. When presented to the House of Commons, it was turned down because of Parliament's reluctance to engage in such an innovative project.

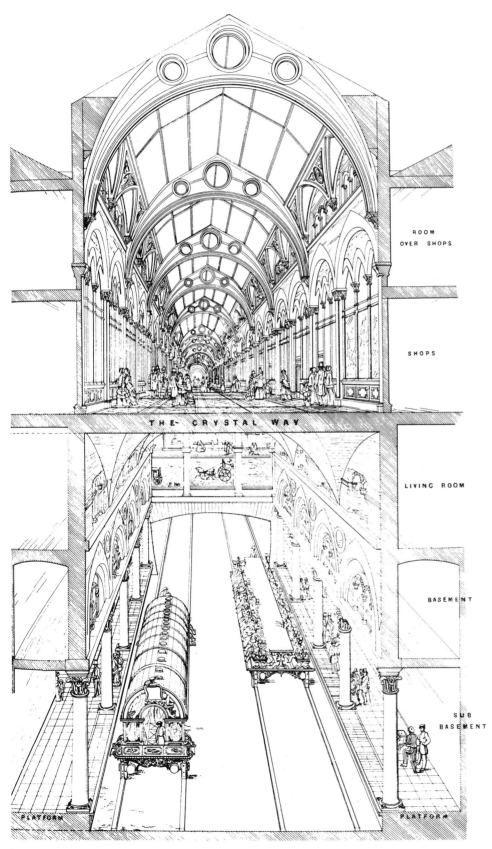

ROOM
OVER SHOPS

SHOPS

THE CRYSTAL WAY

LIVING ROOM

BASEMENT

SUB
BASEMENT

PLATFORM

PLATFORM

private and public interests intermingle and contributions are made from both sides. The private sector can only be expected to participate when it will materially benefit in some way, such as through reduced capital costs, improved depreciation potential, increased potential value, lower assessments, or reduced taxes. These are exchanged for the commitment of capital, management talent, land resources, and the determination that is found in private enterprise at its best. Some joint development strategies are slowly and painfully being worked out in towns, cities, and at the federal level on a case-by-case basis. What is needed is a defined national strategy, one which observes real estate investment and tax realities, to induce private interests to join in joint development projects with cities, towns, and public authorities. Today, the design concepts and development models are available. The problem is implementation—of the necessary laws, regulations, and economics. And these must be tailored to our political and social system so that the desirable urban design concepts that will make movement and life in cities more desirable can be realized.

What are some of the possibilities? Certainly, a more comprehensive understanding of the *three*-dimensional character of cities, incorporating connections between enclosed space and access to it, is a critical matter. *Land* must be forgotten as the basic resource in cities to which all institutions of finance, ownership, and regulation are tied. In its place, *space*, enclosed, usable space, should be considered the critical element. Today, as it has for centuries, land still controls urban financing. Mortgages are based on land and the improvements thereon. Parcel assemblage for construction generally requires purchase of land. Access to city parcels is almost universally conceived of principally in terms of roads at ground level.

This preoccupation with the land, with the two-dimensional base in which buildings are anchored, has caused a predominantly two-dimensional concept of cities. If this technologically and economically

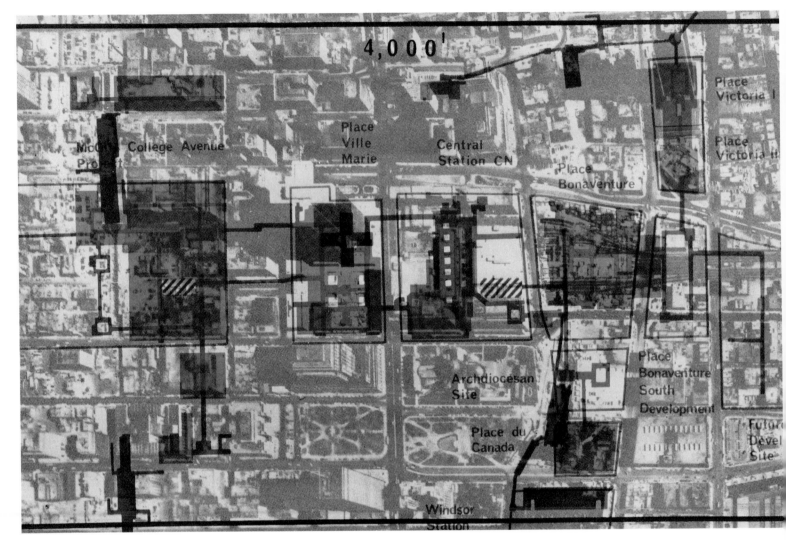

4,000'

Place Victoria I

Place Victoria II

McGill College Avenue Project

Place Ville Marie

Central Station CN

Place Bonaventure

Archdiocesan Site

Place Bonaventure South Development

Place du Canada

Future Devel Site

Windsor Station

90. Plan of 200-Acre Downtown Core of Montreal, 1956–67. Vincent Ponte

Six miles of shop-lined pedestrian promenades link a wide variety of shops and major buildings to one another and to the new metro line constructed for Expo '67. At the metro level there is also provision for parking, truck docks, and suburban train platforms. Much of this network, which began with Place Ville Marie, is now built. Ponte initiated the entire redevelopment with his widely appreciated Place Ville Marie plan of the late 1950's. Subsequently, he extended the network with a plan for Place Bonaventure. The first segments opened for business in 1962, and by 1963 their success was evident. Since then Ponte has charted the continuing evolution of the 200-acre downtown core redevelopment. The potential for climate-controlled pedestrian areas (which are very important in this and other climates that vary from extremely cold to very warm), light and bright arcades which look into sunken garden plazas, easy access to transpor-

tation, and an integrated urban system, has now stimulated development along the entire network. The linked pedestrian concourses and development nodes are shown in dark grey on the illustration against the map of downtown Montreal.

Now, increasingly, face-to-face communication, places of entertainment and shopping, successful commercial enterprises, and places for people to relax at the center of a growing, viable central city are emerging around this well-thought-out plan that integrates people, places, and motion. This highly accessible, climate-controlled multi-level commercial center has proved capable of extension and expansion. Enclosed pedestrian ways, free of automobiles and environmentally pleasing, are susceptible to integrated growth along with buildings and transit, and have been proven as sound commercial devices.

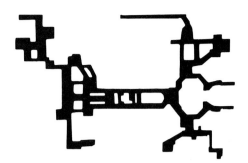

91. Pedestrian Networks. Rockefeller Center (top); Downtown Montreal (above)

The diagram compares the pedestrian concourse under Rockefeller Center to a plan of the existing and planned pedestrian passage system which links 200 acres of downtown Montreal with new metro mezzanines, shown as rectangles. The Montreal system is about three-fourths complete. Both are still growing.

The notion of linking transit directly to buildings by lively, attractive commercial arcade pedestrian passages, even in older urban centers, is confilmed by both as economically wise, as well as socially and environmentally desirable. Commercially viable and convenient density becomes possible without human congestion and unpleasant competition for public open space among people, trucks, and other vehicles. Unfortunate and relatively new problems of urban crime and policing needs are increasingly encountered in such private or semi-private pedestrian streets. These must be considered as well as the calculation of overall maintenance costs of such passageways in the design.

outmoded attitude can be broken, possibilities for more convenient and more successful urban clustering will be evident.

One of the very few examples of liberation from the restrictive concept of land is also a very ancient one. Condominium ownership, usually reserved for residential space, recognizes the inherent value of space as an entity. The condominium apartment which does not generally include land ownership can be mortgaged; and its value is not directly dependent on the land on which it exists. It is worth considering the implications of this form of ownership and financing of urban space as an alternative to our conventional land-dominated basis. It would permit segments, levels, in fact layers of space, to be separately owned. It would even allow the complex interpenetration of public and private ownership to occur as needed, and where appropriate. But condominium ownership is only one possible new conceptual basis for legal and economic formats that would assist implementation of desirable urban design concepts. Why not think further in terms such as:

What alternatives are there to the conventional street as the organizing network for at least the busy central core of cities?

Could a pedestrian mall or a well-designed transit spine serve as a more effective, more promising, more useful central element?

What more flexible ways are there to finance high-density, transit-linked urban development?

What ways are there to partially finance transit operations from tax on values created by the existence of transit itself?

What new concepts of design and finance would be possible if alternative levels and locations existed for access to built urban space?

What would be the implications, even in older cities, of reserving horizontal rights-of-way for public access at various uniform levels throughout the central business district to be incrementally developed as renewal and redevelopment occur?

Many of these and other questions could and must be asked if we are to progress. And they must be dealt with many years before results are realized in new movement systems and in new and improved interlinkage between open space, enclosed urban space, and the movement network of the city center.

At the very least, a better city and a better life in the city are only possible if new and more comprehensive directions are taken in an effort that integrates transportation planning with urban planning. The movement of people, not the movement of vehicles, in appropriate ways to appropriate places must be recognized as the essential goal of transportation. Transit has to be accepted as a public service to which all are entitled, and thus financed or at least subsidized as a legitimate public cost on the basis of the widest understanding of public benefit.

In terms of design and urban organization, transit ways, pedestrian routes, and roads can form a meaningful, pleasant, and rational organizing skeleton for the city. But the space for movement must be reserved in advance. Expensive long-term investments must be accelerated in engineering, hardware, and maintenance of transit systems. And a comprehensive system for implementation—including zoning, finance, legal requirements, and design—must be developed to permit improved and more comprehensive connections between movement systems and destinations in the city. Montreal shows that it is indeed possible. And worthwhile.

New Directions

Public transit, the key to the future vitality of cities, must be planned and developed in concord with urban public and semi-public space and buildings.

City land will give way to space as the planning, financing, and legal basis for urban redevelopment.

Transit and pedestrian corridors through urban space must be reserved long in advance of development. Controls for access, urban design, and land value regulation must be incorporated into initial planning.

New transit technology for both fixed guideways and existing streets, although already available, will be slow in coming. Loop systems in busy districts which require minimum investment will be the first lines affected.

Transit services must be expanded to serve outlying areas of metropolitan regions.

Urban and interurban transit construction and operations should become a continuing federal and state financial responsibility. Subsidies, administered by regional authorities, should be delivered as an incentive bonus for increased ridership.

92. Crystal Palace, London
Inauguration of the Building, 1851
Sir Joseph Paxton

Made of prefabricated glass and iron components, this immense exhibition hall covering
800,000 square feet was completed in less than
six months. One of the first site-assembled,
large-scale, prefabricated component buildings,
it was recognized in its own day as a revolution-
ary achievement in the history of building and
the use of materials.

Housing

During the past decade, for the first time in American history, the public, the government, and everyone in the building professions became aware that more housing is needed—and simply isn't being built. The economics of contemporary housing construction and the failure of innumerable, inadequate public programs have coincided to bring about a generally recognized housing crisis, especially in the public sector. Most of the problems related to how to *build* more housing remain entirely unresolved. And yet some progress is evident in the search for a means to *design* better housing.

In public housing during recent years, administrative, conceptual, and financing inadequacies produced programs that failed, such as Urban Renewal and Model Cities. In addition, in many cases, even before an astonishing and unconscionable moritorium was placed on all new public housing by the federal government in early 1973, due to misplaced funding priorities, public housing agencies had such limited funds that construction hardly kept pace with abandonments. In other cases, publicly assisted housing could not be built at all because constantly escalating construction costs exceeded outdated regulations governing legally permitted housing unit cost maximums.

Because housing is generally unprofitable, the commitment of business capital is usually unwarranted for new private housing in cities, except for luxury units. The costs of land and financing, combined with conventional construction requirements, force a completed package whose cost in urban areas is often excessive when related to obtainable rent or sales value.

Because construction costs are so high and still climbing attempts to update and invent new construction technology and methodology abounded by the end of the 1960's. Men have walked on the moon.

Yet housing is still built by methods relatively unchanged since the medieval guilds institutionalized specialization in the crafts. The result is that housing, one of the necessities of life, is still made and priced more often than not as if it were a luxury handcrafted sculpture.

A more progressive approach to building was tested and publicized in England as early as 1851. That year the Crystal Palace, an exhibition hall covering 20 acres (four times the ground of St. Peter's Cathedral) was erected of prefabricated iron, glass, and wood elements in six months' time (Figure 92). Over a century ago the Crystal Palace made it quite clear that prefabrication was a viable, progressive approach to construction.

Today, fascination with prefabrication persists in industrial, administrative, and academic circles. But the fascination has still to be converted to very useful information and very successful technique. The impressive advances in prefabricated housing types, patents, techniques, and transport of housing elements that occurred between 1860 and 1890 remains unmatched in this century. During the second half of the 19th century, the new rail lines were used to transport houses to the American frontier and cottages to summer resorts. Housing systems were invented, patented, and marketed with interchangeable parts, stressed skin panels, varying types of folding structures. A sectional house and the first disposable buildings were presented.

During the 20th century, much progress has been made in the application of the world's newer technology to automobiles, ships, airplanes, and armaments, but seldom to the process of building ordinary structures. A notable exception is Buckminster Fuller's Dymaxion House of the late 1920's (Figure 93). Fuller, one of the few poet-philosopher-engineers of our

age, displayed the Dymaxion House at Chicago's Marshall Field department store in 1927. It was a portable home composed of light materials and filled with structural innovations adapted from emerging aircraft technology. For instance, it incorporated air conditioning, plumbing, and prefabricated kitchen and bathroom units into a central structural mast. The Dymaxion House remains a prototype, but not an influential one.

In 1946 Fuller built an expanded prototype, the Wichita House that was to be mass-produced by the Beech Aircraft Corporation as its postwar transition into peace-time industry. But costs and labor difficulties stifled the enterprise. Since then, Fuller's Geodesic Domes, structures based on the cellular organization found in nature, which gains maximum strength from minimum material, have been widely accepted and built when long spans at low cost are required (Figure 64).

Both the Dymaxion House and the Geodesic Dome contain promising components for the housing dilemma, as well as for the potential rebuilding of cities. Both attempt to reduce the amount, weight, and waste of material in the provision of shelter. Both work to discover a minimal structuring device to provide maximum enclosure. Both, however, are dependent on a fixed geometry which in itself severely limits massing potentials.

Fuller, perhaps more than anyone else in the last several decades, has forced examination of the issue of the application of contemporary technology and materials to the old problems of providing shelter. Free of a physical design obsession, Fuller was able quite early in the century to see through some of the pseudo-science of the so-called Modern Movement of the 1920's and 1930's and its attendant, International Style architecture. Indeed, in spite of the emphasis on efficiency, struc-

93. Dymaxion House, 1927. View of model, Buckminster Fuller

Lightweight, sturdy materials used in the emerging aircraft industry are the basis of this proposed dwelling. A central duraluminum mast houses all mechanical services and supports a double skin of plastic that is differentiated to respond to various lighting needs. Partition walls and outer skin are hung by wires from the apex of the service core. This leaves flexible living spaces along the exterior of the structure to be arranged in any way suitable to the owner.

"Dymaxion" is a word which combines "dynamic" with "maximum" efficiency, qualities that describe Fuller's central inventive principle

and particular areas of subsequent influence. The Dymaxion House, Fuller calculated, could have been sold at the time for $3,000 per unit if produced in volume. Fuller's proposal for a rational dwelling made of modern components anticipates the current thrust in research and development by the aerospace industry in its search for new markets in housing. His suggestion that lightweight, air-freightable housing be built to solve the mass housing needs of the world recognized long before it was generally evident that transport limitations would affect the range of factory-built housing.

tural clarity, and modern materials, Bauhaus and International Style architecture was preoccupied with surface and end-product design, not with reorganizing complex fundamental building systems and structural sub-units of buildings. Le Corbusier was hauntingly aware of the same inherent inadequacies in Western application of advanced technology to the age-old problem of building when he remarked in 1923, "There is a formidable industrial activity at present in progress, which is inevitably and constantly at the back of our minds . . . (but) the machine that we live in is an old coach full of tuberculosis."

Recently, especially in England and America, whole cities and their sub-units have been imagined by a variety of people and groups as potentially susceptible to completely scientific building. Light, inflatable materials and regularized components that plug in if needed and can be ripped off to discard, are seen as innovations of fundamental significance. In England, for instance, inspired by ideas advanced by Reyner Banham and others, the Archigram Group proposed, by the mid-1960's, projects for modular and mobile cities which, like their Futurist predecessors, were dynamic and temporary (Figure 95). The intriguing potentialities of instant architecture, inexpensive materials, and inflatable spaces led to the postulation of instant cities, often filled with Fuller-like domes. Throughout the United States, Europe, and Japan, groups with exotic names such as Ant Farm, Drop City, Works, Chrysalis Corp., Zomeworks, Haus-Rücker, Archizoom, Superstudio, The Metabolists, and others, intrigued by scientific and pseudo-scientific possibilities and romantic imagery, began to explore the edges of possibility with light membranes, air-pressure support, and catalogue-component service elements.

These often romanticized excursions into technologically advanced building possibilities are still generally neglected by actual builders. In many technical respects, most of them remain inconclusive and unproven. In time, as a result of this experimental work of the last decade or so, new space-enclosing methods and materials could be developed. However, as the work involved is innovative and not yet capable of satisfying an existing market demand, these groups must continue to depend on and to receive support from corporations, foundations, public programs, and international competitions and expositions.

For ordinary use, the totally scientific city or house is unnecessary. Indeed, most people seek a more ordinary place to live. Over the years, generally in periods of national crisis, occasional efforts have been made in America to produce an economically sound, flexible, relatively conventional manufactured dwelling.[20] During World War II, for instance, the federal government initiated a crash program at Indian Head, Maryland, to produce demountable prefabricated residential structures.

Recently, as housing completions fell drastically behind need in the 1960's, the federal government again sponsored a demonstration program, Operation Breakthrough. Now, five years later, about 20 privately developed new construction systems are being tested on nine sites, although the program is far behind schedule and languishing because of inadequate funding. In addition, despite some government reports to the contrary, there is little current evidence that Operation Breakthrough is meeting its objectives, which were principally to: produce economies in housing production technique; encourage a unification of building codes around the country; and reduce shortages of skilled labor in the housing industry. Indeed, since its much-publicized inception in 1969, many participating companies have dropped out of the Operation Breakthrough program. Some have even gone bankrupt. Those few still remaining have not, in most cases, produced important prototypes that exceed accomplishments outside the program in terms of building systems, financing, labor code, or design.

Indeed, by the beginning of 1973, the entire federal public housing program, hard on the optimistic official polemics of the late 1960's, ground to a suprising halt. Scandals within federal financing agencies, massive resistance by influential community groups, the residual power of anti-integration Southern forces and a growing segregationist mood of the North, together with strong rural and suburban interests, succeeded in pressuring a conservative federal administration to halt all new commitments to the entire federal public housing apparatus. In addition, the scope, purpose, and structure of the United States Department of Housing and Urban Development, including all its programs in urban development, such as water and sewer grants, urban renewal, model cities, open space programs, and public facility loans, were halted in the first half of 1973.

The specter of one of the world's major industrial countries, one of the world's major urbanized countries, and the world's wealthiest single nation having no federal housing and urban development program cannot long be tolerated. Substitute organization and housing programs must and no doubt will be developed. But to have halted essential government responsibilities and services in the financing and subsidizing of public housing is an unprecedented withdrawal of government assistance, especially to cities. It must be anticipated, unfortunately, that in the long process during which substitute mechanisms and programs are devised, refined, and finally accepted, that a profound disruption in serving the people, and particularly the housing needs, of the United States will have occurred.

Outside of publicly supported programs and projects, new technology and methods of fabricating housing have been under evaluation by private companies and independent architects for some time. All materials, all means of assembly, all ranges of size and price are being investigated. By the end of the 1960's, the lure of a large housing market combined with the hope of substantial eventual government support to the housing industry provoked the most massive private inquiry ever undertaken in the United States into the potential of technologically advanced housing. In Europe, of course, such a necessity has been evident for years and numerous methods are now perfected and widely used.

Prefabricated housing has not generally been acceptable to American taste until recently, especially in the private housing market. But recent attention to its possibilities by a number of architects in well-publicized schemes may have turned the tide. Moshe Safdie's Habitat, a stunning assembly of prefabricated rooms and room components at Expo '67 in Montreal, convinced a wide range of people to whom systematized, modular, and prefabricated building sounded alarmingly mechanistic that prefabrication processes need not ruin the appearance of the product (Figure 96). Habitat revealed the design potential of using and expressing the dwelling unit itself as a basic component of structure. Since 1967, Safdie, an Israeli-born architect who lives in Canada, has gained academic and critical acclaim as well as professional prominence. Thick concrete framing used at Montreal proved too heavy to make the scaled-down project of only 158 dwelling units at Habitat economically defensible. This serious flaw has been corrected in Safdie's current work for Puerto Rico and Israel. In these later schemes, factory-produced thin-shell concrete modules are designed to satisfy unit construction cost requirements of moderate-income housing programs.

A number of established architects other than Safdie also began in the last decade to work seriously with rationalized, functional systems for single buildings or even clusters which leave the structural bay far behind as the basic organizing principle of building. In recent projects by a number of seasoned architects and planners such as Paul Rudolph, John Johansen, Frei Otto, Kenzo Tange, Noriaku Kurokawa, and others, whole walls, entire rooms, combinations of plumbing, wiring, plaster, and structure are new fundamental, often factory-in-

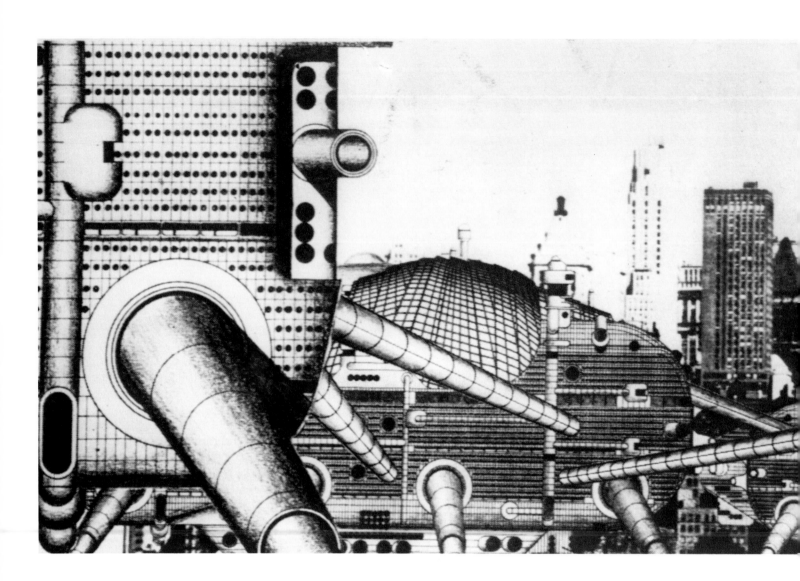

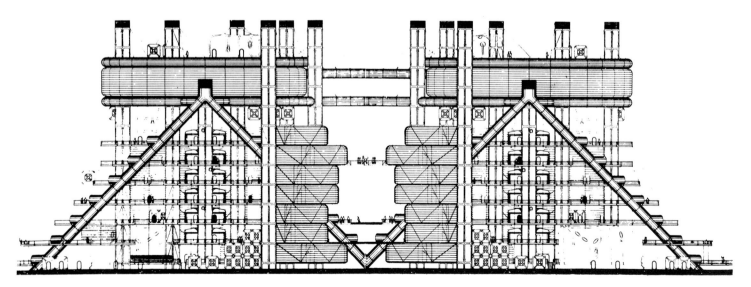

94. Cities-Moving Project, 1964 (above). Ron Herron
95. University Node of Plug-In City, 1965 (left). Peter Cook

Herron's hypothetical building units, functionally and physically related to space landing capsules, can unhook their links to the city and move away (Figure 94, above). The mobility of people and the impermanence of settlement are translated directly and somewhat naively into design and building forms.

Within the city, in whatever its temporary composition of these units, people and things move about in channels that are extended members of contained enclosure. The street is internalized. And circulation tubes, channels, stacks are all developed beyond the encumbrances of grade. Herron, a leading member of the Archigram

group, proposes a building type and urban organization to make a radical, eye-catching statement about new materials, new forms, new awareness of the impermanence of cities. But his proposal is devoid of consideration of its implications for the quality of man's life and even of how people might use such large, impermanent structures. Conditions in the city do shift incessantly. But the city would be totally chaotic without some guarantee of a reasonable amount of permanence, which permits necessary capital and human investment in city services, utilities, and social organization.

In Peter Cook's proposal for a university node,

the structure is designed for random addition or reduction, for plugging into or pulling away from (Figure 95, left). Its component elements are designed for potential functional metamorphoses. The University Node is conceived as a center of communication, of feed-in and feed-back of people and information. Thus its supports are also access tubes, some for movement of people, others for conveyance of information. The precise purpose of the extensible and reducible building units may change, ways of using structure may change; only the central node, the communications core, remains fixed in form and purpose in this proposal.

96. Habitat, Montreal, 1967. Moshe Safdie

A complex of 158 modular apartment units made of concrete elements bolted together on the site convinced spectators at Expo '67 that prefabricated housing could be attractive and offer desirable amenities of private open space, convenience, and dwelling type choices. The heavy material, complex design, and construction of only one-sixth the original number of planned apartments caused higher costs than desirable. But these constraints are being overcome in projects designed for Puerto Rico and Israel. Inside the apartments, innovative construction, especially of bathrooms, revealed how attractive a totally prefabricated, continuous-surface, molded plastic unit could be. Safdie's Habitat expresses physically with both clarity and design sophistication the transition of the building block from traditional subcomponents such as brick or lumber to the dwelling unit itself.

stalled building components. Rudolph's mid-1960's investigation of such potentialities revealed in his Graphic Arts Center project for New York of 1967 (Figure 97) was extended in a number of subsequent projects and further refined in the housing and structural component scheme of his Lower Manhattan Expressway proposal mentioned earlier (Figure 51). It has been Rudolph's contention for a number of years that a new building block must be recognized. The 20th century "brick," as he calls it, must be the entire dwelling unit, seen and used as an integral, compact component of large, multi-unit aggregate forms. And the dwelling unit, or "brick" Rudolph suggests, might very well be derived from the one continuously successful manufactured housing type, the "mobile home." Enlarging the basic unit of building makes sense and is used by Rudolph, Safdie, and others who are trying to get at fundamental means of revamping the conceptual and physical basis of the building process.

A number of advanced building methods are already in use in America. Wood and concrete housing composed of stock catalogue items has been evolved over the last 20 years by the architect Carl Koch, the inventive designer of the Acorn House (1947) and the Techbuilt (1954) and Techcrete (1963) systems. The wheeled trailer is now seen fixed in place all over the country as is the so-called mobile home. Last year over 20 per cent of all new single-family dwellings in the United States were fully equipped and furnished modified trailers, sold at costs unmatched by any conventional on- or off-site fabricated housing. And the proportion is growing. So is research into ways of stacking, arranging, extending, and grouping trailer modules to gain variety, flexibility, and responsiveness to essential concepts of land preservation and aesthetic quality. If these can be worked out, modular units of various types would offer some promise for planning and urban design.

All these experiments with building technique unfortunately offer only mini-

mal potential resolution of the housing crisis. The main problem is cost; and housing cost, when thoroughly evaluated from the occupant's viewpoint, is not based so much on the cost of materials, or even the cost in labor, as on the cost of financing, taxes, and maintenance. The whole point of Operation Breakthrough and private investigation into industrialized or systems building techniques is to reduce the cost of on-site fabrication of buildings. These savings in material and labor are very important to the original developer, who finances and owns an apartment building or house for only a brief time.

To the consumer (the home or apartment occupant), on the other hand, construction costs represent a surprisingly small component of the total long-term monthly cost of occupancy or ownership. For example, on-site labor in conventional residential construction accounts for about 20 per cent of total *construction* cost. However, the total cost of *building* a house represents only about 25 per cent of total monthly *occupancy* costs, which in addition consist of interest and debt retirement (about 25 per cent), utilities (about 15 per cent), and taxes (about 25 per cent). In the final analysis, if a remarkable breakthrough were to reduce on-site labor costs as much as 25 per cent, and few think this is possible, then the total annual occupancy cost of a home to the consumer or homeowner would be reduced only by about one per cent. Thus law and finance emerge as the most promising disciplines through which housing costs may be brought within reach of more of the population. Community subsidy to residential properties through more generous real estate tax policies would be helpful. Local, state, or federal direct or indirect mortgage subsidies could reduce occupancy costs dramatically. State or federal laws requiring a higher proportion of limited-interest loans distributed into long-term mortgages are a possibility. But each of these legal and financial devices, to become effective, depends on a national commitment to reduce the cost of residential shelter. In an economy with

competing demands on every dollar, more extensive housing assistance depends on revised national and state priorities—with a greater proportion of public and private funds allocated to housing.

A few very limited changes in administrative organization to redirect priorities toward achieving massive amounts of needed publicly assisted urban housing at reasonable monthly ownership cost were evident by the early 1970's in spite of a near-complete withdrawal of federal assistance. The most important of these was the creation in 1968 of the New York State Urban Development Corporation (UDC) under the direction of Edward J. Logue. Its purpose, in part, is to satisfy a substantial part of the demand for moderate- and low-income housing in New York State. To perform this complex task, the UDC was initially granted a number of unprecedented powers. These include the right to issue its own tax-exempt bonds and the right to ignore local zoning codes. The UDC was conceived as a conduit and catalyst. Private companies still do the planning, designing, engineering, and building. Now, for the first time in the United States, a public benefit corporation exists to investigate and overcome legal, economic, and technical blockades to the provision of subsidized urban housing; and for the first time the necessary state-level financing, marketing, and legal powers have been assigned.

It is useful to know, if only in outline, how an agency such as the UDC can help assure that more public housing gets built. The UDC has independent, tax-exempt bonding powers. Thus, it can borrow money at lower-cost, tax-exempt rates and use it to reduce the overall cost of holding land, planning, and construction. It can offer a developer calculable economies by underwriting site acquisition, site holding costs, planning, and architectural expenses. These savings can in turn be passed through to the tenant. Thus, public money on which no profit is expected is used to pay for some costly aspects of the development process.

Since its organization in 1968, the UDC has had more than 32,000 dwelling

97. Graphic Arts Center Project, New York, 1967
(View from the West) Paul Rudolph

In Rudolph's proposal, a single large integrated complex is suspended partially above New York's West Side Highway along the Hudson River. There are parking and unloading facilities, office structures, apartments, six floors of loft-type space at the base forming a manmade, terraced hill, schools, a recreation center, a marina, and connecting boardwalks along the river. Apartment units are prefabricated and suspended high in the air from cantilevered trusses; the roof of one apartment forms a terrace for the one above. Public spaces including kindergar-

tens, elementary schools, service, commercial, and recreation facilities are placed on every tenth floor. Here Rudolph expresses one of the early examples of his continuing search for a habitable modular unit which can become the "twentieth century brick," as he calls it. Rudolph seeks to develop such a unit, one which can be manufactured off-site, transported to the site, erected by crane or airlift and, with simple joining, create a basic structural building element and simultaneously a usable enclosed space.

units completed or under construction; a massive planning program is in advanced stages, and implementation of much of it seems certain, including the immense Roosevelt Island development and innovative low-rise housing in Brownsville, New York, discussed later. Projects in major cities around the state are already occupied. This is a remarkable record for a single agency in so short a time.

The New York UDC is presently unique in the United States. But other states contemplate a similar strategy. And so do some cities. However, no federal program of comparable scope is in the works. In fact, federal programs on which the UDC and other state and local housing agencies depend currently remain undeveloped.

Indeed, as the UDC is itself dependent for the great bulk of its building on federal rent subsidy and mortgage subsidy programs, continuing production of housing in volume is directly dependent on renewal of appropriate federal programs.

The UDC has already proved effective as a catalyst to building, as a means of implementing development. It is less clearly effective in promoting and maintaining the highest standards of planning and design in some instances. Responsibility for production of an average of 6,000 to 10,000 dwelling units per year over the last several years is a huge burden, and one accomplished by the UDC through understanding how to work effectively with developers. Thus, the usual compromises in favor of conventional development economics occurred in many of the projects. As the agency matures, it should place more emphasis on maintaining planning and design quality throughout the development process. In this way it could serve as an example of not just how to get public housing built, but also how to make it more desirable and more related to tenants' needs. These concerns are evident in the low-rise urban housing, discussed below, which the UDC is now building.

The concept of the UDC remains sound and progressive from a legal and financial viewpoint. One of its initial powers,

the ability to ignore local zoning, has recently been rescinded except in urban areas. The statewide privilege to override local zoning was initially mandated for the UDC so that public housing could be provided by the agency wherever it was needed. But this power opens up a profound social controversy which is itself a central element in the contemporary American housing situation, and one not often mentioned. This is the issue of *sites*. Building sites. How can they be obtained for public housing? Where can they be found? Who controls them? These are critical problems.

By the late 1960's and early 1970's, as workers followed industry into the countryside, public housing became a very real need in suburban and exurban communities. But this potential is viewed as a threat by most residents outside the central cities and even by many neighborhoods within city centers. Public housing is viewed and indeed actually experienced as a threat to property values, a threat to local education, a threat to the safety of communities, a threat to low social service budgets. Residents everywhere in cities and in suburbs whose vested interests, whose children's education, whose American dream of a standardized safe, secure life have fought this "threat." One way for them to assure that public housing does not threaten these sought-after and cherished qualities is to be certain that no sites are available for public housing. And zoning to exclude multi-family housing is the easiest way to control sites.

The fight is dramatic and will rage on in many forms for years to come. Maverick companies, such as Sterling Homex, which perfected prefabricated housing systems to satisfy an immense market for low-cost public housing in the cities and suburbs, are now famous financial failures mostly because in community after community, approved sites could not be found on which to place the housing. Materials, workmanship, design were all satisfactory. Housing authorities around the country agreed to purchase massive numbers of the factory-produced townhouses. But not enough adequate sites

were made available. Residents resisted. And the acres of prefabricated housing wrapped in immense plastic "baggies" rotted in the fields between the factory in Avon, New York, and the railroad siding.

More recently, in 1972 and 1973, the Urban Development Corporation lost its own long and bitter battle to build public housing in rural towns in northern Westchester County. Public opposition to the Westchester program was so intense that town governments balked; sites were not made available. Finally, in the spring of 1973, the New York State Legislature rescinded the UDC's power to build outside of urban areas. Thus another regressive action in the housing field was achieved by rural and suburban social and economic interests.

However, in scattered locales around the country an effort is still being made by political and legal groups to "open the suburbs." With manufacturing jobs, office jobs, and commercial enterprises now firmly established in many suburban areas, the need for nearby housing of every kind, including public housing, is evident. Thus, large-acreage zoning, which excludes the ordinary single-family house as well as multi-family dwellings, is being challenged in courts by groups such as the Suburban Action Institute. The challenge is based on the claim that zoning laws are generally discriminatory and that housing sites for low- and moderate-income people should be available throughout the suburbs, as well as in the cities.

In some cases, unfortunately, there may be a conflict of interest between the claim to egalitarian housing rights and the potential for developers to benefit financially from new housing which "opens the suburbs." An alliance is more and more often found between conservative, profit-motivated, large-scale development firms and smaller civil liberties groups such as the Suburban Action Institute. The mixture of socially oriented progressive housing development mingled with strong profit-oriented business incentive has a long pedigree, extending to the late 18th and 19th century industrial towns and Garden Cities themselves in Germany and England.

Contemporary efforts to build public housing outside of city centers will, I suspect, continue and will meet with moderate success in some communities. But most suburban towns, through the carefully guarded privilege of building codes, zoning ordinances, and sewer and water control, have impressive powers to resist unwanted development, to say nothing of the high and increasing cost of privately held land in most thriving communities.

At the same time and for altogether different reasons, development of any sort, whether it be industrial, commercial, or residential at anything more than a very modest scale, is becoming increasingly less desirable to many towns and even to some cities, as discussed in the following chapters. Today, costly public improvements are often required of private developers in exchange for the privilege of building—and the demand for these concessions is increasing. In the early years of conventional suburban development just before and after World War II, population and tax ratables were sought by most towns. Since

the mid-1960's, the reverse has become true in well-located, average-size suburban communities throughout the country. In many towns, more people, more roads, and more services are being actively resisted for the first time. This trend, based on growing environmental awareness, new attitudes toward the past, and a complete generation's experience of the American suburb, is expected to continue. Public housing, seen within this overall anticipated evolution of attitudes and local policies, will quite probably remain the most resisted type of development outside the city.

Within urban centers another pervasive problem exists concerning sites for building public housing, even when the site is vacant and appropriately positioned. Sites produced through often brutal and sometimes misguided demolition aspects of the Urban Renewal and Model Cities programs have remained vacant, in some cases for a decade. These sites are in the centers of major cities, such as Newark, Philadelphia, and New York, throughout the country. Why is this so? Why is this the case when urban sites for public housing are in short supply and when

demand for public housing is great?

Part of the answer, of course, has to do with insufficiently funded housing construction programs, inadequate rent supplement programs, and other economic impediments. But some of it has to do, strangely enough, with the premium value that *empty* sites have to the community groups and committees which have authority to dispose of such sites. The site becomes a commodity which, when vacant, possesses continuing value for those who oversee its future. It represents access to power; it represents access to funds for studies, for planning, for community consultants, for grants, or merely for meetings to discuss these measures. When and if a development proposal is accepted and implemented, the site is lost to those who once possessed it. This subtle, complex situation must be recognized; the deterrent which it represents to the use of open sites for badly needed public housing must be resolved in new community control policies and in new approaches to the allocation of sites for housing in urban centers.

In the private sector, specific discernable trends in housing promise to accel-

erate in coming years. Each of these, finally, reflects new land development and real estate business options relevant to current planning, finance, and tax practices.

In the conversion of rural land to housing, the tendency for clustering and for townhouse development is likely to grow. Each uses less land than a conventional single-lot subdivision to create the same number of dwelling units. As a consequence, from the developer's point of view, less land may be necessary at the outset. In addition, the number of utility lines, roadways, and other improvements is minimized. Thus cost can be reduced somewhat. From the point of view of users, the larger-scale cluster development or townhouse community often contains desirable social and recreation amenities such as golf, tennis, and community facilities. These are shared, semi-public facilities maintained not by the homeowner or tenant, but by a management group. The same is true of gardens, walkways, and in some cases even dwelling exteriors. Thus much of the burden of continued maintenance, though paid for by the resident, usually as a separate monthly

carrying charge, is not actually the on-going physical responsibility of the tenant. This convenience combined with the recreational facilities has wide appeal, and both remain crucial marketing points in cluster and townhouse projects. From the viewpoint of the community at large, cluster and townhouse developments, if they are built without increasing otherwise permitted density, have other advantages. Less of the land is actually used. Housing may be placed *on* a parcel at an appropriate spot rather than consuming the total parcel in semi-repetitive houses and streets. Through careful site control and the use of cluster planning concepts, it is possible for a community to manage its physical appearance far more conclusively than would otherwise be the case. In the residential land conversion process, if housing must be built, cluster planning provides advantages to developer, user, and community. When all relevant interests are carefully evaluated the advantages of cluster planning as opposed to the conventional, single, small-lot subdivision, so outweigh the few disadvantages that communitites and citizens should insist that this form of land settlement occur.

98. Voisin Plan for Paris, 1925
Perspective view
Le Corbusier

A city grid is proposed for Paris in which large towers line straight, wide thoroughfares. This powerful image of urban places by one of the great architectural polemicists of the 20th century has exerted a continuing influence on subsequent planning and building. Infatuation with the automobile, to which so much of the city is dedicated in this proposal, and obsession with a startling formal undifferentiated sequence of towers produced a model in urban design which ignores people's needs, patterns of living, and especially requirements for family dwellings in urban areas. And yet the model became pervasive in public housing schemes for large families in many cities. This image is one of the century's great self-fulfilling urbanistic prophecies, and one we are just beginning to muddle out of.

In private sector urban, suburban, and resort multi-family buildings, another significant trend is clear. Owners are trying to get away from residential building ownership. The idea is to ''sell'' the building in pieces, as either a cooperative or condominium, to the tenants. The tenant becomes an owner with certain tax advantages and the satisfaction of owning the place in which he lives. He may also view the apartment as an ''investment'' that will appreciate in value over the years or that he can rent out for profit. The original owner is thereby presumably capable of making a profit on the piece-by-piece ''retail'' sale of the building which he bought or built ''wholesale.'' In addition, his income may be taxed only at favorable capital gains rates rather than as regular income and he is relieved of the burden of sharply increasing operating costs and often annoying management responsibilities. Of course, if rents were rising rapidly all around the country, if tenants were not increasingly organized and militant, if owning residential buildings—in short—were still easy and very profitable, it is less likely that the condominium-co-op trend would be so evident. But the trend will remain evident and of increasing importance in private sector apartment housing because of social, economic, and tax factors of the most fundamental kind.

Important and substantial new directions in the design of housing have occurred in recent years. During the 1960's, professionals in the social sciences in America became interested in the housing issue, as they had been for quite some time in Europe. In ad hoc groups, they often teamed up with architects to try to work out rational criteria for urban housing. Indeed, the exercise of generating new housing criteria, standards, and user-needs analyses became the rage in the mid-1960's and remain in vogue today, Multi-disciplinary teams of sociologists, urban anthropologists, psychologists, and design professionals; university groups; students in Europe and America, all rushed in recent years to develop housing criteria and user-needs standards.

Strangely enough, only a limited number of these groups bothered to ask tenants themselves what they thought, what they experienced, what they liked.

Nevertheless, some promising new design and planning directions are noticeable as a result of so much analysis, especially in the design of public housing. Many problems, it was learned in the 1970's after a long history in America of stacking urban public housing in high-rise towers, had to do with the format of the tower itself (Figure 101), although European and especially English architects recognized this problem at least five years before it was clear in America.

By the early 1970's, it was finally realized in American cities that neighbors in lower, surrounding buildings found the high-rise tower visually offensive and, one suspects, partially unacceptable because of the density of new residents. Tenants and professional analysts of housing found that the high-rise apartment, given trends within the society in general, produces a breeding ground for crime and an atmosphere of insecurity and danger. A notable study by Oscar Newman, *Defensible Space*, published in 1972, produced a statistical basis for and codified many of the critical attitudes to high-rise housing that surfaced in the late 1960's and early 1970's.[21] The high-rise residential tower model, it became clear, is likely to produce an environment in which tenants have no sense of belonging to a community, in which tenants cannot easily or even adequately observe their children at play, in which very little usable semi-private open space is available and in which the crime rate because of these circumstances and others is higher than in socially similar nearby low-rise housing.

In terms of architectural and planning models, this research discovered that the wrong path had been taken as far back as the 1920's, a period when public housing was also of major interest to theorists and designers. By the mid-1920's, both potential models existed—the low-rise tower placed in a park as Le Corbusier suggested; and the low-rise, clustered and linked units which enclose or define com-

munally used semi-private open space, as the innovative American architects Clarence Stein and Henry Wright built in Sunnyside Gardens, Queens, New York, 1924–28 (Figures 99, 100).

But Corbusier's model and its European sources prevailed, especially in New York. It requires somewhat less land per dwelling unit. The freestanding self-contained unlinked slab could be placed on any site. And at the same time it seemed an innovative—even bold—way to develop urban housing. Thus the massive public housing programs in most of the larger American cities from the late 1930's to the present have been tall towers placed in open parks. These park spaces are often underutilized and unmonitored, a condition which has proven to be conducive to crime. At times they are even paved over into parking lots (Figure 101).

By the early 1970's, it became plain to many that a different urban housing model was needed. Planners knew it. Architects knew it. Sociologists knew it. Public development and housing agencies knew it. Aspects of the new model were developed jointly in 1972–73 by the Institute for Architecture and Urban Studies and the New York State Urban Development Corporation (Figures 102, 103). Through research, analysis, and site planning studies came generic proposals for low-rise (no more than four stories), public housing for New York City which is still dense enough to satisfy urban economic requirements. In addition, various types of open space are created in relation to each dwelling where its use can be visually monitored, and in relation to the urban street which is observed as an organizing and informing element. The elevator is nowhere to be seen. And each dwelling has a private door, entered from the street.

The return to low-rise potentials for clustering and planning of urban housing is partially made possible when it becomes clear that density itself is not an issue. Well-planned low-rise housing can accommodate about as many people per acre as conventional high-rise-in-the-park towers. The issue, rather, when one considers urban economics and the lamentable fate

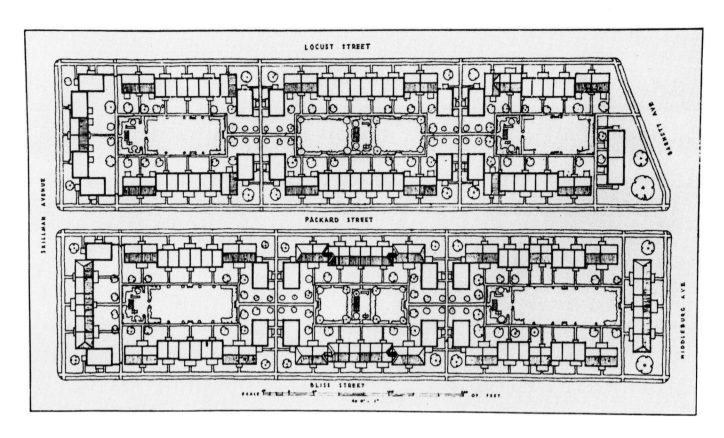

99-100. Sunnyside Gardens, Long Island, New York, 1924–28
Plan of Blocks Built in 1926 (top); Photograph of the Court, 1949 (above)
Clarence Stein and Henry Wright

The block is designed as a whole and the street is seen as a service element (Figure 99, top). Within the block, private and semi-private spaces are created. Private gardens are proposed throughout; semi-private open space is provided in three clusters. This arrangement, one year after Corbusier's Voisin Plan for Paris, offers a compelling alternative to the conventional high-rise superblock perimeter building or the tall tower in the center of the block. The buildings are kept low to the ground so that families and children have access to the surface

for play. Enclosed communal spaces provide a measure of physical safety and emotional security (Figure 100, above).

Many of the opportunities of the city grid are understood in this scheme which respects traditional residential desires for light, air, play space, and the potential for personal interaction and association at all times during the life cycle. The scheme also provides requisite densities, building economies in repeated units and acceptance of the city's infrastructure which is necessary if housing is to be produced at all

in older urban areas.

Stein and Wright, in spite of their exceptional and even influential work at Sunnyside Gardens, Radburn, New Jersey, Chatham Village in Pittsburgh, Pennsylvania, and elsewhere during the 1920's and 1930's, never achieved the national and certainly not the international prominence of their contemporary Le Corbusier. Their influence on urban planning and especially on planning for housing is now emerging. Much is to be learned from a careful analysis of their work.

101. Alfred E. Smith Houses, New York City, View toward Downtown. Eggers and Higgins

This low-cost public housing of the late 1940's is much like middle-income housing such as Stuyvesant Town of about the same time and like most large-scale large-city housing projects into the mid-1960's. The high-rise tower dominates. Around it public open space sprawls at the base. The street is denied, ignored as a fundamental and desirable aspect of the housing itself. A patch of grass which is often transformed to parked cars, is visible from up in the air. But the open space is not usable by young children who must be observed or by people of all ages who seek safety and some relief from the noise and smell of traffic. The expediency of high-rise construction, the goal of packing the most people possible into each city acre, publicly administered building codes, zoning ordinances, and financing programs all collaborated to produce the tall residential tower, which most of the people never wanted and never liked. Today, in many urban areas, abandonments of public housing tower units are commonplace; tenant maintenance is rare; crime is rife; the street is ignored as a communal and commercial resource.

of so much existing urban terrain, is how to keep the built environment desirable; how to provide places where people want to be, and that they consequently will be willing to maintain. If these crucial issues can be taken seriously, then design of housing in cities and in the suburbs can proceed with the occupant, not the rule book or public authority, as the real client. The so-called "low-rise high-density" prototype recognizes the issues and signals the UDC's recognition that redirection of concept and design will benefit the holder of long-term mortgages as well as provide more desirable housing.

The low-rise high-density prototype is indeed sufficiently responsive to need and to public housing program economic requirements that one large development is now underway, based on the prototype on parts of ten contiguous blocks in the Brownsville section of Brooklyn; others are planned for a variety of other types of sites (Figures 104–108).

Quite recently, insistence on a low-rise housing alternative is emerging around the country for large housing projects both publicly and privately financed. For example, a well-planned eight-story condominium for downtown Charleston proposed by a developer was opposed in the fall of 1973 by a citizens' group which gathered financial support from every state except Alaska. As an acceptable alternative the Save Charleston Foundation intends to put low-rise housing on the site for about the same number of people.

This is not to say that low-rise housing is the best alternative in every case. High-rise towers and their attendant convenience of elevators remain sensible when single people, young couples, and especially the elderly are the intended occupants. High-rise solutions also remain a compelling option when absolutely unique views can be obtained in those rare cases when obtaining such views would not also restrain others from the same pleasure. High-rise buildings still make sense when very small building plots are available in prime locations. Here people of all ages are anxious to live who very often have second homes, sufficient leisure time for numerous vacations, and adequate disposable discretionary income to compensate in every way for the limitations imposed by high-rise residential living.

The range of alternatives with a continuing emphasis on better quality and more amenity has been most thoroughly studied recently by the Urban Design Council of New York, directed by Alexander Cooper. In their recently released primer-manual-report, *Housing Quality: A Program for Zoning Reform,* flexible performance standards are detailed with points assigned so that proposed plans can be developed, reviewed, and rated according to neighborhood, environmental, design, and amenity standards. Within this design and evaluation tool a renewed interest is evident in low-rise building, flexibility, and street level amenities. This valuable and progressive proposed program is of crucial importance as it sets city-wide zoning goals for housing which transcend the individual building lot and which recognize the primacy of neighborhood quality and coherence as well as tenant needs. It is tempting to think that the stubborn problems encountered in designing and producing housing can be swept away quite simply by using impermanent structures as proposed with considerable eloquence recently in a very good book by Martin Pawley.[22] Even the mobile home park reveals that this is not the case. People do not really want to keep moving, to settle when night falls in the nearest field within their totally contained trailer. In housing, likewise, people seek continuity but are often unable to obtain it. Forced job relocation, economic independence from the land and from a place, changing economic circumstances, changing social and environmental conditions in a neighborhood—all of these produce a society more mobile and transient than ever before. But it is misreading this mobility to see it as voluntary and misconverting it to a housing policy and theory that ignores the pervasive human instinct for order and permanence.

Indeed, by and large, people seek permanence, and so long as choice is available, they also seek relatively homoge-

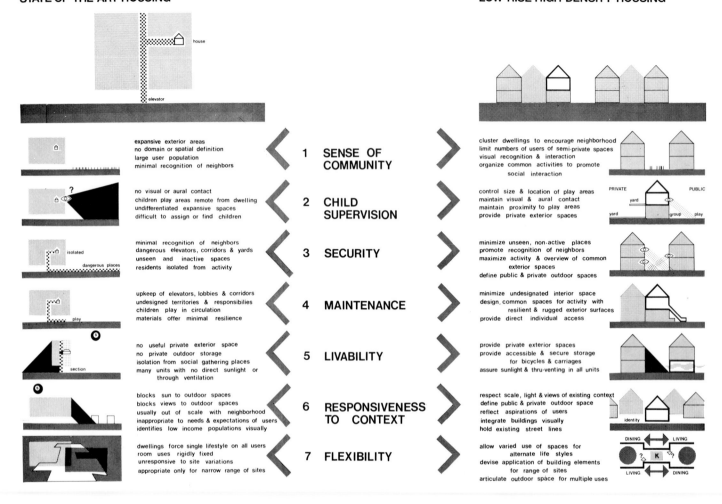

102. Low-Rise High-Density Housing Organizing Issues, 1972–73
The Institute for Architecture and Urban Studies
The New York State Urban Development Corporation

In this diagram the potential for low-rise housing as opposed to conventional tall residential towers with elevators was analyzed to isolate essential organizing issues and amenities which low-rise housing could provide. It was determined that about as many people could be housed with either high-rise or low-rise solutions on the same amount of land. But, in most cases and especially where families are involved, the low-rise alternative, when carefully designed, offers substantial advantages in the crucial matters of sense of community, small child supervision, total community security, maintenance, livability, responsiveness to context, and flexibility.

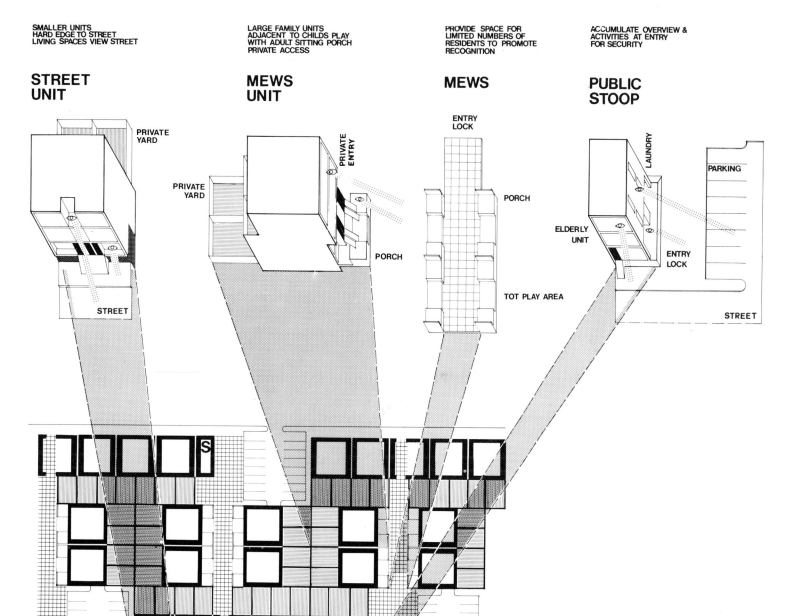

STREET
UNIT

SMALLER UNITS
HARD EDGE TO STREET
LIVING SPACES VIEW STREET

PRIVATE
YARD

STREET

MEWS
UNIT

LARGE FAMILY UNITS
ADJACENT TO CHILDS PLAY
WITH ADULT SITTING PORCH
PRIVATE ACCESS

PRIVATE
ENTRY

PRIVATE
YARD

PORCH

MEWS

PROVIDE SPACE FOR
LIMITED NUMBERS OF
RESIDENTS TO PROMOTE
RECOGNITION

ENTRY
LOCK

PORCH

TOT PLAY AREA

PUBLIC
STOOP

ACCUMULATE OVERVIEW &
ACTIVITIES AT ENTRY
FOR SECURITY

LAUNDRY

PARKING

ELDERLY
UNIT

ENTRY
LOCK

STREET

103. Low-Rise High-Density Housing Prototype Elements, 1972–73
The Institute for Architecture and Urban Studies
The New York State Urban Development Corporation

These prototype housing elements and site design for low-rise housing were derived to fulfill the greatest general promise of this housing type. These elements include: private entrances from semi-private stoops for each dwelling unit, a private yard or balcony for each dwelling unit, semi-private mews spaces at the interior of blocks in which children may be observed from within the dwelling and in which small children can play together safely, common stoop entrances from the street for four to six dwelling units to allow for socialization along the street, but not directly on it, interior arrangement of all dwelling units to assure maximum visual surveillance of street, stoop, parking areas, and mews so as to promote security and a continual sense of community well-being.

104–105. Low-Rise High-Density Housing Scheme, Marcus Garvey Urban Renewal Area, Brooklyn, New York, 1973
Street Façade, photograph of the model (top); Interior Mews, photograph of the model (above)
The Institute for Architecture and Urban Studies

Parts of ten blocks in central Brooklyn are now being redeveloped for low-rise public housing according to organizing principles and proto-typical housing elements developed in previous research and analysis. The elements are modified by specific site requirements into a scheme especially suited to blocks interrupted by a city street grid. The large site will also include convenient commercial facilities, day care centers, and a large recreation park. Each apartment has

either a garden or a large balcony. Units for large families are clustered around internal mews spaces as shown, where younger children can play under visual surveillance from within the apartment. Each apartment has a private entrance from a collective stoop along the street. The stoop continues to function as it traditionally has in urban areas for observing the activities along the street and socializing in the neighborhood. Within the buildings no one walks more than 2½ flights to his own

apartment, many of which are duplex. And yet the density of about 60 units per acre with an emphasis on large-family apartments permits sufficiently economical use of urban land to make this a prototype scheme for older urban areas already developed along street grid patterns. This scheme recognizes persistent social, emotional, and amenity problems in high-rise housing and signals a viable redirection of urban housing schemes.

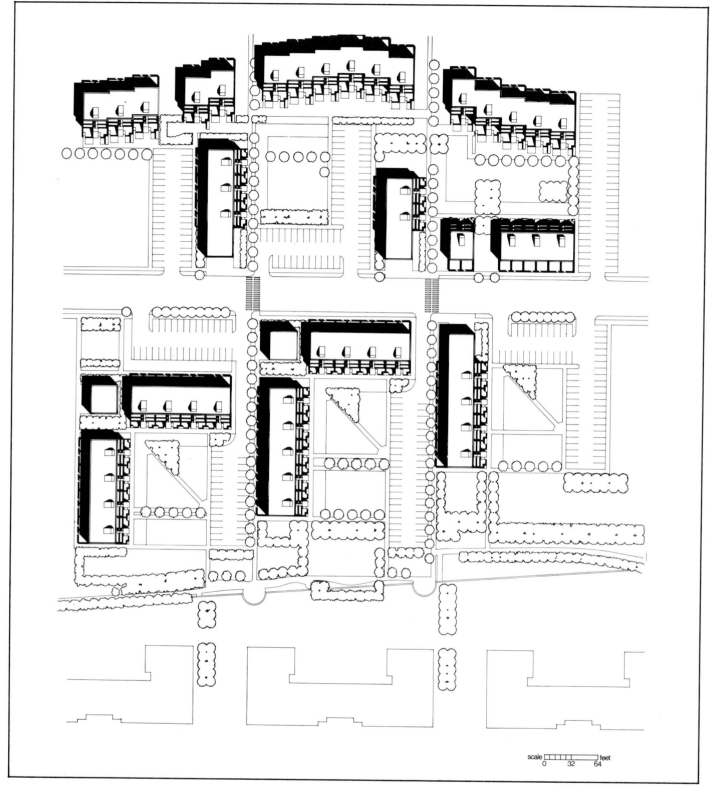

scale | feet
0 32 64

106-108. Low-Rise High-Density Housing Proposal, Fox Hills, Staten Island, New York, 1973. Site plan
The Institute for Architecture and Urban Studies

Most of the same principles which contribute to the Marcus Garvey project are incorporated into this proposal for an open, undeveloped suburban site. But without the imposition of the street grid, semi-private open space can be collected in communal greens and developed selectively for play, recreation, and other purposes. Automobile parking areas, a suburban necessity at present, form a well-landscaped edge to the community green. The massing of the aggregate dwelling units and open space offer a living area with which residents can personally identify while at the same time presenting a reasonable alternative to the land-wasting, socially isolating conventional single-family housing development sprawl at one end of the scale and the ever-increasing suburban town house or garden apartment complex at the other. About 40 dwelling units are placed on an acre, as opposed to two to four in the conventional single-family subdivision and 10 to 15 in most garden apartments.

neous racial, social, and economic surroundings in which to live. It is perhaps more progressive to accept these sometimes forgotten realities about man than to try to inflict new and unwanted settlement patterns and theorist-imposed life modes on people. Many of the political events and dynamic social movements of the 1960's and early 1970's are telling us these things, if we are only patient enough to listen. Success in housing placement and design for those who really need housing has more to do with the architect, planner, and builder listening carefully to the people and to the society than in madly inventing—and thereby imposing—a new order.

At the same time, there is no reason to abandon the search for a lighter, technologically superior, and more efficient dwelling. A quest for lightness, for reduced cost, for improved life support systems, for greater operating economies and efficiency in housing and in building is essential. This quest is linked by some avant-garde theorists and groups, as discussed earlier, with the necessity for transience. It is linking the two that misdirects and essentially misunderstands the great potential in the use of new energy systems, miniaturization, and advanced scientific discoveries of all sorts.

But most important of all—if real progress is to be made in the provision of better housing for more of the people in years to come—national, state, and local financial and legal resources will have to be redirected so that shelter obtains a higher priority, and a greater proportion of these national resources. The problem is first and finally political. Architects, planners, and others in design and development can only help in the middle.

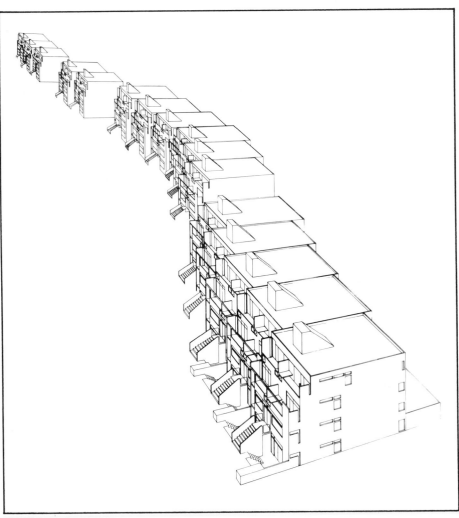

107. Perspective sketch

108. Façade, photograph of the model

New Directions

Meaningful economies in occupancy costs of new housing will be found in methods of finance and tax policies, not in design or building technology, although technologically advanced housing will be built increasingly as new processes are proven and institutionalized.

Building sites in city and suburb must be made available for publically assisted housing by an objective and socially responsible process based on need, job proximity and balanced community development.

More housing should be clustered or attached in new developments.

Amenities and semi-private shared spaces will increase in private and public housing.

Multi-unit residential buildings will be increasingly sold to occupants as condominiums or cooperatives.

Low-rise non-elevator buildings must be provided for most family housing, even in urban areas.

109. Air Pollution, Sacramento River, California

Many of the essentials of urban life such as transportation, electricity, and machinery cause massive and persistent air, water, and sound pollution that severely diminish the quality of urban life. This unpleasant fact is not a perpetual necessity. But only in recent years has public pressure caused a process of control to begin. Fortunately the air, the water, and even the land contain inherent powers of regeneration if man will only use his technological capabilities with restraint respecting the earth's natural resources. This restraint and respect, when exercised, will do a great deal to make city life once again quite agreeable.

The Urban Environment

In the late 1960's, for the first time in the history of man, negative qualities within the environment became an overt urban design determinant. The sources of urban environmental problems stimulated social, political, and legal reaction. During the 1960's, the disparity between the illusion of progress and the reality of a linked disintegration of the physical context of life was recognized in all of its irony for the first time. For many people, more gadgets, more disposable goods, greater consumption of energy, higher gross national product, and other traditional signs of national well-being were shattered as acceptable measures of "progress." The myths of industrialism were shaken, and a society unprepared for the post-industrial age in which it had been operating for some time was exposed. It seems scarcely possible that it was as recently as 1970 that the Environmental Action group organized Earth Day—and catapulted environmental issues into the national consciousness.

In the urban context, for instance, in recent years planners and the public focused for the first time on the invisible structure of the city. Power and utility lines, drainage conduits, and the transportation network, all elements of the "infrastructure" which has been ignored and taken for granted for so long, gained a position of prominence that far outweighed aesthetic considerations. Open space, light, the air, the streets and corridors through which people and noise travels became focal points of major concern to the public, public agencies, and professionals who work with city issues.

Why so much sudden attention? Simply because information about the environment became available just as the infrastructure broke down for the first time and sensory impacts became unbearable. Normal obsolescence and excessive de-

mand on old systems in cities across the country combined to cripple capacity. Electric power was limited, often at critical periods, a circumstance that brought into question the long-range future of older cities. The absence of sufficient supplies of water and fuel began to be viewed as a severe potential limiting factor to urban and suburban life and development.

The quality of city space and air, sometimes called the "urban ecological ambient," was associated for the first time with the infrastructure of the city. Automobile-clogged roads simultaneously inhibit pedestrian movement and render city air increasingly lethal. Electric power, necessary for heat, cooling, business, industry, office machines, and public transportation, sustains the life of the city. It is also the product of a process which itself consumes large quantities of energy and destroys the air and water upon which the city depends (Figure 109). Our incremental micro-scale interventions in the development of cities has produced an accumulation of macro-scale problems which we find ourselves ill-equipped to predict or control, and until recently, almost without means even to measure.

In a single decade our awareness of these stubborn ironies has emerged. The city, for the first time in history, is viewed as a complex "ecological" system. Only recently have we recognized that any proposed major intervention must be evaluated in terms of its impact on the infrastructure; and that in spite of our relative sophistication, this impact remains rather uncertain. Urban environmental resource management is urgently needed; but we scarcely know how or where to begin.

Yet the impact of invisible processes and energy forms, such as sound waves and chemical reactions, must now be evaluated as part of any reasonable planning effort. Never before in the history of cities

has public space and the unseen and generally unconsidered infrastructure been the focus of so much study and so much potential transformation. A new set of environmental opportunities and restrictions is imposed by our emerging awareness. By the fall of 1973, this awareness has grown so dramatically that Russell E. Train, head of the federal Environmental Protection Agency, could remark with some accuracy, "The environmental and quality-of-life issue is the major issue ahead for the remainder of the century." The issue itself is, at the same time, inexorably tied to and interlinked with new directions in land use control and regulation, as discussed in Chapter 8.

Emphasis on environmental issues, which has grown so rapidly in all fields, has led within the planning professions to strong interest at the macro-scale in regional and national land use planning and, on the micro-environmental scale, to a number of efforts to improve the urban ambient in which we live.

In planning and building, development of "controlled urban environments" has become an increasingly strong tendency in recent years. Enclosed shopping malls, pedestrian concourses through buildings, and pedestrian passageways to link various significant structures are regularly suggested, and occasionally implemented as a way, in part, to shield man from the undesirable urban environment. Planning responsive to external environmental conditions and desire for commercial success by client-developers has much to do with such schemes, especially in completely new projects around the country such as Philip Johnson and John Burgee's immensely successful and well planned IDS Center in Minneapolis and Houston's Post Oak Galleria. Both the IDS and the Galleria contain numerous specialty retail shops, a major department store, an

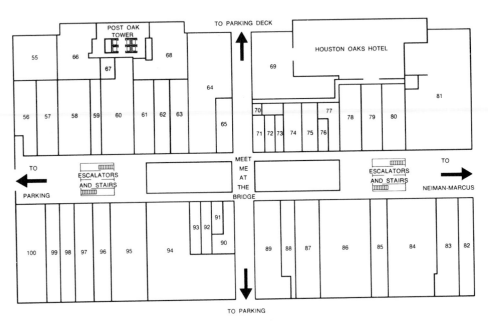

LEVEL 1

TO 3-LEVEL PARKING DECK

TO 3-LEVEL PARKING DECK

POST OAK
OFFICE TOWER
LOBBY

HOUSTON OAKS HOTEL
LOBBY

ESCALATORS
AND STAIRS

ICE RINK

ESCALATORS
AND STAIRS

CINEMA I

CINEMA II

PARKING

LEVEL 2

TO PARKING DECK

POST OAK
TOWER

HOUSTON OAKS HOTEL

TO

ESCALATORS
AND STAIRS

PARKING

MEET
ME
AT
THE
BRIDGE

ESCALATORS
AND STAIRS

TO

NEIMAN-MARCUS

TO PARKING

110-111. Galleria Complex
Houston, Texas, 1970
Plan (left); Interior perspective (right)
Hellmuth, Obata & Kassabaum

This three-level covered shopping mall is completely enclosed and connected to a 22-story office tower, a 21-story hotel, and a Neiman-Marcus department store (Figure 110, left). To make shopping more interesting and profit potential greater, there are entertainment and recreation facilities such as art galleries, restaurants, and cinemas as well as a large ice skating rink at the center of the lower level (Figure 111, right). Parking, which surrounds the complex, is shared among all users as are heat, air conditioning, and light, to gain maximum round-the-clock use of space and equipment. The variety, usage mixture, and sheer scale of the project distinguish it from a conventional mall shopping center.

The Galleria, beyond downtown Houston, is a satellite center at the intersection of two major freeways fed exclusively by automobile traffic. Its linked structures are surrounded by acres of parked cars. Parking space is certainly the most important single amenity this kind of complex must offer. Yet this plan succeeds because it frees the individual from his car, from the strip shopping street to which he is accustomed, and allows simulation of an older, more urbane world of leisurely pedestrian activity that predates the automobile and the American sprawl city. The Gerald D. Hines Interests, developers of the Galleria, are sufficiently aware of the markets that are freeing people from the car that they plan to extend the complex and integrate its extension with a system of public transportation.

The enclosed-mall suburban shopping center is of course the influential prototype upon which major, large-scale central city urban redevelopment now depends. The difference is access and parking. But many of the other elements are the same, including enclosure from the surrounding environment, linkage between multi-level and multi-functional uses, tendency toward dramatic flair, and dependence on joint public-private cooperation.

office tower, and a luxury hotel arrayed around a tall, generous multi-level semi-public space. To enhance and facilitate pedestrian use, IDS is linked in four directions to the street and skyway systems of downtown Minneapolis. The Galleria, isolated as it is at a highway intersection, creates its own central space activity with an ice skating rink (Figures 110, 111).

Most of these enclosed enclaves, linked building complexes, regional shopping centers, and such protect the individual from the noise and foul air generally experienced at the city center and along its auto routes. They also provide a sense of place reminiscent of traditional urban enclaves like the *place* or *piazza*. Additionally, they shield contemporary man from natural climatic extremes of heat, cold, humidity, and precipitation. This climate-controlled world, of course, requires more energy and each similar complex fails to recognize the adverse impact of this demand multiplied manifold times throughout the nation.

On a much larger scale, some cities with inclement weather and deteriorating downtowns have recently tried environmentally astute planning schemes to revive and improve the commercial center. Minneapolis and Montreal are leaders in this movement. Minneapolis has begun to fulfill a plan developed by its progressive City Planning and Development Department for mid-block glass-enclosed second-level pedestrian "skyways" throughout the central business district (Figures 24, 25, 26). Skyways span city streets at mid-block to link the second-story level of buildings throughout the central business district. In this often cold and windy city, a connected network is emerging between major downtown buildings of heated, air conditioned, and well-lighted glass passageways, which are expected to grow through the city center linking the interiors of old and new buildings to one another and to various underground concourses, transit stations, and fringe parking docks. The IDS center tops off this noteworthy achievement by creating

at its mid-block multi-level and multi-faceted central space, known as the Crystal Court, an urban intersection for people and pedestrian-linked activities.

Lawrence Halprin, an American landscape architect and planner whose special concern with the double problem of environment and movement make his practice an interesting manifestation of the last decade, prepared comprehensive studies for the redevelopment of downtown Minneapolis. His emphasis on urban public space design from highways to fountains, perhaps the outcome of his training as a landscape architect, mingled with his interest in activity patterns of people in cities, has made his 1960's environmentally sensitive designs, such as Ghirardelli Square shopping and entertainment center in San Francisco (Figures 119, 120), Nicollet Mall in Minneapolis (Figures 25, 26), and the fountain block in Portland, Oregon, particularly successful.

The Montreal plan by Vincent Ponte (Figure 90) provides enclosed pedestrian passages as a comfortable, attractive link between transportation, commercial, and business centers. Its wide corridors, which offer views to exterior gardens and protect people from inclement weather, noise, and poor air, are proven successful as well by revitalization and redevelopment at the city center.

In fact, Vincent Ponte represents a new direction in the planning profession as well. For the first time, the profession is attracting men from the private sector who are relatively independent in their judgment and relatively sophisticated in law, finance, and marketing. The traditional planner today is still the adequately trained public official or private consultant with a good grasp of local politics, local soil conditions, and local ordinances. He generally reacts rather than initiates. But with men like Ponte in the forefront, this is changing.

John Portman's stunning success as architect-developer in the past decade grows in part from his early recognition of environmental design determinants and

opportunities—and his ability to meet these with dramatic, action-filled, architecturally original interior spaces. In addition, he represents another new type of professional, in this case an architect-developer involved with the whole building process from planning and design through finance, construction, ownership, and management. Portman, and a few other architects with a similar attitude, argue that being one's own client has advantages for the architect, for the developer, and for the project. His hotels and development concepts are successful in Atlanta, Chicago, San Francisco, and elsewhere. His services are in demand around the country. For the Times Square area of New York he proposes a hotel with glassed-in cafés at ground floor, an interior seven-story retail shopping center, revolving restaurants, and a 35-story-high central court through which circular glass elevators travel (Figures 112, 113). This is the external world brought inside with flair to make a commercial venture succeed. It is also urban design working against the city in a certain sense, against the existing street, and against what is out on the street.

Portman's instinct is proven. His judgment of what people want has been tested. Most of all, he is willing to overcome the role of architect as servant. The role of architect-developer permits a new type of practice—a new model of importance to the architectural and planning professions. In coming years, as competition for dwindling commissions intensifies and as economic rewards for planning and especially architecture become even less satisfactory, a greater number of capable professionals should consider expanding their work and role to become their own client.

If the urban environment is not radically improved in years ahead by planners, architects, and developers, the dense connective tissue of the city is likely to continue to loosen. Major environmentally sophisticated enclaves such as Portman's Atlanta Peachtree Center, Ponte's downtown Montreal, and others will meet contemporary environmental demands, especially for acceptable commercial facilities. But much of the city will continue to languish and continue to be replaced by the suburban office center and shopping mall which are, after all, the generic model for many environmentally successful recent urban redevelopment schemes.

Protection from pollutants combined with enhancement of environmental quality for the individual are likely, then, to continue to be goals which stimulate large numbers of city center design proposals and planning concepts in the coming decade. Linkage to existing and new public transit will become a primary direction as suggested in Chapter 4 and as exemplified in a proposed concourse arrangement of the new Washington, D.C. subway accompanied by micro-environmental redesign of the street above (Figures 114, 115).

Uncontrolled infatuation with the environmental predicaments of our age has also appeared in urban design proposals. Theorist and visionary Buckminster Fuller suggests covering a large portion of sound-loaded, air-polluted midtown Manhattan with a great translucent dome; similar suggestions have been made for smaller cities (Figures 116, 117). How any of these could be built, maintained, or even ventilated is never stated. And the impact on man of packaging his life in a large volumetric celluloid container is something worth considering. Fuller's considerable achievements and contributions to urban science, urban planning education, building technology, environmental awareness, and understanding of world resources are still not fully appreciated. He is one of the great men of this century and one of the great American contributors to engineering, planning, and design. But his suggestion for covering New York with a great, clear dome can only be seen as a way to dramatize the potential of the dome rather than as a serious suggestion about how modern man might in fact cope with the environment.

Nowhere, however, has the specter of a species systematically destroying itself through its own building efforts produced

a more curious response than in the work of Paolo Soleri. His conviction is that land must be conserved, and that microminiaturization and the technology of building ought to be combined to produce a new and viable environment for man, as expressed in his compact "arcologies" (Figure 118). Soleri's arcologies might be described as entire cities for a vast number of people meant to sprout on the mesa. The acclaim which Soleri has achieved in the last decade is both a tribute to his own formidable perseverence and evidence of the mind-numbing fear shared by many people that we may be unable to save our physical environment in rational ways.

While proposals and projects of varying usefulness for physical responses to our environmental problems reveal the range of thinking that is going on, other efforts are being made to resolve these problems at their source.

For instance, it is now recognized that the internal combustion engine is the most destructive urban environmental force. Air composition analysis, which was scarcely undertaken a decade ago, now demonstrates that 85 to 90 per cent of all pollutants in city air are a result of the internal combustion engine. Smog, principally caused by engine exhaust, can kill trees, destroy crops, and harm people. Experts believe that the day of reckoning is not far off. Dr. Kenneth Watt, a zoologist and director of the Environmental Systems Group at the University of California, says, "If pollution keeps building up in the Los Angeles basin, by the winter of 1975–76 it will be at levels where mass mortality incidents are possible. The weaker ones will go during an inversion."

It has taken a decade of intensive research and publicity to reveal the magnitude of urban environmental danger. Toward the end of the 1960's, intensive control efforts began for the first time. But the beginning of the 1970's must be recognized as the time when the slowly accumulated evidence of the potential for the destruction of human settlements by pollutants of all sorts culminated in a vast

national redirection, initially of legislation and subsequently of some commitment of resources.

In January of 1970 the "National Environmental Policy Act" was signed into law. This act required a vast assessment of the environmental effects of all projects with a federal interest. By this Act, the Environmental Protection Agency (EPA) was established. The new agency consolidated regulatory powers that had been by and large ineffectually vested in a dozen bureaus and special-interest oriented agencies within the federal government such as the Departments of Agriculture and Interior, the Atomic Energy Commission, the Federal Power Commission, and others. The importance of this new agency and its continued independence cannot be underestimated. Its responsibility is to see that all projects with a federal interest are properly assessed in terms of impact on the environment and to see that these potential impacts become public information. As William D. Ruckelshaus, until recently head of the Environmental Protection Agency, correctly pointed out in early 1973, "it is the first systematic attempt to change the pattern of ecological *laissez faire.*" If the federal government can successfully and rigorously regulate its own massive enterprise environmentally, a huge step forward will have been achieved. Thus far, most of the evidence is in proposals, new regulations, and verbal commitments. Rigorous implementation of and adherence to new criteria and standards is the essential next step. The next several years will set the pattern. And it is likely to be set in the courts. *If* the EPA asserts its authority, and *if* the courts around the country generally uphold the EPA's demands, then a dramatically improved environmental situation will prevail within a decade. But both *ifs* are very important. It is too early to know.

Congress itself overrode the National Environmental Policy Act to expedite the trans-Alaska pipeline quite recently, and continuing revision of standards may very well occur during the

112–113. Proposed Hotel
Times Square, Manhattan, 1973
Photograph of the model (left)
Interior perspective drawing (right)
John Portman & Associates

The proposed 54-story, 2,020-room convention hotel includes a 35-story-high atrium or lobby-court through which round glass elevators travel, a seven-story self-contained shopping center, a "legitimate" theater, a revolving restaurant, ground and roof level cafés, and other major design and development features. The proposal expands concepts already used in successful Portman projects in Atlanta, Chicago, and San Francisco. It illustrates how a forceful, aware architect-builder-developer who recognizes the environmental wasteland of our cities is able to respond with a successful commercial formula. City amenities are brought inside; the convention-going guest is contained in a micro-universe. The older, existing city is closed out—its noise, dirt, crime, and bad air forgotten.

This pattern of urban redevelopment, stimulated in part by environmental problems and linked to competent urban planning and programming, could accelerate the already-perilous decline in the amenity offered by public spaces within the city. Enclaves of enclosed, protected urban spaces replace the street, the older public meeting place and shopping artery. And where linkage to transit and long-range transportation is provided—as it will be wherever possible—people will be able to *use* the city as a central, regional meeting spot or cultural and shopping resource without ever really *being in* the city. This is already possible at Gateway Center in Newark, one of America's first registered urban casualties, and one still declining by all reasonable measures.

On the other hand, major redevelopment projects with strong and even flamboyant commercial and retail elements create needed vitality in urban centers. Portman's $200 million Peachtree Center helped rebuild the heart of downtown Atlanta, his $250 million Embarcadero Center in San Francisco (financed jointly by Portman, Trammel Crow, David Rockefeller, and Prudential Life) has been a commercial boon to its district, and the projected $500 million Renaissance Center in Detroit is being sponsored by the Ford Motor Company and other local Detroit investors for profit and also to restore a languishing downtown to economic health.

114-115. Proposed G Street Pedestrian Concourse, Washington, D.C. 1969
Perspective section (above); Perspective drawing of concourse level (right)
Wallace, McHarg, Roberts & Todd and Conklin & Rossant

One of the few new subways in the planning stage in the United States is in Washington, D.C. In this proposal, the existing street above the subway is roofed over by a simple structure and converted to a climate-controlled pedestrian mall (Figure 114, above). Below street level, but open to it, a new shopping concourse is connected to the rapid transit level below.

The implications of eliminating traffic, double decking, and enclosing a section of a major existing street are explored. With relatively sparse use of resources the public space now devoted principally to auto traffic, fumes, and noise becomes a desirable two-level, climate-controlled, commercial promenade, integrally related to existing buildings which abut the original street (Figure 115, right). Removal, redevelopment, and relocation of utilities pose the major problem.

A tendency to enclose public space in the city to make it more comfortable and to change its character radically from automobile-dominated to people-dominated has emerged in many urban-scale redevelopment proposals, especially in recent years. The emergence of urban environmental impacts as one aspect of the problem in our cities responsible for a self-destructive situation is reflected in these proposals to contain and recondition the space, place, and air in which urban man lives and functions. This scheme also reflects the growing importance of transportation as a stimulant to urban design. In many cases without the funds associated with new transportation projects and the physical changes which they require, large-scale redevelopment and planning would not be undertaken.

**116. Two-Mile Hemispherical Dome
for Manhattan, c. 1955** (right)
Buckminster Fuller
**117. Domed Spaces for Poughkeepsie,
New York, 1963–64** (below)
Conklin & Rossant

The environmental issue has even provoked
superscale techno-romantic imagery. The
dwindling number of residents and job holders
in midtown New York could be encapsulated
under a hemispherical dome for about $200
million, according to Fuller, who claims that savings to the city in air conditioning, street cleaning,
snow removal, and lost man-hours from colds
and other respiratory ailments would soon repay
the initial investment (Figure 116, right).

Redevelopment of older industrial communities beneath area domes is envisioned for
Poughkeepsie by Conklin & Rossant in a prototype study (Figure 117, below). Besides
problems of exhaust removal and maintenance
of the dome (even keeping it clean), people
would probably abhor living in a completely
contained and controlled environment.

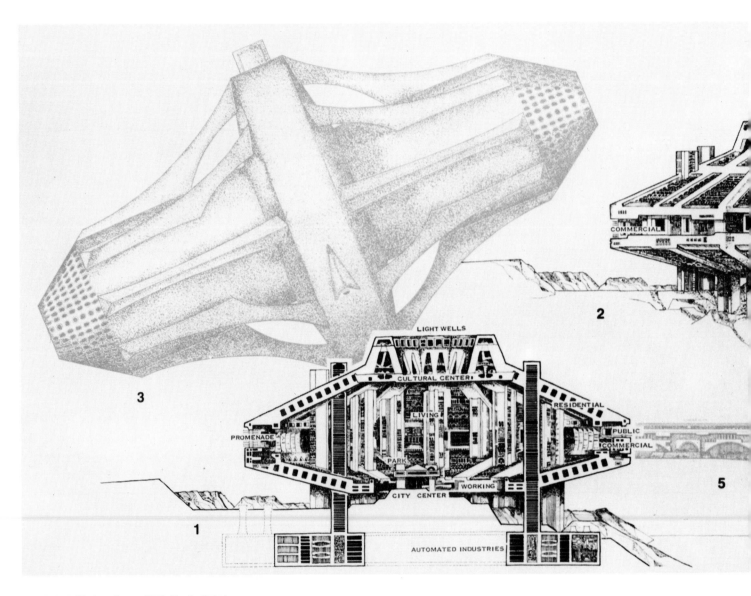

118. Babel IIC Arcology, 1969. Paolo Soleri

Soleri's "Arcologies" (Arcology = Architecture + Ecology) are total cities in which he imagines modern man, the man of the future, to live. Certainly our decade's preoccupation with the environmental question is exposed and explored in Soleri's diagrams for a massive redirection of city building. But in indulging in a public preoccupation he has lost sight of man himself. If people did not want to even shop in the convenient interior commercial street at the center of Corbusier's *Unité d'Habitation*, it is doubtful that they would be willing to live, work, promenade, and relax all in a massive interlinked compound raised high above the ground and dug deeply into it. Sprawl has certainly been a disaster to the community life once enjoyed in cities. But for the city

to function as a warren for up to half a million people is a doubtful proposition which for all its visual complexity must finally be recognized as an unacceptably simplistic solution to *la condition humaine*.

Through its complexity of detail, encumbrances of symbolism, and seemingly mechanized rationalism of space arrangement, and urban process, Soleri claims his focus is toward regaining contact with the natural order, toward preserving the land, toward assuring the continuity of urban, national and world resources, toward using potentialities of miniaturization to produce a complex, compact environment for man that approaches the coherence of natural order. Soleri's "Arcologies," diagrams to represent his theories of urban process, call for a

"transfiguration of the earth without defiling or disfiguring its own cosmic aspects." In Soleri's judgment, "the performance of the professionals, engineers, architects and planners are doodles on the back of a cosmic phenomenon and will not do. Unlimited doodling produces squalor. This work seeks a definition of the problem in its more general terms, an environment suitable for the species of man . . ." However, his suggestion that we build gigantic mechanistic cellular structures on open land as the cities of the future omits substantial understanding of what most people seek, how they would like to live. It also abandons the city that is for a strong image of a mechanized city that we may hope never is.

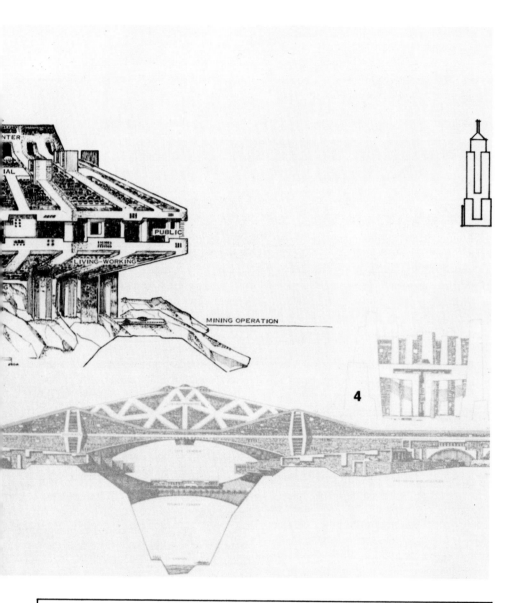

4

Babel IIC

Population	340,000
Height	1,396/hectare; 565/acre
Diameter	850 meters
Surface covered	1,750 meters
1. Section and elevation	240.8 hectares; 595 acres
2. Scale	1:10,000

COMPARATIVE ARCOLOGIES

Asteromo

Population	75,000
3. Elevation: scale	1:10,000

Theodiga

Population	20,000
4. Elevation: scale	1:10,000

Stonebow

Population	200,000
5. Elevation: scale	1:10,000

initial years of the program as strong industry groups lobby successfully for more time and less costly requirements. On the other hand, by 1973, three years after promulgation of the Act, very considerable progress has been made in producing a legal and regulatory framework capable of providing a dramatically improved environment in this country within a decade or so. Implementation of programs must now be assured by progressive and responsible administrators and by aware citizens who insist that the framework which took so long to develop produces, in fact, a very much better environment. There will be no substitute for continued effort and vigilance on the part of concerned officials and citizens to assure the realization of this goal. It will not occur easily or automatically. Without a lot of work and persistence, it will not occur at all.

In addition, current standards for required environmental impact statements must be expanded. Primary impacts must be quantified to the extent possible; secondary and tertiary impacts which are now ignored on natural resources, on land development, and on transportation, among other elements, should also be required considerations. Attempts to develop a systematic matrix for environmental impact analyses have been initiated recently.[23] More work must be done to require proper and thorough evaluation of the environmental impact of large projects.

The federal government also recently committed itself to confronting the problem of air pollution. The federal Clean Air Act of 1970 directs the Environmental Protection Agency to set acceptable air quality standards for the nation's air. The problem is centered in the cities where electric power is needed, where many factories are still clustered, and where automobile exhaust is concentrated. A 90 per cent reduction in automobile exhaust pollution by May 31, 1975, was a primary goal declared in the Act. By 1973, at the insistence of automobile manufacturers, the deadline had been pushed back to 1976. And that issue is far from closed.

The ability of most very large cities to meet federal air quality standards set in the Clean Air Act, even by the end of the decade, is already questionable. However, most cities and regions claim they will try, and all are required to by federal law.

As a result of the Clean Air Act, for the first time, proposed large developments which effectively concentrate automobiles in one area, such as a regional shopping center, must comply with federal environmental standards. Whereas once zoning was the principal inpediment to the realization of such projects, the arena has now expanded to include environmental concerns as well. Indeed, as a result of the Clean Air Act, a number of major regional shopping centers and other big projects have already been delayed or cancelled.

Other new public initiatives are likely to occur as a result of the Clean Air Act. Gasoline sales may be rationed in certain areas, not because of shortages, but because of environmental control standards. Urban parking facilities may be systematically reduced; tolls may be placed on bridges which were once free, or at least levied progressively against cars with the fewest passengers; traffic restrictions may be intensified; a selective ban could be imposed on taxi cruising; off-hours truck deliveries and even staggering of work hours are all possibilities now being considered by public agencies to cut urban air pollution. And a number of them may very well be implemented in especially polluted areas such as Los Angeles, Houston, Detroit, northern New Jersey, and New York within the next several years. The fuel and gasoline shortages experienced across America in the fall and winter of 1973–74 could facilitate reaching the goals and standards set in the Clean Air Act if other standards are maintained, especially those related to the quality of permissible prime energy sources.

According to the Clean Air Act as it now stands, cities and regions in the United States are expected to meet federal standards for air quality by May, 1975,

with a two-year deadline extension to 1977 possible in hardship situations. If air quality standards are held at current levels, and if the nation's local public environmental protection apparatus takes adequate initiative and is given adequate political support, much improved conditions, especially in the cities, will become evident. For instance, the use of public spaces would again be pleasant. With national de-emphasis on urban automobile traffic, increased attention should be given by the public and by public agencies to public transit and all the benefits it could bring.

Water pollution control also became a major federal concern very recently. Under the Water Pollution Control Act of 1972, all sizeable discharges of fluid wastes (for instance, from industrial establishments and municipal sewer systems) need permits and are subject to increasingly stringent standards. The Act anticipates that by 1985 there will be "zero discharge" of pollutants into the nation's waterways.

Out of this law could come reclaimed lakes and rivers usable again by urban people for swimming, boating, and fishing; available again as desirable sites for public open spaces, promenades and municipal facility development. The current trend in cities around the country of building and rebuilding along the old industrialized and all but abandoned edges of rivers and lakes anticipates these possibilities. It also signals an important trend in recognizing as desirable the water-edge spaces along rivers, lakes, and canals, lost for decades to general public use because of industrial development patterns and concomitant pollution of all sorts. Their loss to the people of the city is unacceptable and unnecessary. The waterfronts of New Orleans, San Francisco, New York, Chicago, and other cities around the country are coming back to life for people. This tendency will accelerate in the coming decades along the canals, creeks, lakes, rivers, and inlets that were in many cases the initial *raison d'être* of many cities.

Noise pollution, another aspect of urban outfall, is also now being identified and

dealt with in a systematic way, for the first time. The 1972 Environmental Noise Control Act contains the first federal efforts toward identification and regulation of maximum noise levels permissible for human health and welfare. As a result of this act, Environmental Protection Agency standards are now being developed for construction and transportation equipment, motors and engines, and all electrical devices. Airplane noise was made a joint concern of the EPA and Federal Aviation Agency with the FAA required to explain publicly any rejection of EPA control recommendations.

In several cities, new noise control efforts also occurred in recent years. Mayor John Lindsay of New York, for instance, appointed a Task Force on Noise Control in 1968. (Emphasis on such a subject by local government was unthinkable before the mid-1960's.) After a three-year study it was reported that noise in New York City has "reached a level intense, continuous and persistent enough to threaten basic community life."

Specific Task Force recommendations issued in 1970 suggest that:

"(1) Vehicular traffic, especially truck traffic, is the single constant source of pervasive noise in the city.

"(2) The city should seriously consider routing truck traffic away from noise sensitive areas.

"(3) Noise control must be recognized as an essential element of basic city planning and development. The physical environment—homes, roads, parks, subways, factories and offices—must be thought of as indivisible from the total organic system which makes up the community. Consequently, noise abatement, like air or water pollution control, must be regarded as an environmental problem integral to the complex urban life.

"(4) The Environmental Protection Administration should be given wider powers to regulate or prohibit noise disturbances from sources whether fixed or movable."[24]

In April 1971, as a follow-through, 150 spots were scientifically tested all over

New York to pinpoint exactly what makes the unacceptable noise—and what can be done about it. The first Noise Abatement Code in New York was passed as Local Law No. 57 in 1973. It is administered by the Bureau of Noise Abatement, a part of the Department of Air Resources, both founded in the 1960's. However, the effectiveness of the enforcement code and procedures is still uncertain.

In cities and states around the country, efforts are also underway in many different programs to deal with the environment—and to improve it dramatically. Of the 43 state legislatures which met in 1972, at least 35 of them enacted environmental quality measures. The process has begun. Environmental control has become a part of the legal and administrative mainstream of federal, state, city, and town government.

There will, of course, be resistance to the growing network of environmental regulations. And the touchstone of the resistance by the private sector, government departments, and taxpayers is likely to be cost. But how burdensome is the cost, really, of building and assuring a more acceptable environment? Between 1972 and 1981, the Council on Environmental Quality estimates that some $275 billion is needed, or roughly $27.5 billion per year, for all federal, state, local, and private programs. This compares to a current annual Defense Department budget of about $79 billion, or nearly three times as much as the environmental budget. Environmental funds allocations comprise 40 per cent for water control, 35 per cent for air control, and the other 25 per cent split between solid waste, land reclamation, noise control, radiation protection, and a number of other items. All of these budget numbers, of course, are based on rough estimates of the meaning of massive data being examined, in many cases for the first time. Significant revisions from time to time may be expected. But the shape of the problem, in terms of cost, is becoming roughly visible.

The annual environmental control costs, as currently estimated, represent about 2.5 per cent of the value of the nation's annual production of goods and services. The bill will be split, under current regulations, with about 37 per cent paid from public sources with the remaining 63 per cent paid about equally by private citizens and by private industry. The average cost of this immensely important effort to the average family in 1976 is currently estimated at about $250 per year, or roughly 1.8 per cent of income.

By the year 2000 the gross national product of the United States is likely to be somewhere in the vicinity of $2-2.6 trillion per year. If a very active national pollution abatement policy is in effect by that time, it is estimated by the national policy organization Resources for the Future, Inc., that annual costs will range between $34 and $47 billion dollars, or somewhat less than 2 per cent of the GNP. Such a cost is clearly within the scope of our national resources and must be accepted if sound national planning and resource management policies are to be followed.

Public officials and politicians are beginning to jump on the environmental bandwagon. Favoring a good environment has become an acceptable political position. Indeed, favoring an improved environment is replacing old-fashioned nationalism (due to Vietnam, Watergate, etc.) and Motherhood (due to zero population growth, the Pill, etc.) as an indispensible, safe political position. It is also becoming a prudent political stance. In the 1972 gubernatorial and congressional elections, for instance, 43 out of 57 candidates supported by the League of Conservation Voters came out winners, and some who were opposed vehemently on their record as environmentalists, such as Wayne Aspinall, the former head of the crucial Interior Committee of the House of Representatives, were defeated.

The public is even voting money for environmental control in an era when few bond issues for other purposes are passed. In 1972 New York State voters approved a $1.15 billion bond issue to combat air and water pollution, to control solid waste, and to acquire recreational lands. Washington State voters approved $265 million and Floridians $240 million in bonds at the same time for roughly the same purposes; out of 10 environmental bond issues presented around the country in 1972, the majority were approved.

Awareness of the urban environmental issues discussed above has influenced urban design and planning proposals for some time, as previously discussed and illustrated. Until very recently, however, physical design responses have been based on acceptance of urban environmental pollution of many sorts. The projects and proposals have attempted to shield people from the urban environment without attempting to improve the environment itself. Recently there has been evidence that some architects and planners are anxious to cope with the problem at its source. They seek to reduce the amount of energy consumed in the operation of buildings and other aspects of urban life. In 1972, for example, Richard G. Stein of New York determined that "architecture, through its product, the manmade environment, has a greater influence on energy use than any other major component of GNP except transportation and the military." He went on to point out in a thesis presented to the American Association for the Advancement of Science in Philadelphia and subsequently printed in the Journal of the American Institute of Architects (AIA) that the mindless use of overdesigned heating and cooling systems in buildings of sheer glass walls, which themselves produce unnecessarily high demands on power, should be reconsidered by architects.

Such a comment at another period in our history would have been ignored. However, in the early 1970's, such sensitivity to the issues of environment and the demands for power exist that Stein's work was also described in the *New York Times* by Ada Louise Huxtable, an influential and aware commentator on architecture, planning, and urbanism.

Among the displays at the Paris Fair in May, 1973 was a five-room solar house built by Jacques Michel, a Harvard-trained French architect, who believes that approximately 70 per cent of the space heating requirements for private homes in France can be provided by solar energy. It is indeed likely that the limited supply of energy will become an increasingly important restraining and perhaps eventually positive and creative influence on designing, developing, and constructing buildings. It is already a fact that electrical energy and gas are in short supply in certain urban areas. This fact itself limits the potential for building new structures and rebuilding older neighborhoods. Even the rationing of power by utility companies in certain areas is imaginable. One of the new responsibilities of any competent planner or architect is to determine what energy source is available. One of his new responsibilities should also be to decide how to limit the required use of power and still produce a comfortable, desirable, attractive building. From an economic point of view, as the cost of energy rises rapidly, it is even likely that a more desirable building complex will be partially defined in terms of economic use of energy resources.

I would suspect that the limitation on energy, which is itself a result of growing environmental awareness and supply shortages in this country, will soon begin to affect aspects of building and planning heretofore entirely exempt from such considerations. One can imagine certain materials being favored because of their ability to retain heat or cold. Less glass is likely to be used. When it is, new types or better grades of glass which are less susceptible to climatic changes will be specified; an emphasis on insulation of all sorts will be evident. It is not inconceivable that at the intermediary scale of urban intervention, somewhere between the single building and the entire city district—which is the most promising physical size for significant and successful urban redevelopment—that small, substation, independent, and perhaps new types of power plants will become a part of development and redevelopment costs. In this way, new projects may function with efficient new equipment that is "clean," that is sized to need, and that is independent of older and less reliable municipal systems.

Science, government, and citizens are unaccountably late in recognizing the systematically destructive patterns of urban life that our culture has been allowed to assume. In the cities, as a result, insupportable environmental conditions are, in part, responsible for outmigration of residents and jobs—fundamental trends with the potential to destroy the city as we know it. Sound, air, and water pollution must be coupled with physical, economic, fiscal, social, and administrative decay for the first time, as matters basic to the life—or death—of cities.

This recognition is likely to signal a turning point in the history of Western cities. We have begun to recognize that urban development processes are, as Raymond Dasmann wrote in 1968, "susceptible to understanding, increasingly predictable, and capable of being managed."[25] The impact of this new awareness will certainly lead to implementation policies within a decade. Whether these policies will have adequate force is a social and political problem of the most profound urgency.

Our newly gained understanding, developed slowly in the early 1960's and with increasing intensity recently, is also certain to be the foundation for increasing sensitivity to physical and sensate experience in urban design. Rearranged priorities in which environmental considerations are given unprecedented emphasis will encourage a wide variety of urban design responses. These will affect transportation's relation to public space as well as climate, light, and sound control within structures and in the public space of the city. Large-scale new and redeveloped areas may be provided with new types of mechanical systems and waste disposal devices. The evolutionary rearrangement of dense urban areas into more varied, more compact clusters may occur according to new principles of environmental planning.

Certainly the change in attitude that accompanied construction of urban freeways in the last decade (see Chapter 3) will affect future urban form significantly, and is partially a consequence of public and political attention to the environmental impact of the freeway on the city. Just as certainly, new attitudes toward uses of the urban street which surfaced in the 1950's and 1960's (see Chapter 2) are integrally bound to the environmental understanding and sophistication gained recently.

Urban planning as a legitimate discipline was not fully accepted by most people in America until recently. Its acceptance is based in part on belated recognition of the large number of interdependent physical and life support systems which compose a city. These can no longer be either ignored or conveniently manipulated by architects involved in a conventional practice or alert public officials and builders primarily interested in urban development as we have known it in the past. The urban planner and urban designer, professionals who intersect and interact actively with urban-scale social, economic, environmental, transportation, political, and design questions, will be increasingly important in government and in the development process as the complexity and the manageability of the evolving city is recognized.

The environment is amazingly resilient. Treated with only a modicum of respect, it is able to self-regenerate and sustain itself remarkably well. Indeed, the environment may prove much more resilient than cities whose qualities have been so severely diminished during long years of unmitigated resource waste and pollution. Cities certainly will not come back unless the air, water, sound levels, and built environment, in the widest sense, are improved. Many of them may be in irreversable cycles of decay and degeneration, partially as a result of over a century of environmental mismanagement in the building of America. At least now, for the first time in our history, the environmental issue is very visible and a process toward regeneration has begun.

New Directions

Enclosed public and semi-private spaces will become part of more private development schemes.

River, lake, and canal city edges are now desirable spots for urban redevelopment.

The city must be handled as a fragile ecological ambient in which all forces and interventions are interdependent and interrelated.

More thought and money will be devoted to the long ignored urban infrastructure—utilities, transportation networks, and streets and environment (air, space, and light).

New air, water, and sound pollution control programs will take longer to be effective than was anticipated.

Environmental issues will influence building materials and design, urban design, the economics of development, the location of development, the nature of new building, and the maintenance cost of public and private spaces and structures.

Environmental impact statements must be made more rigorous to include probable secondary and tertiary effects of new development on natural resources, land use, and all modes of transportation.

Historic Preservation
Urban Conservation

Throughout the 20th century, until very recently, consideration for the urban past —its spaces, structures, and patterns of life—has been largely ignored as a source of information for bettering the city. Most real estate owners, public administrators, urban planners, and even architects have been more than antihistorical; they have been ahistorical. Sturdy and often very fine older structures are persistently demolished when tax-sheltered depreciation periods expire; older parts of the city, even though well serviced by utilities, roads, and public open space, are allowed to languish with shifting focal points of activity. Old and forgotten urban commercial, residential, and industrial districts exist around the country in tattered disarray.

What has made this happen? In part, it is the economic basis of urban development in the United States and the tax system that accompanies it. The rewards are higher for "putting. together a new package" than for redevelopment of existing older buildings, especially when it is possible to recoup more than 100 per cent of the cost before a new building is occupied by "mortgaging out" of it. And it has been possible to entirely or partially mortgage out in large-scale development throughout most of this century. The tax laws also encourage new building by offering fast depreciation—that is, the right to deduct the cost of the building from current income over a relatively short period. In addition, they discourage investment in older buildings and rehabilitation of older buildings because these costs cannot be subjected to the same favorable accelerated depreciation treatment.

The causes of this remarkable indifference toward history, as expressed in the laws and tax rules of the United States, go very deep into the national culture and

into 20th century Western thought about cities. They are expressed in the philosophical presumptions which have been commonly accepted by most architects and planners throughout this century.

The first major pronouncements of this century of importance to the physical future of our urban culture were published in 1909 in Italy by Filippo Tommaso Marinetti as *The Foundation Manifesto of Futurism*. In this euphoric, ringing proclamation of unparalleled optimism in a future of fast machines and lightweight materials, Marinetti proclaimed that each generation must build its own city. Following this lead, Antonio Sant' Elia, the principal Futurist architect, announced in 1914, "we must invent and build *ex-nuovo* our modern city . . ."[26]

Infatuation with change, with the machine, and with industrial imagery then led the great theoretical efforts of the Bauhaus and most progressive European architects into a long sequence of planning and architectural excursions dominated by new materials, new technical potentials, and rather superficial efforts to translate scientific and engineering precepts into building. The ethos of the Industrial Revolution, and the product promotion which has come from it, persisted unscathed into architectural and planning theory and practice. Confidence in progress—faith in a future shaped by new materials and new forms—is perhaps the essential ingredient of commercial advertisement. It is not, however, a suitable basis for the maintenance and shaping of a culture, which is the job of the urbanist.

It was not until the very end of the 1950's, with the formulation of concepts central to Team 10, as discussed previously, that new philosophical and theoretical directions sympathetic to the urban

past emerged. Aldo van Eyck expressed a fundamental attitude of Team 10 members when he wrote:

"Man is always and everywhere essentially the same. He has the same mental equipment though he uses it differently according to his culture or social background, according to the particular life pattern of which he happens to be a part. Modern architects have been harping continually on what is different in our time to such an extent that even they have lost touch with what is not different, and what is always essentially the same."[27]

Team 10 members were mostly Europeans living in cities where the physical past remains in most places an organic part of the present. In the United States, however, there has always been less interest in history and less interest in the physical form of our culture than in Europe. Among architects and planners, until very recently, there was little understanding of the history of cities and the relevance of that history to current and projected needs. Nonetheless, Team 10 did exert an enormous influence on progressive architects and urbanists in the United States during the 1960's.

But it was not out of the meager coterie of historically minded architects and planners that a recent and now growing interest in conservation and preservation of older buildings and places emerged during the 1960's. And it was certainly not as a result of beneficial legal and tax policies which could be used to influence development itself. Rather, it has been the persistent and often eccentric alliance of historians, preservationist societies, a conservative urban aristocracy, and "little old ladies in tennis shoes" that has actually made the difference. These loosely federated interests which stood so long outside the mainstream of planning and development are now moving closer to a central position. They are assisted, of course, by the recent interest in the environment (see Chapter 6) and in land-use control (see Chapter 8). This interest has brought the sudden realization that certain preservation and conservation oriented alternatives to conventional patterns of urban and suburban development are not only desirable but urgently needed.

By the mid-1960's, a new movement was underway in this country, one dependent upon unprecedented disillusion with the old trinity that dominated America: increased growth, increased prosperity, increased power. The fall of this secular trinity is still not generally recognized. But it has occurred. And as a result, the possibility of a major new direction has emerged—one long needed as a national priority in urbanism.

Cultural awareness linked with interest in preservation of buildings and districts opens new opportunities for programs to save and use whatever is important and substantial from our past. Research and analysis of our own and other cultures to understand the desirable attributes of urban life in the past can provide suggestions for the use of these attributes in a contemporary context to improve urban life today and in the future.

These potentialities are just emerging. They will grow, I suspect, to major importance in years to come to encompass resource allocations, the deployment of imaginative and progressive professionals, public requirements, political support, in fact a new direction with emphasis on the adaptive redevelopment of older urban places. Strong signals of this trend are already present in the form of recent and proposed federal, state, and local programs; in political strategy; in actual projects; and in legal, economic, and physical planning now underway. What programs are there? How have these been effective so far? How limited are they?

In 1966, the Historic Preservation Act, the first federal program to preserve *and* protect places and districts of historic importance within the country, became

law. The Historic Sites Act passed in 1936 had simply produced a list of properties worthy of preservation for their historic value, but these properties were not protected. Moreover, single buildings were the exclusive focus of the listing. The concept of districts, areas, the entire context of older settlements was ignored. The Historic Preservation Act of 1966 is of great importance because it is not limited to single properties but in fact emphasizes districts, sites, and areas of archeological importance, as well as buildings and structures. Thus, federal legislation permitting preservation on a meaningful scale and in a way that will permit the recall of a historical situation rather than a single historical fragment exists in this country for the first time.

As a result of the 1966 Act, a property or site, once listed in the National Register, cannot routinely be invaded by any other program—such as a highway, airport, sewage treatment plant, etc.—to which federal funds are committed. Although the Act is still deficient in having no injunctive power to halt federal undertakings that threaten historic properties and sites, it makes dealing with these areas so difficult that alternatives are generally sought. However, the listing of a property in the National Register still offers no financial assistance to a private owner and does not restrain him from using private, town, county, or state funds to modify or even destroy a property or site. The lack of financial resources on the one hand, and the omission of legal, economic, and tax devices on the other, are serious weaknesses in the attempt to induce private cooperation with the National Historic Preservation Act of 1966. More will be said below of recent efforts to remedy this flaw.

A measure of growing concern about the physical past is obtained from the record of listings in the National Register itself. Today there are over 4,000 buildings and sites in the National Register, including all historic areas in the National Parks System, and all properties eligible for designation as National Historic Landmarks. In 1969, when the Register first appeared, there were about 1,000 listings. By the end of the decade, the Department of the Interior estimates that the number will exceed 100,000.

In 1972, as a further indication of growing interest in the need to preserve properties and sites of historic significance, the Advisory Council on Historic Preservation, established by the Historic Preservation Act of 1966, issued a booklet, *Guidelines for State Historic Preservation Legislation.* These guidelines propose a comprehensive legislative program concerning involvement in preservation for both state and local governments, including administrative structure, legislation, and procedures to guide agencies in the conduct of their activities so that the objectives of historic preservation are best served.

Even though interest in preserving large sites and districts as well as buildings is growing, there are very few federal programs that have adequate funds to be of major financial assistance. When the Department of Housing and Urban Development is reorganized, it should include adequate budgets for national preservation of historic sites and buildings. The same must be done at state and local levels if an extensive and successful preservation effort is to be undertaken.

In 1973, the need for priority attention to historic preservation was vividly expressed by the influential Citizens' Advisory Committee on Environmental Quality. Though a private organization, this Committee reports to the President of the United States and the Council on Environmental Quality. Its findings and recommendations, which focus on land use control and historic preservation, include the following statements:

"(1) Historic areas need protection, too. Many communities have important or unusual buildings or whole streets and neighborhoods with historic integrity, where the buildings, by their age, design and scale form a unit of visual continuity and character. Such areas may already be registered historic districts, as in Charleston, Boston and Santa Fe, or they may be

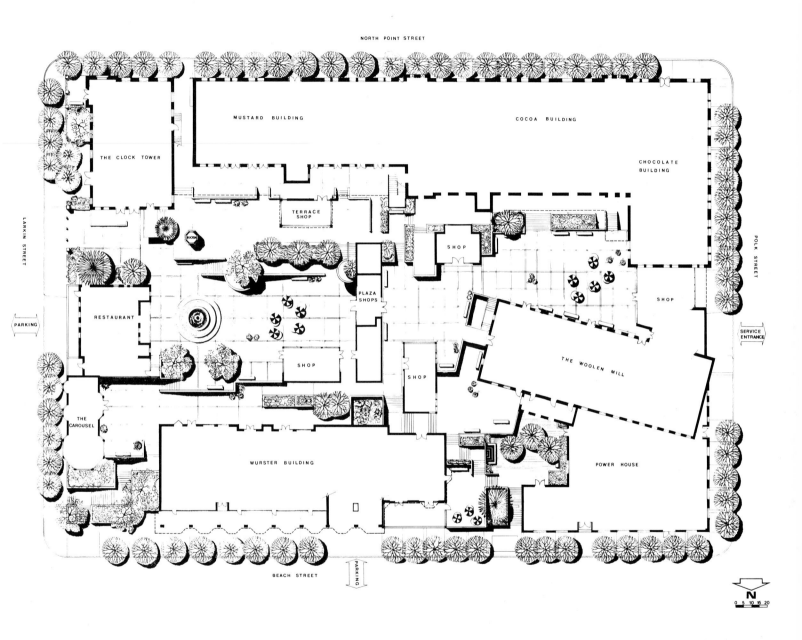

NORTH POINT STREET

MUSTARD BUILDING

COCOA BUILDING

THE CLOCK TOWER

CHOCOLATE BUILDING

TERRACE SHOP

KIOSK

SHOP

LARKIN STREET

PLAZA SHOPS

SHOP

POLK STREET

RESTAURANT

PARKING

SHOP

SHOP

THE WOOLEN MILL

SERVICE ENTRANCE

THE CAROUSEL

WURSTER BUILDING

POWER HOUSE

BEACH STREET

PARKING

N

0 5 10 15 20

120. Ghirardelli Square, San Francisco, California. Plan
Lawrence Halprin & Associates (Urban Designers)
Wurster, Bernardi & Emmons (Architects)

A group of waterfront industrial and factory
buildings is renovated into a complex of shops,
restaurants, and public open spaces (Figure
120). When fine older buildings are successfully
preserved and reused, gains accrue to the city.
Some variety is made available to people and
interesting and appealing spaces, reminiscent
of older, people-oriented urban organization, become once again available (Figure 119). Complete transition of use such as occurred here is
tricky. Success depends on sound economic
feasibility, understanding of the potential of the
location involved, and appealing design.

stylistically varied areas lacking any significant single buildings but forming units of pleasing proportion and providing a sense of the past. Such historic properties are vulnerable to the same threats as open space, and their preservation often poses the same 'buy it or lose it' dilemma to local authorities. We see historic districts and buildings benefitting from the same approach and many of the same techniques we recommend for protecting privately owned open space, an approach based primarily on regulation, not purchase.

"(2) For historic preservation, as for open space protection, the first requisite is a framework for regulation, preferably a statewide system for registration of historic districts and properties and a clear policy favoring preservation. States should enact appropriate legislation to implement the *Model State Guidelines for Historic Preservation recommended by the Council of State Governments among its 1972 suggested legislative proposals* (emphasis theirs). Such legislation would establish a state institutional structure for the review and regulation of historic sites, structures and districts and would enable local governments to take special measures to ensure that the integrity of historic sites is protected."

Among the few national financial resources available for historic preservation today are Federal Preservation Grants, administered by the Department of the Interior. These funds, established by the National Historic Preservation Act of 1966 and released on a 50 per cent matching basis, are generally restricted to $2,000 to $40,000 per grant. Thus, hardly enough is made available to assist in most land or site acquisition or adaptive re-use projects.

The real potential for historic preservation in terms of legislation and funding programs is the increasing linkage of preservation activities to environmental, recreation, and conservation programs. Through this natural alliance between all resource conservation programs, it is likely that historic preservation itself will receive legal, political, and financial support.

Even without adequate public assistance, in recent years many adaptive re-use preservation projects using older buildings have succeeded, especially when commercial potential was involved. The commercial rehabilitation of The Cannery, Ghirardelli Square, and Wharfside in San Francisco (Figures 119, 120); Old Town Hall in Pittsfield, Massachusetts; Henry Hobson Richardson's Glessner House in Chicago; Canal Square in Georgetown, Washington, D.C., all are recent notable examples. These would not have been initiated a decade ago. No one cared. The opportunities were invisible. Today private individuals and developers are beginning to recognize that many fine older buildings can be purchased at reasonable cost and that they can be re-used in imaginative ways to produce unusual places and districts which are attractive to a people whose physical history is rarely apparent. The economic feasibility of private renovation and conservation of older and often historic structures is just becoming apparent in many places, in many different ways.

More important, the economic penalties associated with rehabilitating buildings—as opposed to the advantages of building new structures—are now being recognized and revealed. Currently, tax and financing rules encourage demolition, site clearance, and rebuilding. But under a crucial new piece of legislation now before Congress, the Environmental Protection Tax Act of 1973, demolition of registered historic structures would become disadvantageous and economic incentives would be provided for restoration, such as allowing the owner to treat the renovated National Register building as a new structure for tax depreciation purposes, or alternatively allowing him to deduct the rehabilitation expenses of buildings used for business or rental purposes from his annual income over a five-year period. These modified federal tax rules would make historic preservation by the private sector much more feasible than it is in most cases today.

This legislation is badly needed to complement the National Historic Preserva-

tion Act of 1966, mentioned earlier. But its fate in the Congress remains very uncertain. Nevertheless, the existence of this provision in a major piece of federal legislation indicates how significant the issue of historic preservation has become.

There is also considerable recent evidence that pressure from a growing alliance of interested citizens, states, and local communities is diverting some resources into historic preservation. These resources come principally from revenue sharing funds which, being an entirely new source of local money, have as yet no spending precedent. For instance, in Seattle, Mayor Wes Uhlman and the City Council have recently authorized $600,-000 to establish a revolving fund for the city's preservation effort. And in Georgia, during 1972, the General Assembly appropriated $12.5 million, including $10 million in revenue sharing funds, to establish a 15-member State Heritage Trust Advisory Commission to "identify, acquire and protect environmental, recreational and historical areas within the state."

In addition, principally in recent years, growing numbers of districts with special character within older cities have been sufficiently recognized to become protected areas, through local zoning, municipal ordinance, imaginative planning, and/or listing in the National Register. Isolated incidents of joint public-private district preservation had occurred in Charleston, New Orleans, Alexandria, Virginia, and elsewhere before the 1960's (Figure 121). But only in recent years has the trend gained more substantial acceptance. Since the mid-1960's, districts such as the more than 90-block area of Greenwich Village (1969) and the 26-block area of Soho in New York City (1973) have been protected as Historic Districts by local ordinance (Figures 122, 123). Currently, in countless towns across the country, similar moves are under study. In Oyster Bay, Long Island, formed 320 years ago, an ordinance which would protect any designated historic structure, area, or district within a 110-square mile area is being considered. In

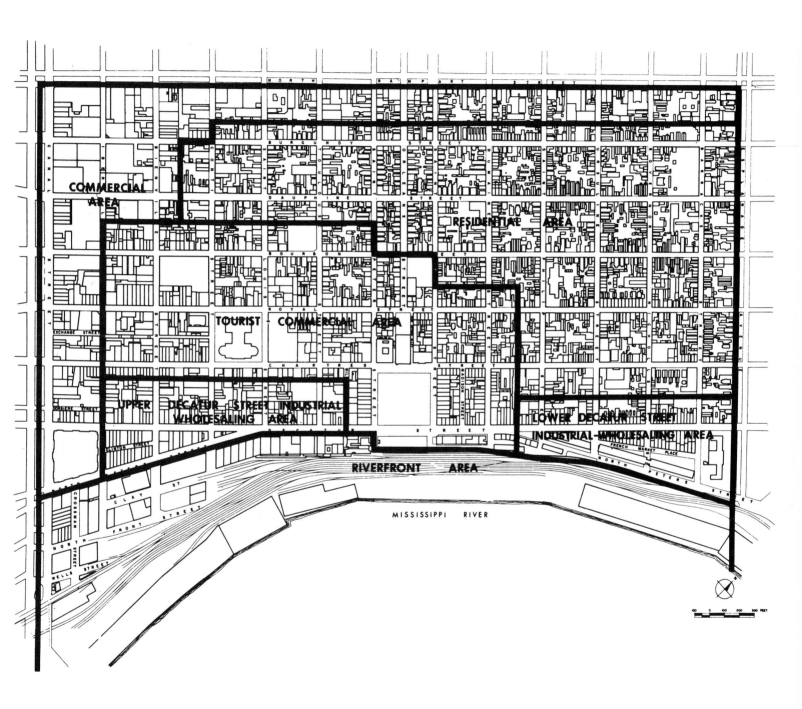

121. Vieux Carré Historic District, New Orleans, Louisiana. Plan

The *Vieux Carré*, more than 24 blocks in all, was the original French settlement in New Orleans. Today, protected by architectural-control and height-limitation ordinances passed in 1937, it functions as a fine ensemble of varied buildings and uses. French, Spanish, and Mediterranean urban architectural styles are mingled. Uses and activities run the gamut from industrial and wholesaling along the Mississippi River to commercial, residential, and intense tourist-entertainment clusters toward the center of the District.

The preservation of the *Vieux Carré* as a self-contained environment of buildings, spaces, and streets has made it a thriving attraction to visitors and an acclaimed, unique national resource. It has also created a stable, vital commercial, residential, and entertainment complex in downtown New Orleans which may very well be largely responsible for the continuing vitality of the rest of that city's downtown area. It is too often forgotten that a major large-scale resource such as an appealing and active historic district can benefit an urban area far larger than its own limited boundaries.

Today, the *Vieux Carré* is almost too successful. Adherence to façade and height limitations is not always rigidly enforced by the Vieux Carré Commission when powerful national developers appeal for leeway. In addition, land use is in transition from mixed uses, including residential, in many of the most accessible and attractive parts of the district, to higher rent uses such as in-town motels, hotels, and shops at a rate which, if continued, will spoil the integrity and vitality of the District.

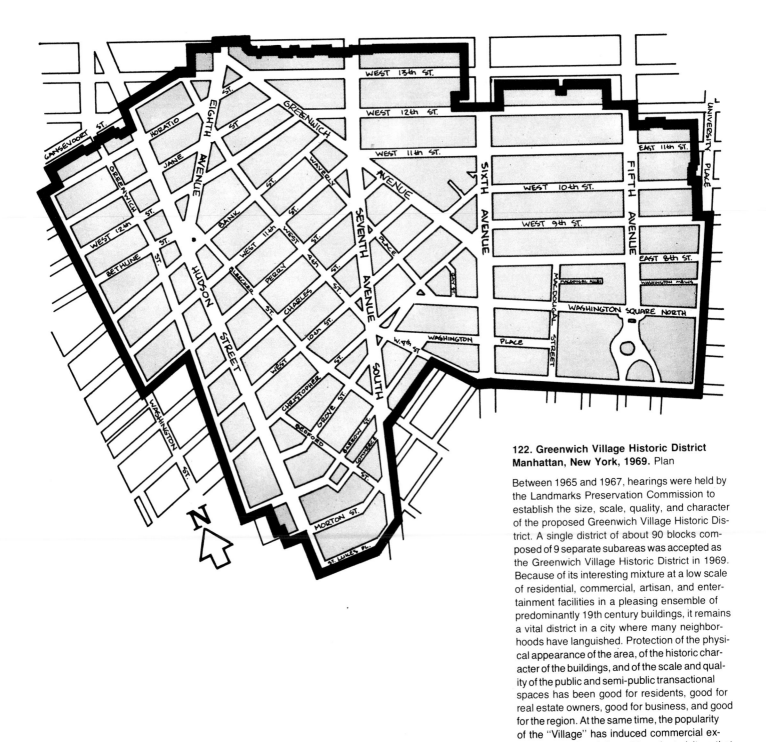

122. Greenwich Village Historic District Manhattan, New York, 1969. Plan

Between 1965 and 1967, hearings were held by the Landmarks Preservation Commission to establish the size, scale, quality, and character of the proposed Greenwich Village Historic District. A single district of about 90 blocks composed of 9 separate subareas was accepted as the Greenwich Village Historic District in 1969. Because of its interesting mixture at a low scale of residential, commercial, artisan, and entertainment facilities in a pleasing ensemble of predominantly 19th century buildings, it remains a vital district in a city where many neighborhoods have languished. Protection of the physical appearance of the area, of the historic character of the buildings, and of the scale and quality of the public and semi-public transactional spaces has been good for residents, good for real estate owners, good for business, and good for the region. At the same time, the popularity of the "Village" has induced commercial exploitation and an influx of transient visitors that compromise the stability and quality of life in the district.

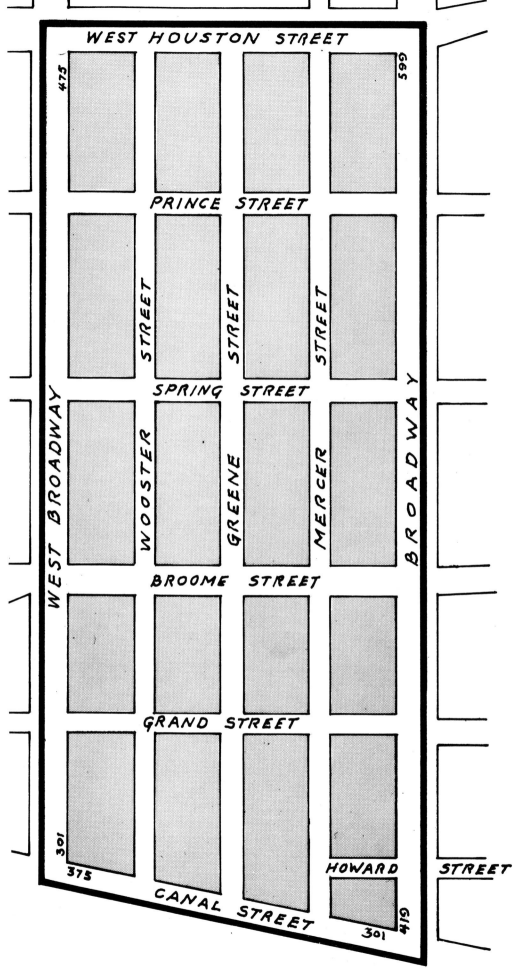

**123. SoHo Historic District
Manhattan, New York, 1973.** Plan

A 26-block area in lower Manhattan south of Houston Street (thus the acronym SoHo), the exclusive domain less than a decade ago of light industry and in-town warehousing, has become an active, lived-in, worked-in artists' residential and studio area mingled with a continuing commercial and small-scale industrial atmosphere. The designation of this area, made up of the largest group of cast-iron structures anywhere, as a historic district, assures its permanence and protects it from conventional land assembly and subsequent redevelopment. The assurance of permanence combined with an appropriate zoning change to permit residential uses has made the upper-level lofts in buildings throughout the district attractive as low-cost working and living studios.

Previously, many of the upper floors in the wide, well-lit, predominantly four- and five-story brick and cast-iron façade buildings had been empty for years. Then artists began to move into the area in the mid-1960's, before it was zoned for artists' residential use and before it was formally considered for designation as a Historic District. Today much of this space is well used and productive. The potential for recycling of older and even nearly abandoned districts within the city to new and additional uses is vividly demonstrated by SoHo.

Phoenix, Arizona, a different but equally promising approach is underway. There, a Special Conservation District is to be established through the proposed new city zoning ordinance. In a Conservation District, conventional single-purpose zoning is set aside in favor of whatever mixed-use activities fulfill the planning goals established for the district. At the national level, within the last year, the 210-acre Old West End District of Toledo, Ohio, entered the National Register of Historic Places.

These large districts offer new and unusual promise to urban life. Within them, sturdy old buildings survive, and the scale of the buildings is often appealing. Quite often, automobile traffic can be effectively and inexpensively monitored to make available more pedestrian ways. The districts frequently benefit from a premier location near waterways, on riverfronts, or adjacent to existing downtown commercial centers. With sensible controls on redevelopment and proper stimulus for rehabilitation, these older urban centers could become desirable mixed residential, commercial, retail, and recreational districts.

The South Street district of Manhattan on the Lower East Side along the East River is a recent representative case of possibilities that can occur. Less than a decade ago the area was a shambles of underutilized warehouses and rarely used docks. Then the South Street Seaport Museum, composed of little more than an old dock flanked by moored schooners was established. Seaport artifacts are exhibited nearby, in Schermerhorn Row—a block of fine Georgian commercial structures at the foot of Fulton Street. Today, a well-conceived and ambitious plan exists to redevelop, through a combination of restoration and new construction, seven square blocks in the area. Over a ten-year period, the plan anticipates that galleries, craft shops, studios, commercial facilities, and housing could be provided. An entire block of unusual historic quality could be restored. Implementation of the redevelopment plan would turn this dreary and ignored edge of the city into an economi-cally viable, lively, and appealing enclave along the water.

From the point of view of a community, the opportunities afforded by the revitalization of older urban districts hardly needs to be stressed: tax yields increase; adjacent areas beyond the district boundary benefit; vandalism and crime diminish; residential alternatives are presented; an urban life style that includes a sense of community becomes possible.

Historic preservation and conservation also create opportunities for imaginative planners, architects, and public officials. In some cases there is also a very interesting potential for private developers and investors who are able to determine economically feasible and aesthetically acceptable adaptive re-uses for well-located buildings and districts of good quality.

This evolutionary approach to historic preservation in urban areas seeks to renovate and productively use older buildings and districts as a continuing enterprise in older parts of existing cities. It seeks to maintain the present ownership base and to improve the existing tax base. This strategy, as opposed to static historic preservation such as that so successfully undertaken at Williamsburg, Virginia, does not depend on massive public investment or complex administration. It requires only recognition of redevelopment potential together with support in ordinances and tax laws.

One signal of the interest in this field is a program, recently initiated by the Institute for Architecture and Urban Studies, which attempts to plan re-use projects for suitable industrial and commercial buildings and sites while maintaining their historic integrity. The goal of the program is to interest public bodies and/or private developers in carrying out the redevelopment program. The Cohoes Mills in Cohoes, New York, a spectacular, massive assembly of 19th-century textile mills, is the first project in this program.

In rural and suburban areas, other historic preservation opportunities exist. Districts with significant historic associations and/or some historic buildings can be

124. Proposed Watervliet-Shaker Historic and Recreation District Colonie, New York, 1973
Peter Wolf

The National Register listing of 27 original Shaker buildings in three clusters and over 750 acres of largely undeveloped surrounding land creates an unprecedented opportunity for a thriving town on the urbanizing fringe between Albany, Troy, and Schenectady. It is proposed that a new mixed-use Watervliet-Shaker Historic and Recreation District of about 580 acres be established. In it about 50 acres are reserved for active recreation while the remaining 470 acres are conserved for open land uses such as wetlands, a model farm, nature trails, and parks. The protection offered by listing this historic area in the National Register in 1973 and strong local public anti-highway sentiment combined recently to defeat a proposed interstate highway segment scheduled to penetrate the Historic District.

Public control of an area which is now 60 per cent privately owned is feasible through a carefully mixed alliance of federal, state, county, and town legal and financial resources which have become available only in recent years through growing interest in historic preservation, wetlands, open space conservation, and recreation. Of fundamental importance is the potential of implementing such a program without court litigation, without requiring private owners to act against their will or at an economic disadvantage. With careful organization, it is now possible to institute financial, tax, legal, and planning strategies that make historic preservation and land conservation of potential benefit to both public and private interests.

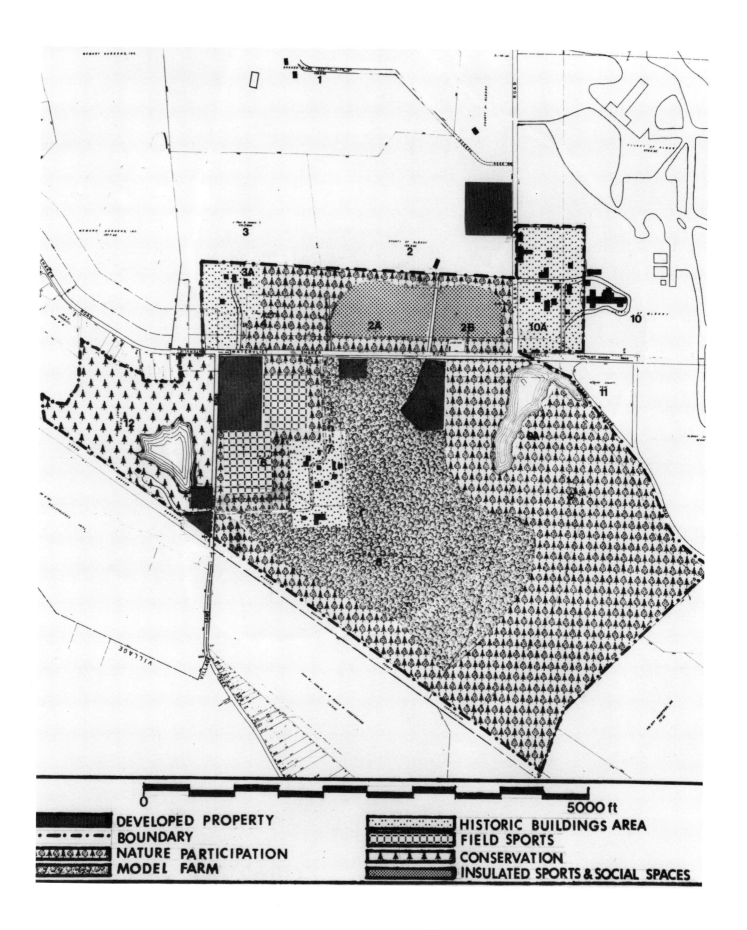

DEVELOPED PROPERTY
BOUNDARY
NATURE PARTICIPATION
MODEL FARM
HISTORIC BUILDINGS AREA
FIELD SPORTS
CONSERVATION
INSULATED SPORTS & SOCIAL SPACES

5000 ft

preserved or imaginatively conserved in many ways, for many public purposes, especially if the districts remain relatively undeveloped. But once developed, or even subjected to ownership fragmentation, the opportunity is generally lost. Progressive town and county administrators are only beginning to recognize the growing need for sound public management in the long-term protection of this country's irreplaceable physical resources. As one example, the Town of Colonie, New York, near Albany, is now investigating programs, policies, and resources to preserve nearly 600 acres of land and three clusters of original Shaker buildings recently entered in the National Register (Figure 124).[28] Other towns and counties throughout the country are considering similar programs.

By combining the newly valued historic character of an area with recent recreation, conservation, and environmental goals and programs, it is now possible, with good planning and creative use of available programs, to create meaningful, active historic districts and simultaneously to preserve large areas of land at little local cost. A growing reverence for the past and an emerging respect for our heritage promise to provide a new basis on which to build and plan for a better life in both urban and rural areas.

In September 1973, because of the growing interest in environmental and historic preservation, the Metropolitan Association of Urban Designers and Environmental Planners, Inc., with *Design and Environment* magazine, jointly sponsored a conference that focused exclusively on the re-uses and new uses of cities. Workshops in this Recycling Cities Conference included "Preservation of Historic Landmarks," "Abandonment" (new concepts for the re-use of abandoned buildings), and "Conversion of Existing Structures." It appears that some professional organizations and publications have caught the scent. Where once architects and planners might have seen no professional opportunity, time, history, and a transition in our cultural priorities now suggest a challenging and satisfying future for planners, architects, politicians, and even investors who recognize new trends in conservation and historic preservation. Urban and suburban people will benefit. And the culture of this country will begin to exert the fundamental influence it must if we are to have a past, a national memory, and an enriched physical future.

New Directions

Emphasis must be on districts, not single buildings.

Historic districts should be identified, protected, and revitalized through public policies.

Older districts in some cities will become highly sought after mixed-use and residential areas.

Evolving tax rules, financing practices, new programs, and awareness of social benefits will stimulate the adaptive reuse of historic districts and will make rehabilitation and preservation increasingly attractive to both private initiative and public interests.

Commercial feasibility will be increasingly recognized for adaptive reuse projects.

Historic preservation will gain financial and legal support through combination with environmental, recreation, and conservation interests.

Rural and suburban communities should seek to conserve and preserve enclaves, districts, and lands of historic and cultural importance for public use.

125. Lakewood Housing Subdivision, San Francisco, California

The conventional subdivision across America is calculated to squeeze maximum value out of the land development process. This process has now been challenged in many places and in many ways and public control of land development is increasing rapidly.

The automobile and exploitative land development have formed the suburb. A bland similitude is imposed so that each dwelling can have street frontage, driveway, and garage. A dispersal pattern across the landscape never before experienced by man is taking place. Some people think the city is becoming obsolete as the automobile eliminates requirements of centralized living, working, and shopping. But is this really the case? Does a small plot filled by a house, a driveway, a garage, and maybe two automobiles substitute for the potential of the city? The experiment in suburban living is now matured but not completed. The results are very mixed. The cities are stabilizing; they are learning how to improve life for their remaining residents. In the suburbs, in many cases, high costs, limited resources, developing racial tension, rising crime rates, and new restrictions on land development indicate that the experiment is far from over, that the balance sheet is still incomplete.

Land Use Regulation

In America, possession of land has traditionally conferred privileges, such as voting and reaping the fruits of the land, and obligations, such as taxation and upkeep. Land has always been acknowledged in the rules that govern our society as a commodity, like any other, to be used as its owner pleases.

Today, the concepts of what privileges and rights accompany ownership of land are beginning to change. Increasingly, land, even when privately owned, is seen as a public resource—a fundamental part of the environment. And the environment is becoming a public responsibility (see Chapter 6). This change in attitude, now visible in advanced legal, social, financial, and planning circles, is of profound consequence. Its impact on the cities, on the suburbs, on rural land, and on human settlement patterns in this country is just beginning.

In the past, cities, towns, and suburbs came into existence as the demand for housing appeared, often induced by commerce and industry. Owners subdivided well positioned land into lots, laying out buildings and streets to afford maximum profit, and ignoring long-term needs, public requirements, and humanistic amenities that would assure an attractive and safe environment for living and working (Figure 125). Settlement patterns, subdivision patterns, and city grids, all calculated to induce the highest land market value, formed the basis for nearly all land development in America. Only in the last several years has this approach been challenged and the challenge has come from forces concerned with the environment, distressed about dwindling land resources in densely populated areas, and anxious to improve the quality of life now and in the future.

The prospect of public regulation that extends much beyond zoning as opposed to traditional private control of land development is seen as a threat by many land owners and investors. They fear the impact of such regulation on land value or potential value. Even zoning is a major determinant of inherent land value. For instance, land that can be sold for housing in ½- to 1-acre lots may be worth 100 to 200 per cent more than land zoned only for 35-acre building sites. And land zoned for residential uses may be worth as much as 500 to 1,000 per cent more than the very same land restricted to agricultural uses. Through regulation, especially zoning, a public authority is thus able to sharply influence land values. But new regulations and new bases of regulation under consideration, as discussed below, go far beyond zoning. They extend all the way to the privilege to use, or develop, land. And these have an even more far-reaching influence on value, potentially. The issues involved are inflammatory and question the basic rights of ownership and control. And a lot of money hangs in the balance. The real estate developer holding land, the land speculator, even conservative long-term investors in land suddenly must ask: What do I really have? What are the rules of the game now? What are they likely to be in five years? For surely the old rules are changing.

In the United States land use control by public authority has a history extending as far back as 1693, when the colonial government imposed certain constraints on the use of public lands in New England. Through the 1862 Homestead Act, great reaches of federal lands in the West became open to settlement under certain regulated conditions. Two-thirds of these public lands were eventually sold or given to individuals, companies, states, and railroads. Sale of them and tax from them became the principal source of wealth for the federal government during the 19th century. The national park system, established in the 1870's, permanently reserved 30 million acres of land, removing it from private control.

Our national land management history is, then, of minimal public control over vast, publicly owned lands. But new public attitudes are bringing pressure for care and management on the federal government. In 1973, for the first time, for instance, the nation's biggest land custodian, the Department of the Interior's Bureau of Land Management, restricted historically, environmentally, and ecologically precious parts of the great southern California desert from the pervasive recent onslaught of recreation vehicles. The idea of public control of *private* land is also a relatively recent phenomenon. The right to impose zoning restrictions was first upheld by the United States Supreme Court in 1926. But zoning, as conventionally practiced in the United States, is less a source of public interference with private rights than it is a way for land owners, town boards, and zoning boards to assure the continuance of desirable development trends and rising land values.

Today, local public land use control of private land is still not very extensive. Even zoning is still far from commonplace in America. Currently, of some 60,000 jurisdictions with authority over land use, only about 5,000 have instituted zoning. And in most cases, zoning is understood, and properly so, as a flexible tool subject to review and change as circumstances require or as needs evolve. However, zoning is also seen as a way to manipulate land value with public complicity. It is all too often used by public authorities for short-term gains—to assure the continuation of local development, income, and jobs in the construction industry. This use of zoning, so long characteristic of land use in America, in the long run has bankrupted towns, congested communities, and finally disillusioned residents in many towns, cities, and counties throughout the country.

The growing trend of public control of land is being accomplished through a change in emphasis rather than through a radical change in ownership base through public taking of land. It is not revolution but evolution, and in most instances, quite rapid evolution that is underway. It is not so much the *means* of control that are changing, but the *degree* of control. These means, which have been in effect in many places for years, can be categorized as: (1) planning requirements imposed by planning boards; (2) building requirements imposed by building departments; (3) zoning requirements established by a zoning plan, zoning resolution, special zoning district, zoning board and/or zoning board of appeals; (4) water and sewer requirements, generally imposed by a health department and/or planning regulations; (5) outright public acquisition. Each of these is being used with sharply increasing vigor by public agencies at all levels of government around the country. The result is increasing emphasis on public control of the land development process.

Out of this emphasis have come requirements that developers, in return for the right to develop land, provide all sorts of "public amenities" such as pre-defined street-level public open space in some cities and suburbs, scenic easements along subdivision roads and frontage roads, improved landscaping, and more satisfactory land settlement patterns.

Cluster housing and development is increasingly promoted nowadays by public authorities as another way to improve land settlement patterns with conventional regulatory tools. Cluster development is sometimes mandated in new zoning ordinances and sometimes induced through the offer of economic incentives, such as increased density, to developers. Cluster housing does save the developer road, utility, and sometimes construction costs. At the same time more open land for watersheds, recreation, or conservation is generally preserved than would otherwise

be possible. When good design and good planning are combined, the clustering principle has advantages which far outweigh its disadvantages. But clustering, like conventional subdivision with amenities, does not generally provide more *public* land. Nor does it generally provide a *town* with resources it would not otherwise have. It is often simply a very dense form of conventional development which might incorporate a number of private recreational amenities.

Nevertheless, while the process of land control in recent years has remained within rather conventional channels, the concept of what land ownership means has, in progressive legal and planning circles in this country, been undergoing a profound reassessment. For instance, responsible groups have suggested that in time "private ownership of open space without urbanization rights should become as commonplace as ownership of land without mineral rights."[29] According to this suggestion, ownership of land may not necessarily include the privilege to develop it. Separating the right to use the surface of the land as it is from the privilege of building on it (or mining beneath it) might very well eliminate the basis for land speculation, thereby predicating an entirely new type of land ownership, one in which the so-called development rights revert to the public domain. This possibility, discussed in more detail later, is of great importance for better urban planning in this country.

Nor is this new concept of land use and land regulation an isolated one. In 1973, after a year of study country-wide, the Citizens' Advisory Committee on Environmental Quality reported to the President of the United States and to the National Council on Environmental Quality on the mood of the nation in regard to directions for land use regulation. Broad press coverage and unanticipated popularity have boosted their report, *Land Use and Urban Growth,* to national prominence. Among the findings and recommendations illustrating the attitudes that have been developing for a decade are the following:

"A new mood in American attitudes has emerged that questions traditional assumptions about the desirability of urban development. The motivation is not primarily economic. It appears to be a part of a rising emphasis on human values, on the preservation of natural and cultural characteristics which make for a humanly satisfying living environment.

"A changing attitude toward land, not simply a growing awareness of the importance of stewardship, but a separation of ownership of the land itself from ownership of urbanization rights, is essential.

"Historically, Americans have thought of urbanization rights as coming from the land itself, 'up from the bottom,' like minerals or crops. It is equally possible to view them as coming down from the top, as being created by society and allocated by it to each land parcel. We think it highly likely that in forthcoming decades, Americans will gradually abandon the traditional assumption that urbanization rights arise from the land itself. Development potential, on any land and in any community, results largely from the actions of society (especially the construction of public facilities). Other free societies, notably Great Britain, have abandoned the old assumption in their legal systems and now treat development rights as created and allocated to the land by society.

"To protect critical environmental and cultural areas, tough restrictions will have to be placed on the use of privately owned land. These restrictions will be little more than delaying actions if the courts do not uphold them as reasonable measures to protect the public interest, in short, as restrictions that landowners may fairly be required to bear without payment by the government. The interpretation of the 'takings issue'[30] is therefore a crucial matter for future land-use planning and regulatory programs.

"Many judicial precedents (including some from the U.S. Supreme Court) date from a time when attitudes toward land, natural processes, and planning were different from those of today. Many judicial precedents are anachronistic now that land is coming to be regarded as a basic natural resource to be protected and conserved and urban development is seen as a process needing careful public guidance and control.

"Ignorance of what higher courts have actually been willing to sustain has created an exaggerated fear that restrictive actions will be declared unconstitutional. Such uncertainty has forestalled countless regulatory actions and induced numerous bad compromises. The popular impression of the takings clause may be even more out of date than some court opinions.

"It is time that the U.S. Supreme Court re-examine its earlier precedents that seem to require a balancing of public benefit against land value loss in every case and declare that when the protection of natural, cultural or aesthetic resources or the assurance of orderly development are involved, a mere loss in land value will never be justification for invalidating the regulation of land use. Such a re-examination is particularly appropriate considering the consensus that is forming on the need for a national land-use policy."[31]

These collective suggestions and recommendations indicate a profound reassessment of traditional assumptions and privileges which may very well affect the economic character of the nearly two-thirds of the nation's 3.5 million square miles of land that are still privately owned. However, the report omits environmental issues, basic planning questions, and most significantly, specific reference to transportation policies which are, after all, the greatest single influence on land use and land development.

Two years before the Citizens' Advisory Council on Environmental Quality released its findings, the Council on Environmental Quality commissioned a study of innovative land use laws and proposals. These findings, published as *The Quiet Revolution in Land Use Control*, also received widespread publicity. After reviewing many of the new land use rules,

regulations, and proposals, principally at the state level, the report concludes:

"This country is in the midst of a revolution in the way we regulate the use of our land. It is a peaceful revolution, conducted entirely within the law. It is a quiet revolution, and its supporters include both conservatives and liberals. It is a disorganized revolution, with no central cadre of leaders, but is a revolution nonetheless.

"The tools of the revolution are new laws taking a wide variety of forms but each sharing a common theme—the need to provide some degree of state or regional participation in the major decisions that affect the use of our increasingly limited supply of land."[32]

The quiet revolution is supported by more than public statements. Across the country a rising tide of land control legislation is becoming law. Most of this new law depends on older land control concepts and newer environmental regulations.

In 1972, on the state level alone, consequential land control measures were passed by Colorado, Florida, Virginia, Connecticut, Michigan, Maryland, and other states. Of all environmental problems, from pollution to overpopulation, reports from all 50 states indicate that land use is now receiving the greatest attention. Within the last several years, landmark legislation has been passed in Hawaii, Vermont, Massachusetts, Maine, Wisconsin, and elsewhere; in many cases it has already been tested in the courts.

Many cities, counties, towns, and regional agencies now have substantial land use regulations where none existed a decade ago. California now requires statements on environmental impact for significant private as well as public developments. In addition, a powerful state regulatory agency must approve all development along the California coastline, and in most cases, 1,000 yards inland. The Town of Ramapo, New York, has imposed a virtual moratorium on development for up to 18 years or until the utility infrastructure has been developed to support new growth. In 1973, the New York State

Legislature approved a Tidal Wetlands Act that will affect 100,000 to 250,000 acres of land along 2,000 miles of shoreline. A moratorium now exists on development or modification of any of these lands without a special permit from the New York State Department of Environmental Conservation. The list continues to grow at an accelerated rate. And the first cases are now in litigation by which the new law will be tested in the courts.

As a result of new environmental regulations and growing public interest in the land development process, large-scale projects that affect land use and the environment are now forced to undergo greater public scrutiny than ever before. Many of these, which would have been implemented without question a decade ago, have in recent years encountered massive public resistance. These include the defeat, after a long and bitter struggle, of the supersonic transport project, the abandonment of a jetport and the blocking of the Cross-Florida Canal, both of which would have disturbed the Florida Everglades, the long delay in the Trans-Alaska Pipeline, the delay or actual defeat of power plants and highways of many sorts, and resistance to construction or expansion of airports. This resistance reveals a strengthening of the link between the often unrecognized quiet revolution in land use control and the more broadly recognized revolution in environmental control.

In addition, for the first time the broad impact of large-scale land development is being understood by the public. This awareness was best symbolized by the remarkable 1972 statewide citizens' referendum in Colorado, which barred the use of city and state funds to support the 1976 Winter Olympic Games. The defeat was based on the conviction that new development of the state's land and recreation resources was undesirable.

Public pressure is increasingly placing demands on political candidates to support environmental and land use control measures. In 1972 virtually the only spending measures approved by voters countrywide were bond issues for environmental improvement and the purchase of endangered lands. In November, 1972, one year after defeating a major $2.5 billion state-wide highway bond issue, the voters of New York State overwhelmingly approved a $1.15 billion environmental bond issue to assist in the immense efforts necessary to control water pollution, to help fight air pollution, for community solid waste recycling programs, and to buy and protect land, especially valuable wilderness and wetlands. At the same time, as mentioned previously, voters in Florida and in the state of Washington approved environmental bond issues in the $250 million range.

Federal legislation now before Congress could significantly accelerate the combined environmental preservation and land use control movements in this country. The Environmental Protection Tax Act of 1973 (discussed in greater detail in Chapter 7) is calculated to encourage private land owners to donate property development rights or other remainder interest in land to public bodies. The Act entitles the owner to a deduction from his income tax equal to the market value of an easement, an option to purchase, or a long-term lease donated for charitable purposes for not less than 30 years' duration, to a recognized charitable organization (including state and local governments). In this way, public control is obtained at no local public expense. Rather, it is the federal government, through reduced tax collections from the donor, which would subsidize the transition from private to public control. This Act substantially modifies recent tax reforms which have generally abolished tax deductions for anything less than full ownership (fee) interests in land, and quite obviously is calculated to make public control of certain private land more palatable to private owners.

The Land Use Policy and Planning Assistance Act (S. 268), first introduced in 1970, is a piece of federal legislation of major potential consequence now under consideration. It passed the Senate in June, 1973, but its fate remains uncertain in the current Congress. The bill provides up to $100 million annually for eight years in grants to states to cover from 66 to 90 per cent of the administrative costs of land use planning programs. The goals of this Act are to finance state land resource inventories and programs and in addition to: develop methods to control large-scale developments; control the use of environmentally sensitive areas; control land subject to developmental impact by facilities such as airports; influence the location of new communities; keep all developments consonant with antipollution laws; and assure citizen participation in carrying out these programs.

The Land Use Policy and Planning Assistance Act emphasizes the realization of these sweeping objectives at the state level in coordination with the Department of the Interior, which at this point has a spotty record in environmental and land use control. Whether or not this Act is passed in 1974, and if passed, whether or not and to what extent it is effective, the progress made by the Act in the federal legislative pipeline over a three-year period is compelling evidence of concern with the physical future of this country.

In the public sector, efforts are now underway in most parts of the country to inventory precious and endangered resources. Unfortunately, these are roughly parallel to the first identification of national historic structures in 1935 which went no farther in preservation attempts than simply listing unusual buildings. An inventory such as this, although a necessary first step, cannot assure conservation. Moreover, land values are already so high in most places where precious and unusual land exists that financial resources are often inadequate to purchase a meaningful amount of land, although these acquisitions should take top priority. Supplementary devices need to be employed and are being developed for the first time.

For instance, in fast-urbanizing Suffolk County, New York, the county legislature, prodded by an enlightened County Executive, has put together a financial and legal package calculated to preserve some 30,000 of the remaining 58,000 acre farmland inventory. This figure is down from nearly 125,000 acres in 1950.

The legislature has recently approved a three-year $45 million bill to buy farmland at market prices. The land is then to be leased back to farm operators. This procedure foresees, in the decade to come, a joint financial and legal means of implementing important farmland conservation.

However, in Suffolk County, and other areas, such programs are still the exception. Most public jurisdictions must seek a means to gain maximum control of important private land at minimum cost. This has led in recent years to both innovation and abuse.

Abuse generally results when carelessly conceived programs confiscate privately owned land. Confiscation may occur in principle if not in fact through imposition of excessively large lot zoning, through unwarranted and unfounded control of utility linkages, or through planning and building requirements which cannot be satisfied. Ultimately, confiscatory programs are self defeating. Meaningful public control is diminished by legal judgments rendered against public amenities. Innovation is much more desirable and has occurred in a number of new land acquisition and legal control programs. Most of the innovative programs seek an equitable agreement between a private owner and public bodies in terms of value and in terms of the owner's ability to continue to live on and use his property. What are some of these innovative programs? And how do they work?

One such program is a new concept of zoning, known as "zoning with compensation," that provides a fundamental new opportunity for an improved and equitable approach to land use control. The approach, upheld in "City of Kansas City v. Kindle" in 1969, provides a legal basis for a public body to compensate a private landowner for the value differential between a value-limiting new zoning and the full development value of land under existing zoning. In some cases, when this value is very small, the approach becomes feasible. In others, the differential could be so large that the compensation required would involve an insupportable public cost, as in the case of trying to convert land zoned for shopping centers into a public park. Thus the approach has merit and is useful, but its application is limited.

Nevertheless, the notion of "zoning with compensation" introduces a new concept into the body of land law. It reverses a very long history in this country of assuming that local governments could validly impose most land use regulations without the payment of compensation, a decision based on the 1926 Supreme Court ruling on zoning. And it is this ruling that has made public bodies very cautious. For when zoning can be defined as a "taking" then a community must compensate an owner for the full market value of land. Under the "zoning with compensation" approach, a community's maximum liability is limited to the difference between the old market value and the new market value of the property.

Another zoning-related device, introduced only very recently, is the "special zoning district" by which a public authority may gain control of specific land use areas to fulfill public purposes or public planning objectives at considerably lower cost than full-fee land acquisition. It is possible, for example, to establish a special zoning district to protect and promote public objectives such as agriculture, conservation, historic preservation, recreation, pedestrian-related amenities or other public purposes. Generally, the owner agrees to restrict the uses to which his land will be put. The public authority, in return, may reduce or omit his real estate taxes or relax height or bulk limitations on the building in recognition of the impact such an agreement has in fact on land value or development costs.

Another very new device for public land control is for a public entity actually to buy an *interest* in private land, but not to buy the land itself. The interest purchased would be, in effect, the development rights to the land, usually for a limited period of time. In this way the public authority pays the owner an appropriate fee, but in every case the payment must be less than the cost of pur-

chasing the property or the device would be senseless. The potential recognized in such an arrangement of separating rights to develop property from property ownership is just beginning to be realized in urban planning circles, although it has long existed in tenant farm agriculture, mineral rights leases, and other business enterprises. It is now becoming clear, for example, that a public authority may accomplish its purpose by acquiring development rights in the form of a lease, an easement, or even a covenant regulating the use of land.

The effective use of the development rights concept depends on a public authority's ability to *require* that the transaction occur. This means that public purpose must be proven so that privileges of eminent domain may be invoked. In most cases, a public agency will not seek to use powers of eminent domain even to condemn land in fee. Using the power to condemn less-than-fee title is a new concept which remains quite untested. The idea has recently generated such substantial interest that the technically sound and innovative American Law Institute investigated the matter thoroughly. Their conclusions are contained in a recently released and already influential proposed *Model Land Development Code*. The American Law Institute asserts that eminent domain proceedings could successfully be used by a local government to acquire leases, easements, and covenants on private land for desired public benefit. Their observations on this delicate matter are worth noting:

"(a) The local government could use eminent domain proceedings to acquire the desired public benefit for a short period of time by condemning a lease for 10 years or some other period of time to the government as lessee. The government would purchase by eminent domain a term of years. Thereafter the government could 'sublease' the land to a person who would agree to use it in a manner consistent with the previously determined public purpose; i.e., a lease for agricultural purposes only.

"(b) The local government could by emi-

nent domain proceedings acquire an interest in the land which was neither a fee simple interest nor a leasehold interest but was a permanent easement, servitude, or covenant running with the land, the benefit of which was acquired by the government, and the land would thereafter as the servient tenement be burdened with the easement acquired by the government.

"(c) The government could by eminent domain proceedings acquire an interest which was a combination of the methods used in paragraphs (a) and (b) above, such as an interest for 10 years of the benefit of a right in the land of another (easements, covenants, etc.)."[33]

The importance of this method of land control, from the point of view of a financially restricted public agency, is that some planning objectives which require land control can be accomplished without the costly purchase of the land itself. To refer back to the three examples above, for instance, the public cost of obtaining a time-limited control of the necessary land would be based on (a) the market value of a term of years, (b) the market value of the benefit of an easement, and (c) the market value of an easement of a term of years.

Just as in a sale and lease-back agreement or special zoning district, under these remainder interest transactions owners remain in possession of the land for the term of the agreement. This allows current uses to continue so long as the uses conform to public planning objectives, and often assures that the land will be well maintained and remain productive. However, unlike a sale and lease-back agreement, since the land remains privately owned, real estate tax income is not completely stopped, though it may be reduced. This too is advantageous from the viewpoint of a local municipality.

Purchase of a limited interest in private property may also be an expeditious interim method for local governments to save a great deal of money if outright purchase is anticipated but funds are currently unavailable. Control of the development rights can, after all, prevent the private development of property in a manner inconsistent with public objectives. And yet, if the development were undertaken, eventual public acquisition costs would have to include the value of any improvements, no matter how unwanted or unneeded.

The use of development rights as a public land use control mechanism is likely to grow in coming years. The approach goes a long way in resolving municipal needs for near-term land use control without necessarily disturbing present land use; an owner is not deprived of present income from the land or of receiving eventual fair market value for his property. In addition it permits a continued flow of real estate tax income to the community. The method is limited by the undeniable need of the community, even at reduced cost, to come up with capital funds for land use control. It also does not eliminate the need, at some time in the future, to renegotiate control or buy the land in question, perhaps at higher market values. And it is limited, at least at the outset, by complex legal and financial agreements that must be developed and negotiated.

What else can a municipality do to try to achieve public land control objectives at reasonable current cost? One of the most obvious moves available is one most often ignored by public commissions, study groups, and legislative research committees. This is to stabilize, and even reduce, real estate related municipal taxes, especially the school tax. The immense impact of real estate taxes on the timing, quantity, and quality of suburban and rural land development is rarely acknowledged by public groups. And yet high and increasing real estate taxes, the revenue source upon which most communities depend for most of their income, are the single greatest forces which drive undeveloped land into conventional suburban and rural uses. Just as the federal government during the early 20th century financed its operations through the sale of two-thirds of the nation's land, today most municipalities survive, year after year, by driving more land into development. A generally unacknowledged irony prevails: municipalities are trying to buy back or restrict development of land now in the private domain, yet at the same time their own tax policies in many cases force increased quantities of land into conventional development and concomitant higher public service expenses. As a result, money raised by increasingly high taxes still remains unavailable for public land development, land management, and sound planning programs.

Federal revenue sharing is one very new program that relieves local government's predominant dependence for income on real estate tax. But the program's future is not absolutely certain. The funds flowing to local communities are still relatively modest and are allocated on a year-by-year basis, making long-term programs and budgeting hazardous. In some cases, however, these funds are being used to immediately offset increases or even reduce real estate taxes. The use of revenue sharing proceeds in such a way is highly controversial. It limits their availability for capital expenditures, for social service programs, and for other general obligations of government. Instead, the funds assist the owner of private property. Ideally, sufficient funds should be available for all worthy programs. But if hard choices have to be made, then first priority must be given to finding some means to interrupt the devastating cycle generated by the conventional land development process. Many of the devices discussed in this chapter are now being considered. Hopefully, as they are tested and become more effective, revenue sharing funds will be liberated. In the interim, however, a share of these funds can be wisely spent by a local public body to directly offset increased real estate tax or to assist in financing public education. This approach would indirectly help restrain sharply rising property taxes, and combined with the approaches previously discussed, would be likely to assist in the implementation of sound, long-term public land management and planning objectives.

Although evident and often desirable change is occurring at a rapid rate in conservation and land control measures throughout the country, and though significant new programs exist and important federal legislation is now pending before the Congress, the energy and verve with which the land use control movement is charged and the alliances upon which it depends suggest a number of difficult social, ethical, and philosophical questions that should be asked.

For instance, who are the real beneficiaries of this movement? And combined with this question is the charged issue of no-growth, controlled growth, and limited growth. Taken together, the two questions are replete with greater irony than is generally acknowledged. For instance, one objective of many local regulations is to explicitly, or at least implicitly, limit new population growth within the community itself. Present residents in these communities have in many cases fled from urban problems and high taxes, and from the many issues and problems induced by living in socially and economically heterogeneous circumstances. They have sought a haven and they have invested money. Basically, they have what they want and they will seek to protect it, even to enhance its quality and value. These people now represent increasingly important voting blocks in the areas in which they have settled, in which they own land. They are aware of what has happened in the cities; they are also aware, even if not in detail, that the post-World War II "baby boom" is now causing the formation of 27,000 new households every week in the United States. Even with downward-revised population growth projections, it is still probable that within the next 25 years upwards of 50 million people must be accommodated somewhere in this country. And most of these people in the future, as in the recent past, will want to settle in existing populated regions which cover less than 5 per cent of the nation's geographical area.

This cumulative experience and growing awareness is shared in prosperous suburban and rural communities by politicians and residents alike. It is mixed with a genuine concern for the future and for the local environment. The result is policies generally based on rational or rationalized arguments related to open space, available public facilities, available transportation and parking, available utility services and water resources, and so forth. These issues provide a rational basis, or at least a justification, for a series of rules, such as large-lot zoning, which both control land use and limit population growth. These very same policies almost always instantly cut down the potential supply of new land for development, new houses for sale, new stores for rent. So, as the old economic formulas predict, prices go up. The beneficiaries are existing vested interests who own improved property, that is, those landowners already installed and voting in a community. Rising prices and a limited supply of places to live mean that poorer families who seek accommodations are increasingly excluded, that marginal or fledgling and potentially competitive business in search of a place to operate cannot get started or survive. At the same time, the programs and policies do relate settlement to resources, numbers of people to public accommodation for them. And so a strange alliance is forged between the idealistic, progressive proponents of land use regulation who want sound environmental management and the economically oriented, often conservative local vested interests.

It is this alliance, so fundamental in many respects to the local land regulation movement, that is being attacked by low-cost housing advocacy groups such as the Suburban Action Institute in Westchester County, New York. It is charged by such groups that decisions effected to limit population growth are calculated, in part, to particularly exclude lower-income residents who need subsidized housing and extensive social services. Such an argument is, in many instances, not without a basis in fact. The thorny issue raised by this argument, however, is whether or not established older communities should become responsible for resolving nationwide social problems and national land settlement policy issues even if their solution might be objectionable to a majority of present residents. In a sense, pervasive home rule versus a dominant federalist system is at issue. So stubborn questions do arise; good planning, sound land management, and worthy public strategies to limit irresponsible land development are also accompanied by exclusionary tendencies.

In other respects the land control movement forces an examination of the privilege of individuals to live in social and economic enclaves of their own choosing. Recently the traditional liberal stance of the 1950's and 1960's which favors unselective racial integration has been open to question—a question raised, in fact, by substantial dissatisfaction found among even these same people when they find themselves actually living in close proximity to others with vastly different economic backgrounds and social habits. But experience among residents in all social, economic, and racial groups during the last decade indicates a new and more positive tendency. When choice is available, it appears that people actually seek to live in relatively homogeneous social and economic enclaves without special emphasis on race. Forcing the opposite, socially and economically heterogeneous neighborhoods in city or suburb, it now appears, is a certain way to both frustrate personal interests and impede progressive, desirable community living and development.

Today, a growing number of communities and neighborhoods are in effect saying to all outsiders: "You may not live here. This place is closed." Across the country, as Fred Bosselman points out:

"The stop-growth movement . . . is becoming an important political factor in every part of the country where rapid growth is occurring. People who formerly felt there was nothing they could do about growth are suddenly feeling a surge of power as they see neighboring communities bringing the bulldozers to a halt. For the first time large numbers of people are beginning to ask, 'wouldn't it be better to leave things as they are?' "[34]

By the fall of 1973, land use control and the linked issues of mobility and population growth control had reached such national prominence that major conferences were held on the subject. One of these was the National Conference on Managed Growth held in Chicago. There, nationwide attitudes were discussed by George Gallup; restrictive action within communities around the country was reviewed; litigation, legislation, and court decisions were discussed; and techniques and strategies to assure managed growth were shared by politicians, planners, lawyers, legislators, editors, and others.

Managed growth is clearly a viable and reasonable stance for a community whose resources are demonstrably overextended or inadequate. But if and when used as a euphemism for highly selective and exclusive growth throughout the entire jurisdiction of the community, the policy must be questioned. A more promising alternative, when growth is possible, is to prepare for a variety of socially and economically compatible neighborhoods and districts within each community. Race is not so much the issue, though it is still an issue. The valid and fundamental progress already made in reducing racial segregation in this country has still to be matched with a well-thought-out and implementable plan to assure stable and viable settlement patterns that encourage racial integration. This goal is elusive. It may be reached in part, it would seem, if the human quest for social and economic homogeneity is emphasized in planning.

New Towns are often suggested as a panacea for the stubborn contradictions inherent in land control, growth/no-growth and municipal finance pressures now faced by existing communities and expressed by citizens around the country. In some instances, a totally new community is a sound idea. But New Towns are slow to develop and are still not a major thrust in America. Thus New Towns are not likely in the near future to relieve the pressure on well-positioned, older suburbs, or rural towns within major metropolitan areas.

Yet New Towns do hold promise and are themselves a new direction of consequence in American planning, land development, and land settlement control. In

1970, as a completely new federal initiative in America, the Urban Growth and New Community Development Act was passed as Title VII of the Housing and Urban Development Act of the same year. In essence, it provided up to $50 million in federal loan guarantees to private developers as financial assistance for an approved New Town. Although a lot of private venture capital was still required, the government offered a tempting inducement to large investors and rich corporations to enter the land development business on a massive scale—the scale of a New Town. As a result of the Act some New Towns are already underway in the United States. These include Flower Mound, Texas; Jonathan, Minnesota; Maumelle, Arkansas; Park Forest South, Illinois; and St. Charles, Maryland. In all, however, as of July 1973, only 15 new communities had been approved for federal assistance. In addition, several New Towns have been started in recent years without initial federal support, including the well-known communities of Columbia, Maryland, and Reston, Virginia.

The premise of publicly assisted New Towns is quite new to America. Most towns in this country, until very recently, have indeed been new towns, but new towns built on a base of business and speculation—not on subsidy. It was not until 1969 that a new direction in national settlement policy was even suggested. That year the National Commission on Urban growth proposed that 10 new communities of one million people each and 100 new communities of 100,000 people each be developed in the United States to accommodate at least half of the 50 million people who will seek a place to live in the next 25 years. But this proposal has not yet become national policy. The approval of 15 new communities for target populations generally under 100,000 since the Urban Growth and New Community Development Act of 1970 is hardly a stunning start, and the movement has slowed substantially in the last year or so. The program is stalled because of diminished funds and disorganization within the Department of Housing and Urban Development, and because of difficulties in terms of economic feasibility already encountered in several New Town projects.

In addition, because of the private capital base upon which most new communities depend, even when they receive federal loan guarantees, they are almost all placed in proven market areas. Thus they are built very close to existing centers of settlement, to existing airports, to existing or planned major highways. They usually fill in well-defined regions of intense existing settlement rather than expand the development potential to the vast majority of open and unused land in this country.

One would expect nothing else of privately ventured excursions into the tricky, long-term and high-risk business of establishing a new place for people to live. But future government programs in which public subsidy is made available should focus more clearly on the need to develop a reasonable national settlement policy and plan for this country. New Towns should be placed in relation to such a policy. There is no land shortage in America. The shortage is of land that people now consider desirable because of location or amenity. It may just be, in years to come, that policies will have to be developed to increase the desirability of new places. This is not hard to do. Recreation resources can be built almost anywhere—even in the desert. Centers for gainful and desirable employment can be established through subsidy and tax abatement programs, as many other countries and even some states in this country know already. Through devices such as these and others, a meaningful New Towns program with adequate funding and workable procedures could be used in the United States, as it has been in other countries, especially in England and Europe, to assist in a national resource deployment and population distribution program. New communities approved in the future should respond more directly to national social needs and national and settlement policy objectives—if these are ever formulated, as they should be. Building New Towns in unpopulated areas is admittedly not the least expensive way to cope with our future. It is less expensive to look the other way, as we do now.

No large-scale new community program will ever be successful unless crucial public assistance is provided. New Towns require a continuing flow of capital, sometimes for over a decade. If these funds are subject to conventional, private market risk-reward investment feasibility formulas, the majority of new communities would never be built; it is unlikely that many would become significantly better communities; and it is doubtful that any would be useful as a rational instrument to assist in improved national land use and land settlement policies. In addition, if governance of new communities remains restricted to the initial investment group for decades, as it is in many cases today to assure no untoward tilting of the cash flow and economic model which the new community is really constructed by its developers to serve and to fulfill, they will remain places of considerable social and political disappointment from the viewpoint of residents who have distressingly little to say about the affairs of the place in which they live. Finally, if the new communities are to arrive at the bottom line of the investment objective that they represent to corporate and private backers, a thoroughly mixed and balanced social, racial, and economic cross-section of the country is generally not feasible. So social goals, too, in terms of national and even statewide land use and settlement planning, are also aborted under the present system of new community planning and development.

The state, in many respects, is becoming the new frontier of national planning policy and the unit of government basically in control of new land use regulation. As federal agencies such as the Department of Housing and Urban Development and the Department of Transportation encounter increasing local resistance and increasing difficulty in self-definition, public power in America is shifting from the federal to the state level. Clear signals of this shift are the state-level primary responsibility under the proposed

126. Lake Anne Village, Reston, Virginia

New Towns will help house some of the 50 million people who will seek a place to live in the United States in the next 25 years. But unlike Reston, most of them will have to be publicly financed or at least publicly subsidized. New Towns should be seized as one of the ways to establish meaningful coordination between state and federal planning objectives as well as a sound national population growth and land settlement policy.

Land Use Policy and Planning Assistance Act; the new distribution of unrestricted revenue sharing funds to the state; and state-level responsibility for environmental protection legislation, enforcement, and budgets. It is therefore increasingly important that each state become aware of its potential role in statewide and coordinated national land settlement planning, which in turn is part of the larger, growing public responsibility for land use regulation. A component of this responsibility is surely to consider, plan for, and continually support New Towns.

Yet only two of the 15 new communities approved for federal assistance between 1970 and 1973, Roosevelt Island in New York City and Lysander, near Syracuse, New York, have public agency sponsors. These are both sponsored by the same agency, the New York State Urban Development Corporation. The Urban Growth and New Community Development Act enabled state and local public bodies to undertake new community development. But the public sector has been slow to enter the field. It is especially unfortunate that more states have not organized public-purpose agencies to initiate new community development as a part of statewide planning policy. In years to come, I suspect, state government will increasingly enter this domain of activity.

It is also too often forgotten that about one-third of the land in the United States is still publicly owned, and the vast majority of that land is federally owned. Appropriate parcels could be turned over to state development agencies for new communities. Too much of this land has been exploited for too long with government complicity for private gain through cheap ranching, agriculture, mining, subsurface exploration, and forestry leases. Of 187 million acres in the National Forest System, for instance, only 10.7 million acres are protected from commercial exploitation today, as wilderness areas (Figure 127). In 1973, as a result of intense and ever-growing pressure from nationally organized environmentalist groups and conservationist societies such as the Wilderness Society and Sierra Club, an addition-

VIRGIN FOREST, 1620

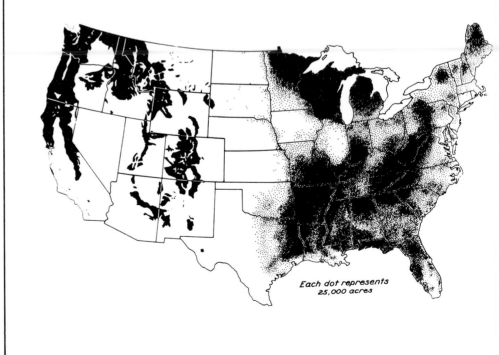

VIRGIN FOREST, 1850

Each dot represents
25,000 acres

127. Forest Areas in the United States

Through private development, sale, and lease of public land and inadequate land management and reforestation programs, the forests in America have been severely depleted. Of the remaining national forests less than 10 per cent are currently protected from commercial exploitation as wilderness areas.

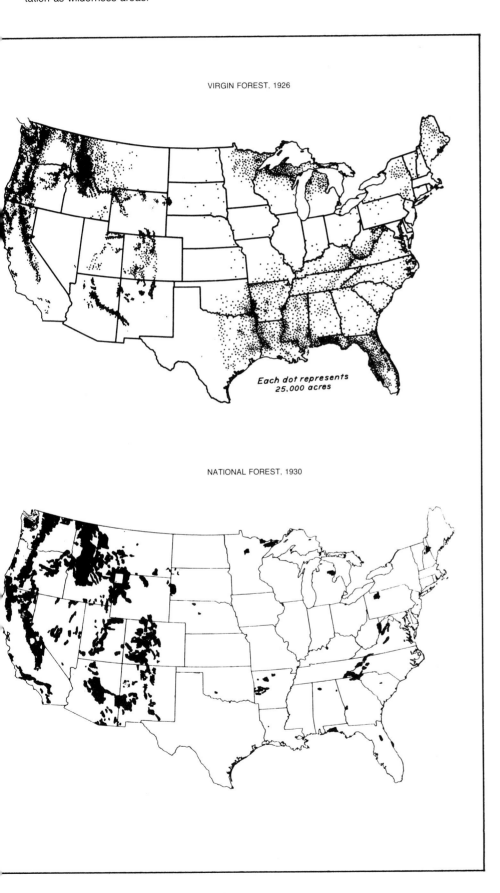

VIRGIN FOREST, 1926

Each dot represents
25,000 acres

NATIONAL FOREST, 1930

al 12 million acres of virgin national forest will be studied for inclusion in the protected "wilderness" category. How much of this will actually be protected is still uncertain.

But most federal land is not especially unique, beautiful, remote, or well-positioned for recreation. An inventory should be produced within each state of potential publicly owned sites for New Town development. On suitable and properly positioned publicly owned sites, New Towns could be developed at greatly reduced public expense. The land would be free, and the incremental growth in land value created by the New Town development could be recaptured by the public sector. Were such an enterprise to ever get started it would be essential to insulate the management of the New Town from external political pressures. It would also be advisable to have private management experts involved so that the profuse waste, time-delaying procedures, and inertia that generally coagulate around most public agency development programs could be guarded against.

In national planning efforts there is at least some scant evidence that a new direction toward rational provision of parks and recreation facilities is emerging. Currently, only 3 per cent of the nation's 490 million acres of public recreation lands are within 40 miles of the center of a metropolitan area with over 500,000 people. Clearly, most recreation land is not where it is most needed. In 1972, Congress set an important precedent and hopefully a new direction in open space legislation by establishing two major national recreation areas in *urban* regions, to which federal lands were contributed—the Golden Gate National Recreation Area, near San Francisco, California, and the Gateway National Recreation Area near New York City. It is now essential to ensure that these urban recreation areas are well administered, well maintained under anticipated intense usage, and made accessible to the people they are most intended to serve, urban residents of moderate to low income, who will need transit facilities to reach them.

There are, then, clusters of very new trends and tendencies that affect the control of the land operating simultaneously and with increasing force in America at every level of government, of law, in study commissions, and in the private sector. The various approaches contain ambiguities and ironies, they contain social, legal, political, policy, and financial questions of the most fundamental sort. There is the entire and pressing question of local and state land use policy's still not being coordinated with any program for a national land settlement policy. Which zoning controls are in the public good, how to define the public good, what public is being considered, and how zoning and other land control measures must be reconciled with uncompensated public taking of private property are other difficult questions.

What is certain is that the trend is here. It is now. And it is growing. A redefinition of property rights is underway. A re-evaluation of public responsibility for the disposition of land is also underway. These very new trends are sure to preoccupy especially suburban and rural communities, their legislators in county and state government, and their representatives in the Congress for years to come. They are trends that touch the rawest nerve endings hidden deep in the core of land development questions; they touch the issues of money and control, of profit and power.

The first emergence in this country of a widely based social and economic alliance of residents united against continued growth of their own suburban and rural areas does signal a new direction in America. Political repercussions of this alliance, so evident in the ecological, conservation, and preservation movements, are just becoming evident in local, state, and national land use policies.

It is my guess that in time, as laws and procedures are sorted out, the development of desirable suburban and rural land will be made very much more difficult and very much more costly than it is today. In some cases a variety of public subsidies may be used to offset some of these costs, but in many instances the new rules, the delay involved, the costs that will have to be risked, and the uncertainties imposed may very well stimulate development of publicly assisted New Towns and make the cities more attractive for redevelopment than they are now. This, after all, is one of the unspoken, underlying goals of the entire movement. And it is a new movement of very great political and economic power—enough power to succeed.

The rebuilding of older cities and the starting of some new ones is likely to result. But the building is likely to be more measured and more rational than in the past. Amenities for people will have to be provided that were ignored the first time around. For the competition is there. The suburb and the exurb exist. They did not exist when the city was first spewed out in a speculative land binge that enriched a few people and rendered many others exceedingly unhappy for a very long time. And so, in spite of great attendant difficulties, it may be expected that new and in many instances altogether desirable and appropriate innovative land control measures will help, in an overall way, to preserve the unusual land resources of this country, to intensify and improve new community building, and to assist in the fruitful rehabilitation and rehabitation of older cities. The cities, most of all, will benefit. They are ready and waiting.

New Directions

Land will be treated more as a *resource* in which the public has an interest and less as a *commodity,* even when privately owned.

Environmental concerns coupled with new concepts of land ownership rights will change the legal basis of property rights.

Innovative public land control programs will proliferate, especially those related to temporary control of development rights through acquisition of a lease, easement, or covenant and use of tax abatement agreements.

Public regulation of the land development process will increase sharply through zoning, construction permit requirements, utility demands, and planning criteria.

Private land development will become a right granted by cities and towns in exchange for increasingly costly required public amenities.

National, state, and local tax and legal policies should be modified to assist private owners in withholding forests, farmlands, wetlands, and coastal shores from development. Tax assessment of underdeveloped land should be based on present use, not speculative potential.

Pressure is growing to limit population growth and new land development, especially in thriving established residential communities near urban centers.

With the choice available, people will seek to live in relatively homogeneous social and economic enclaves.

New Town development must receive greater public support.

New Towns should be located as part of national, state, or city land settlement and land use programs.

Trends in land use regulation will make older cities increasingly desirable for redevelopment.

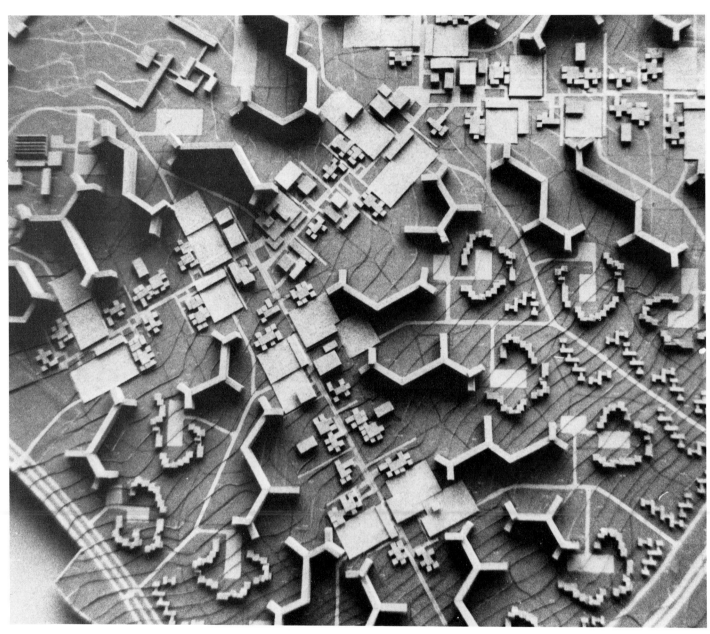

128. Plan for Caen, France, 1961. Photograph of the model
Shadrach Woods, George Candilis, Alexis Josic

This city extension scheme for about 40,000 people near Caen, France, represents a search for a flexible planning tool that would suggest growth possibilities without limiting opportunities or imposing inflexible strictures on the city as it develops. Low-scale commercial and public buildings are clustered along linear pedestrian ways or "Stems," car parks intercept access roads near the grade-level pedestrian streets, taller, elongated apartment buildings are surrounded by green space and link the commercial areas to clusters of townhouses. No specific architectural style is suggested, on purpose, although inevitably, some degree of specific formal design is implied through the architect's rendering or model.

New Directions in Planning

Whereas the previous chapters of this book were concerned with new directions in urbanism itself, this chapter focuses on new directions in the way urbanism is practiced or might be practiced. The focus now shifts from the product to the practitioner and to the tools of his practice.

During the last decade decisive changes have occurred in *how* urbanists function, *where* urbanists function, *what* they produce, and how the society functions in relation to them. Three specific realms of activity delineate the urbanist's work: derivation of a working methodology; preparation of a "plan"; and implementation of the "plan." In all three of these, the practice of urbanism in the United States has undergone important and often unrecognized transition in a very short time. This transition in one way or another has expanded the types of people and disciplines involved in planning, multiplied the procedures by which urbanism is practiced, and varied the product it is producing.

First, consider for a moment changes which have occurred in the urbanist's working methodology. The urban planner, since the origin of the profession in the late 19th century, traditionally operated from a set of visual or geometric presumptions about the proper, intelligent, beautiful, and/or hygienic arrangement of cities. Commercial, industrial, and residential districts were usually distinctly separate. Open spaces with fixed edges (squares, plazas, etc.) and buildings with fixed styles (classical, gothic, colonial, etc.) were used to symbolize purpose and to enrich the cityscape. The urban plan, in short, began as a stylistic conceit derived from a number of selected prototypes which often boiled down to nostalgic cultural reminiscences and transmigrations of physical, city-form patterns. The choice of geometric patterns for both the public

spaces of the city and its principal buildings generally depended on the predisposition of the planner, the government, the era, and the intended symbolism or message contained in the building or plan.

These traditional preoccupations were canonized at the beginning of the 1960's in Kevin Lynch's influential and enormously popular book, *The Image of the City*. In Lynch's book, which has been through at least 10 printings and influenced urban designers throughout the country, issues of "imageability" are paramount and methods for producing certain kinds of visual impact are described. It is Lynch's view that imageability, as he defines it, produces an awareness of cities and an urban environment which is very desirable. As he says:

"Since the emphasis here will be on the physical environment as the independent variable, this study will look for physical qualities which relate to the attributes of identity and structure in the mental image. This leads to the definition of what might be called *imageability:* that quality in a physical object which gives it a high probability of evoking a strong image in any given observer."[35]

The Search for New Planning Methods

The search for a new methodology in planning is taking many forms. A growing interest in obtaining flexibility in the evolutionary process of city development is evident. Zoning is being used in new and entirely different ways. New methods and attitudes are leading to new building types. And research is accelerating into new methodology which could become fundamental to the practice of urbanism.

Flexibility. A new focus now entering the mainstream of advanced planning notions accords increasing attention not to the imageable artifacts of the city itself,

which are discussed by Lynch, but to the many substructures of the city which are crucial to our appreciation of it and to planning and management of the built environment.

The transition in focus began tentatively after World War II, accelerated in the last decade, and was completed during the later 1960's. It was completed in association with a rising tide of rationalism in this country. Serious attention to social need, inquiry regarding patterns of human association, and recognition of the impact of time on the city became significant. The rise of the social sciences is reflected in a new series of plan determinants, in the rise of broader-based political representation and political power, and in an understanding of time as a crucial fourth dimension in which the urbanist must work.

This series of influences gained articulate exposure by the mid-1960's, especially through younger architects and planners who spent a number of years, alone and together, attempting to formulate an understanding of what urbanism could be—and what was meaningful in its contemporary practice. Team 10, one highly articulate and, during the 1960's, progressive association of such individuals and firms, remains today loosely confederated for purposes of international discussion and concept formulation. Alison and Peter Smithson, English members of Team 10, demonstrated the growing tendency away from formalism as a basis of planning in the early 1950's when they defined a town as a "specific pattern of association, a pattern unique for each people, in each location, at each time."[36] From this base they go on to define a town plan as "the method of applying those principles."[37]

Associational networks, as well as indeterminacy of form evolution over the period of urban evolution or through time, are even more at the core of planning concepts that emerged during the mid-1960's from the notable practice of Candilis, Josic and Woods, members of Team 10 then living in France. In their "Notes on the Origins and Planning Methods of the Partnership" they indicate that "in [our] view, the structure of towns is based on human activities and not on geometry."[38] Their principal concern was to "find a minimum structuring system, thereby leaving the maximum possibilities for adaptation. . . . To develop a system of organization which could be recognized gradually and was valid for every stage of growth. Growth and change were the basic conditions of the planning."[39]

These goals were developed in thinking about and preparing city extension schemes for Caen, Bilbao, and Toulouse-le-Mirail in the early 1960's (Figure 128). The plans themselves attempt to present notations for structures, not structural types. They are meant as suggestions for functional groupings on the "Stem" principle, not architectonic prototypes with highly designed, stylized skins assembled to serve as decorative space walls. The "Stem" idea, as mentioned previously, seeks to organize residential, commercial, entertainment, recreation, and parking according to a functional rationale, along a flexible, extensible pedestrian spine (Figures 129, 130).

Much more expedient and direct methods to assure some control over the physical evolution of urban areas have been successfully developed by practicing urban planners in recent years. Control is sought to assure that planning objectives are obtained without inhibiting potential for design and development flexibility. This is accomplished through increased focus on the infrastructure of the city, its utility lines, its street patterns, its transportation network, and the future location of vertical lifts such as elevators and escalators. This method has been seized, increasingly, in large-scale planning efforts to provide a flexible grid upon which changes over time and accommodation to

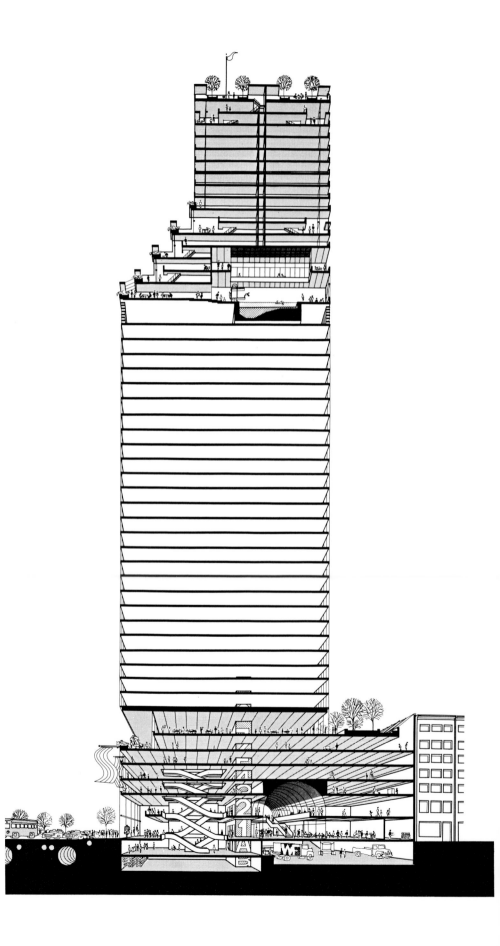

129-130. Special Fifth Avenue Zoning District, Prototype Building, 1971
Cross-section (left); Arcade rendering (above)
New York City Office of Midtown Planning and Development

Between 34th and 59th Streets along Fifth Avenue, one of several New York City Special Zoning Districts is now in effect. Along this traditionally active retailing street segment, transformations and procedures to make new public intervention desirable were taking place under the former zoning rules. Land values and rental requirements escalated. Lower margin, profit-oriented retail operations were forced to close or move. Banks, airlines, and other service operations which traditionally pay higher rent than retail stores moved in. Land assembly became rampant as developers contemplated replacing the low buildings and retail stores with more profitable office towers. Fifth Avenue, perhaps the nation's most prominent urban retail center, began to die.

To stabilize the situation, a "Special Zoning District" was created. In it a developer of a new building must generally include retail store space along the street. In addition, he is encouraged to negotiate with the city for more rentable office space on upper floors than would ordinarily be allowed under the zoning guidelines. It is this privilege to negotiate that distinguishes the special zoning district. The city offers a more lucrative building in return for certain amenities, in this case even more retail space enclosed in mid-block arcades and residential space (apartments or hotels) perched atop the new towers. This way, with induced horizontal layering of diverse functions and development of mid-block enclosed shopping arcades, a more active, more varied district is anticipated which will be used by people over a considerably longer day than the usual 9-to-5 office or shopping span.

The cross-section (Figure 129, left) illustrates the new kind of mixed-use building envisaged in the new zoning district. The bottom half-dozen floors might contain small shops or a larger department store. Above the retail space, office floors are provided and apartments cap the building. Between Fifth and Madison Avenues a three-story pedestrian arcade stretches through the block. These covered arcades, when completed, would be lined with shops and restaurants. The first new building to participate in the Fifth Avenue Special Zoning District is now under construction. Others are expected to follow. The special zoning district is one of the new ways that public sector planning is being used to induce private developers to assist in implementation of publicly established urban amenities and planning objectives without dictating precise building design, location or development timing.

incremental building would be possible.

It is finally being recognized that the arrangement of the primal fixed and generally invisible elements of urban structure should determine where, how much, and how little can be built. It is now realized that the *capacity* of the enclosed environment can be planned, located, and sized long before construction begins. What is necessary is the proper predetermination of location and capacity of vertical elevator cores, escalators, and utility lines and the horizontal location of their linkage to street and to the transport system of the city. Through this strategy, urban areas and suburban districts may be planned without unduly influencing the future appearance of specific structures or even the time frame in which they may be built. At the same time, maximum capacity of all service elements can be defined in advance to prevent future congestion, overbuilding, and poor linkage to streets, to transit, and to other buildings such as now plagues older cities. This approach is graphically summarized in the "Access Tree" organizing principle developed by Frank Williams and Rai Okamoto for the Regional Plan Association's *Urban Design Manhattan* study completed in 1969 and previously discussed (Figure 75).

Vincent Ponte's imaginative and commercially successful planning for Place Ville Marie and its attractive tentacular pedestrian extensions to nearby transit, parking, and growing commercial centers in downtown Montreal illustrates many of the same principles in a vibrant, successful downtown redevelopment which has been steadily growing since the plan was initiated in the mid-1960's (Figures 90, 91).

Zoning. Used in new ways, especially in urban areas, zoning is another means seized only recently to control long-term development through planning without necessarily dictating size, scale, or design of buildings. Traditionally, zoning was used to define *what* specific buildings and building types could be built in every part of a city or town and how big it could be. Because it defined the maximum *building*

envelope, it traditionally influenced the precise form assumed by buildings put up to conform to zoning requirements and yet achieve maximum internal rentable or usable space.

Zoning is conventionally used as a relatively rigid control which may not be altered, theoretically, block by block or project by project. It establishes control, not positive goals, and this control is supposed to be applicable to all development. This leads, one way or another, to considerable back room juggling and private pressure on public officials for changes on a property-by-property basis. Negotiation is initiated by the private sector. The zoning official only responds to overtures, requests, etc.

Only recently, has zoning been recognized for its potential to establish amenities in the public environment and more generally to establish a means of guiding the quality and character of future development without specifically dictating the location and appearance of that development. It is, in other words, now emerging as a publicly administered tool able to assist in the positive redevelopment of the so-called negative space of the city, the city beyond the building skin, the open space used by most of the people in the city.

To these ends an imaginative and in some ways risky use of zoning called "incentive zoning" is being tested in a number of cities. Incentive zoning declares the flexibility of a zoning code at the outset, encourages public officials to negotiate with private developers, and offers an incentive to a developer to provide amenities deemed to be in the public interest. The incentive or bonus available to the builder or developer is the privilege of building a greater amount of rentable space than is authorized by the zoning code. In return the developer provides a pre-established public amenity of some sort, presumably of a value as nearly equal to the city as the bonus in space is to the developer. Thus, a sort of public urban design process becomes available on a district-by-district basis rather than on the older uniform city-wide application of

zoning and building controls.

With this approach, as used in certain locations in New York City for instance, zoning is used as a flexible, negotiable control which permits a financially strapped city to achieve certain planning goals which might otherwise be unobtainable. Goals established by the city's planners thus far involve providing special amenities in special districts. These include new theaters in the Broadway theater area, pedestrian arcades near Lincoln Center on Broadway, retail shops in the Fifth Avenue shopping district (Figure 129), improved pedestrian and traffic circulation throughout the special Greenwich Street Development District in lower Manhattan, and retail and commercial spaces in new buildings, limited to 13 or 14 stories for the most part, along the proposed Madison Avenue Preservation District. In addition, a similar approach is now recommended by the Urban Design Council in New York to achieve more varied, more tenant-responsive and neighborhood-oriented housing in both private and publicly assisted development.

Some of the amenities selected in New York are questionable, such as an excessive number of new theaters and certain windswept public plazas. In certain instances the plazas have produced a senseless and useless array of spaces which are not actually of public benefit, or of value in maintaining and improving the character of the street, district, or city. Furthermore, it seems clear that the city gave away too much in some trades in the early years of special zoning districts when great additional bulk was produced in the commercial real estate boom of the 1960's without adequate planning of services and with inadequate return to the public. But overall, the procedure has provided great gains to the city. It holds immense promise and is likely to be used with increasing sophistication. In Chicago, planners, lawyers, and city officials are using a modified form of zoning manipulation to preserve fine older buildings in the Loop.

The practice of negotiated zoning for amenities as well as for the exchange of building rights above fixed land parcels is functioning, and can be improved. But special circumstances are needed. A real estate industry willing to build is a prerequisite. A planning commission willing to work is necessary and difficult to find. The tricky responsibility of negotiating special favors to a special interest group in the alleged public interest opens up every conceivable opportunity for skullduggery. Thus, strength and integrity, qualities not universally displayed by city planning commissions around the country, are necessary unless the public is again to be bilked.

The creative and honest use by government of economic leverage through devices such as special zoning districts in the course of urban redevelopment, should be recognized by more cities as an available and valuable resource. The cities do not have money themselves to provide many amenities which could make urban life more desirable. Nor do cities have title to much of the usable land within urban areas. The privileges of ownership together with the single basic goal of all real estate development—profit—can be used by alert and intelligent city planners (as it has been thus far by and large in New York) working with city administrations to accomplish coherent and relevant planning programs in the city, programs which should be devised to improve the quality of urban life. Time is short. The city center is still losing its population and its political clout. New ways to make life better for people must be found and implemented if people can reasonably be expected to stay in cities. The owners and developers of urban real estate know this. That's why they cooperate. But city governments across the country must also become aware.

More extended and more informed investigation of negotiated urban amenities contained within defined districts is likely as other cities review the progress and problems encountered in New York and Chicago. The use of public power will become a tool increasingly used to exact from private developers concessions that benefit all people in the city, as it has been for some time and is increasingly

in suburban and rural development. The privilege of building in the city, of using the city, its utility system, its transportation system, its resident worker population, will more and more often be exchanged for provision of required amenities to the city. None of it will work, however, if the price is too high, or if commercial activity at the city center diminishes so that new investment is not undertaken.

Some cities, of course, such as Houston, have decided that zoning is entirely unnecessary. Market forces are allowed to determine what is built, where it is built, and when it is built. However, restrictive covenants are generally incorporated into residential deeds to protect property values. Such a system may indeed produce a city and a region not very unlike one with traditional zoning, as it is often argued. But it also means that the opportunity to plan for the ultimate implementation of certain types of public amenities through imaginative and negotiated use of the new types of zoning is largely lost.

Mixed-Use Buildings and Districts. Planners in the United States have recognized with increasing clarity and only in recent years that the mixed-use building as well as the mixed-use urban district is desirable. This recognition is reflected in the Special Fifth Avenue Zoning District discussed above. It is also revealed in the increasing number of multi-purpose, often horizontally layered or closely juxtaposed mixed-use buildings now being proposed and built. These do indeed signal new and promising trends in planning and programming for urban areas.

Throughout most of the industrial and post-industrial building experience in America, the single-purpose, free-standing building has been the unchallenged norm. Churches, offices, factories, houses, stores, government buildings, and institutions commonly stand alone. Washington, D.C., is the symbolic prototype. Each department of government has its own discreet building site, often surrounded by expansive open space and fenced in by wide traffic-filled streets. The building as monument is proclaimed,

insistently. It is as if the theoretically sound principle of constitutional dissociation of power had been accepted as a practical and desirable building and planning principle as well. The White House is majestically separated from the legislative and judicial buildings with which it is supposed to be intimately concerned. In cities throughout the country the single-purpose building lot filled with the single-purpose building has prevailed.

Occasionally, a free-standing building actually responds to programmatic and symbolic requirements, as in a church or a cultural or institutional structure. But most often it is simply the result of accepted cultural attitudes, mixed with the requirements of zoning and the predilection of mortgage lenders, both of which are themselves based on long-accepted, culture-bound normative rules by which urban form and building type are shaped. As a result of health precepts developed during the factory era of the industrial revolution, which have retained their currency in a post-industrial age, housing in urban America has been especially restricted by zoning from all other types of urban development.

This pattern of monumental, free-standing buildings, long accepted in America, is by no means commonplace. Throughout most of the world, from ancient settlements to the present, the varied activities of urban life commonly have taken place in complex, interlinked structures in the centers of cities. Commercial enterprises and residential life are traditionally juxtaposed in the same building. The pattern of multi-use complex structures zoned horizontally for different uses (such as shops below, dwellings above) has sources as ancient as the classical periods of Greece and Rome. Mixed-use patterns, often based on convenience for people and a logical association of interconnected activities, show promising signs of reappearing in the United States.

In the last decade, planners, architects, and developers have come to recognize that the reintegration of residential activity with social, recreational, and commercial life is desirable. In a number of highly

131–132. John Hancock Center, Chicago, 1969
Section (right); Exterior (far right)
Skidmore, Owings & Merrill

This approximately 100-story structure is the largest single multi-use building arranged in horizontal layers. Commercial spaces and parking are intermingled at ground level. The next 30 levels of office space are served by an independent bank of elevators from a separate lobby. Near the top, about 45 floors of luxury apartments command views across Chicago. A restaurant and observatory cap the very tall building. This horizontal layering of activities breaks with the old American tradition of one building, one function. As the inconvenience of travel within cities becomes more pronounced, as the conventional street is progressively avoided, as the horrors of commuting are fully experienced with the maturation of the suburbs, new urban building types are being sought. Greater efficiency, heightened activity, and new convenience result. The European-type medieval house above the shop reappears at a new scale and new level of complexity based on, among other things, real estate economics for institutional investors.

The specific form of the building, placed on a well positioned but small three-acre site, was determined by computerized analysis to achieve optimum functional, structural, and economic efficiency. As is unfortunately characteristic in venture capital building, particular accommodation to context—the surrounding urban environment—was not a form-determining criterion. This tower reveals what a well-programmed computer working with well-trained economic feasibility analysts may come to. Good planning, complex structural solutions, efficient construction, all may have been achieved, but in the process a scaleless monolith unrelated to its site was produced.

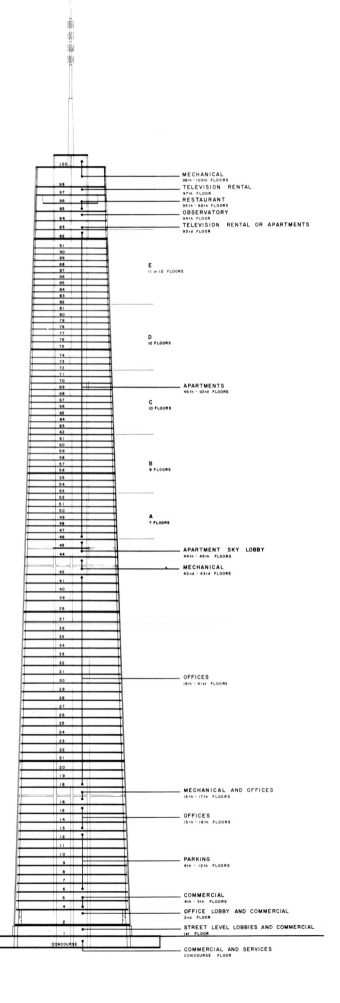

MECHANICAL
98th-100th FLOORS
TELEVISION RENTAL
97th FLOOR
RESTAURANT
95th-96th FLOORS
OBSERVATORY
94th FLOOR
TELEVISION RENTAL OR APARTMENTS
93rd FLOOR

E
11 or 12 FLOORS

D
10 FLOORS

APARTMENTS
46th - 92nd FLOORS

C
10 FLOORS

B
9 FLOORS

A
7 FLOORS

APARTMENT SKY LOBBY
44th - 45th FLOORS
MECHANICAL
42nd - 43rd FLOORS

OFFICES
18th - 41st FLOORS

MECHANICAL AND OFFICES
16th - 17th FLOORS

OFFICES
13th - 16th FLOORS

PARKING
6th - 12th FLOORS

COMMERCIAL
4th - 5th FLOORS
OFFICE LOBBY AND COMMERCIAL
2nd FLOOR
STREET LEVEL LOBBIES AND COMMERCIAL
1st FLOOR
COMMERCIAL AND SERVICES
CONCOURSE FLOOR

specialized instances, such as the Fifth Avenue Zoning District model discussed previously, this reorganization is attempted within a single building, itself often a free-standing monumental structure.

A prominent recent example developed without zoning guidance but in observance of market forces is the new John Hancock Center in Chicago completed by Skidmore, Owings & Merrill in 1969 (Figures 131, 132). Superimposed over more than 40 floors of shops, garage, and office space are about 45 floors of apartments. Although the building is severely flawed in terms of its relation to the street and to the surrounding city, in the Hancock Center, the physical and economic concept of a multipurpose building is explored as a way to vary the urban *milieu* and partially to subsidize free-market housing. High land and foundation-laying costs are paid for by high-economic-return office space; as a result, retail spaces and luxury housing becomes economically feasible in urban areas where it might not be otherwise. Besides, it is finally becoming evident that housing in areas now devoted solely to eight-hour-a-day commercial activity offers a sensible way to revitalize urban centers, to improve safety in central areas, and to offer people an opportunity for convenient urban living near their jobs. The rigid exterior skin of the Hancock Tower (worked out by computer printout) and the overbearing scale of the Hancock Center leave much to be desired; but the spatial relationships and planning concepts by which it is organized internally are promising departures from the conventional downtown office skyscraper.

Integrated mixed-use planning in a single building was rare and even unacceptable in America a decade ago. Today, with city transportation difficult, and with acceptance of apartment living and the economies of shared land, foundations, power plants, lobbies, and so forth over the 24-hour cycle rather than the eight-hour work day, this approach is increasingly attractive, convenient, and economical. Certainly new problems are also associated with integrated mixed-use space planning. Questions of land ownership, allocation of shared costs among a variety of entities, and new problems in structure require resolution. These have retarded implementation of many schemes. But potential far outweighs problems. Much more vertically integrated planning and development is sure to take place in years to come. It will appear in city centers and in suburban centers—wherever activity, vitality, and economic conditions warrant joint use of built space and land.

The search to find an economically and socially viable way to intermingle residential uses with commercial, retail, entertainment, and recreational activity is not limited to single buildings or to luxury housing. In almost all subsidized housing development these days, an effort is made to assure the presence of convenient commercial and retail as well as day care and recreational facilities. But more important as a very new trend in planning concepts in this country is the ever-increasing attempt in new development, and especially in urban redevelopment, to plan an active, vital, multi-functional district, rather than a traditional separate commercial, industrial, retail, or residential district within the city.

A recent public housing scheme by Gruzen and Partners for 300 acres of land now pre-empted solely as railyards in Sunnyside, Queens, New York, illustrates this growing trend (Figures 133–135). An entirely new urban "subcenter" is proposed above a massive transportation complex which continues to operate and serves to link the center to the rest of the New York City metropolitan area. The center, as proposed, would provide substantial subsidized housing within a multifunctional and multi-layered retail, commercial, office, industrial, entertainment, and transportation complex. Indeed, there is a specific link intended between the jobs created, especially by the badly needed industrial loft space, and the housing provided.

The goal, increasingly evident in redevelopment schemes, especially in urban areas, is to bring together people and their

activities within the city. This single goal has tremendous benefits which have been ignored for far too long in the arrangement of cities and even of towns. What are some of these benefits? The reduction of transportation requirements liberates both the people and the systems. Urban areas are given a multiple purpose, and used day and night, to effect a more efficient use of the city infrastructure, buildings, elevators, sidewalks—everything. Increased and continual activity is a strong deterrent to crime, thus fear and violence are both mitigated. And people enjoy more vibrant, more active areas in which to live and work, so the experience of the individual within the city tends to be heightened. All of this can be accomplished with good planning, awareness of needs for quiet and privacy as well as activity and vibrance, and most of all when the scale of development is large enough that it approaches the "intermediate scale" discussed later. Finally, it must be considered that most of the intensively used areas in most cities in this country are contracting in size. City populations, businesses, jobs are all stable or declining. A tightening up is occurring in that strong centers are growing more desirable—stronger—while the weaker areas are obliterated, abandoned, or simply slowly decaying. The process of regrouping is incrementally underway in most cities. This is a positive trend, one which signals the contraction of the city to a more manageable size and shape. The regrouping, if done wisely, will be in multi-use, multi-functional buildings and districts. We should know enough to be clear about this by now. The development, maintenance, and business economics of urbanism work better this way. The social objectives of most people and most enlightened programs can be better served in this way. Together these will make the city more desirable to more people and will link its survival to a promising economic and social basis.

A new building type has also evolved in recent years as a result of changing planning concepts. The new type, sometimes called the "megastructure," may

be described as a generally elongated, continuous building in which a variety of functions is served, but on whose exterior these disparate functions are not necessarily evident. In a conceptual sense the megastructure is the skyscraper turned on its side. But use of more land and lower building mass opens up an opportunity for more variety in the form of the building itself.

The linear integration of buildings and spaces is a planning method that has been used, especially by architects, with increasing success in recent years to reduce building cost and to enhance large-scale public areas. Seen in the context of this recent trend, the much-acclaimed and architecturally seminal Boston City Hall by Kallmann, McKinnel and Knowles is a recent monumental free-standing public building that summarizes older planning tendencies in a neo-brutalist style. In the same city a building of approximately the same date, Paul Rudolph's irregularly patterned Boston Government Service Center, illustrates more recent planning tendencies behind a more conventional architectural skin (Figures 136, 137). In one continuous structure, the Boston Government Service Center contains the Department of Health, Education and Welfare, the Mental Health Building, and the Social Security Department. Its differentiated, linked functional units in turn surround an interior public court space shielded from street noise, parked cars, and traffic hazards. Here, many different functional units share one continuous multipurpose building. The Boston City Hall, on the other hand, proclaims its absolute independence in the conventional fashion from other units of government, from other parts of the city, by isolating itself in a large, urban plaza.

An analogous trend is apparent in university campus planning. Traditionally, each university department or school has had a separate building, linked by walls and roads. In recent years, multi-use linked linear structures that combine purposes and functions have become commonplace. The trend was signaled and notably influenced by the winning of a much-publicized international competition for the Free University of Berlin in 1963 by Candilis, Josic and Woods. Their design, a complex continuous structure for many departments and functions, is modulated internally and externally to human scale and in relation to activity and space use requirements along four circulation spines (Figures 138–140). At Scarborough College in Toronto, another influential multifunctional structure designed by John Andrews was recently completed (Figures 141, 142). Andrews' work, however, as compared to the Berlin scheme, imposes choice limitations, problems of inflexibility, and a high degree of formal monumentality of which the Candilis, Josic and Woods scheme is liberated. These and other new university compounds and institutional facilities around the country signal a new and sensible trend in large-scale linked institutional planning and building.

What are the motivating economics and urban design gains involved in such megastructure schemes and how may they be especially useful in cities? The continuous building, as compared with a number of scattered buildings, allows more economic utilization of site, structural materials, and time. Some exterior walls are eliminated; land needs and thus land cost are reduced. Valuable land reserves can be conserved for expansion or preservation. In many cases savings are also realized by paring down external roads, utility conduits, and service areas. Climate control is facilitated. Above all, convenient places are built for people to use. In the foreseeable future integrated multi-functional horizontal and vertical megastructures will play an increasingly strong role in building design and economics. They are one of the ways that housing costs can be reduced and that urban clusters of all sorts can become more vital, more viable, and more varied.

Intermediate Scale. Larger building complexes and district-wide planning signal the new scale at which the city is to be organized and incrementally rebuilt. The single house or even single major public

structure cannot continue to be the focus of most financing, planning, or building. At the other end of the scale, massive urban clearance in anticipation of rebuilding is not a viable way to proceed. In the former, the effort of intervention exceeds the impact possible from the effort. In the latter, the scale of operation is so large that disruption of families, of neighborhoods, of the settlement pattern itself, makes the long-term risk of final redevelopment for improved public and private benefit an unacceptable—and in recent experience losing—gamble.

Thus a new scale of activity, a scale larger than the single conventional building site, but smaller than an entire district, should be recognized as the area of maximum potential. Very roughly, the optimum range for intervention in urban areas should be 5 to 50 acres.

On this *intermediate* scale, complex, multi-functional buildings and areas are capable of preserving the diversity and vitality of an urban environment while also producing an economically viable construction package. In this way the combination of model planning and building used at a relevant and manageable scale creates an opportunity for people to do many things of very different types in a constricted space; the opportunity to do them without use of the automobile or even public transportation; and the opportunity to spring from the trap of the conventional eight-hour day and its rigid zoning of human functions.

In the continuing search for a way to stabilize the American city, it appears that a sensible scale of possible intervention has been found in recent years, even if inadvertently. With the pragmatic evolution toward the complex multipurpose tall structure, megastructure, and district, it appears that building types suitable to urban needs and a manageable yet economically and politically defensible scale of intervention are in the early stages of recognition and development. Both tendencies—when fully recognized and carefully explored—contain substantial promise as a means of confronting a number of the forces which have successfully

diminished urban life and form in recent decades.

Computers and Research. Important new trends are also emerging in the way planners work within their offices, especially in the way the myriad, varied, variable data that must be absorbed is analyzed and the way that potential plans are tested for their impact on people, places, and over time. In much of this work, for the first time, computers are being used.

Computers have been proven to be reliable storage centers for information. More extensive use of them as data banks for planning is long overdue at a municipal or regional level. Unfortunately, in the few cities and regions which do have computerized planning data, the blatant limitation of such information has become evident. The information is rarely in the form needed, it is rarely relatable precisely to the area under study, it is often expensive to retrieve, and most grievous of all, it is generally not kept up to date. All of these limitations lessen the usefulness of the computer as a planning data bank source, and yet it is clearly a good device for storage and retrieval of the enormous quantity of statistics that have become a necessity for the planning profession. But its information must be used with greater circumspection, with greater cynicism, if you will, than most planners are willing to exert.

The computer is an especially tempting and lethal device for producing *projections* into the future from data gathered in the past. Planners must make these projections to plan properly for the future. But they are often too willing in every type of planning effort to make straight-line projections directly from an observable past trend into an inadequately considered future situation. This single shortcoming in planning methodology goes a long way to explain many inaccuracies in planners' projections, ranging from the flagrant errors made in highway demand analysis to the often very flawed estimates of future demand for housing, commercial, and retail space. Variables need almost always be introduced. These may

depend on an intimate understanding of local circumstances, or on an awareness, so often lacking, that what is changing is more important to isolate and understand than what remains constant. These and many other opportunities for insight in planning invalidate the too often relied upon, mindless use of the computer. The ability to see what is not yet there, to grasp the potential, to uncover the variables, to realize the opportunities for a place distinguishes the better planner from the ordinary technician.

The computer is also being used experimentally in research centers around the country by planners and others to try to understand ways that it may be applied more creatively in the planning process. For instance, since the mid-1960's Christopher Alexander has worked with computers to investigate new analytic means to penetrate unchallenged assumptions and formal procedures commonly used in urban analysis. Much of the approach depends on translation of subtle information to a numerical format acceptable to the computer. Alexander has worked in recent years to develop a computer-compatible design system which incorporates the complex net of human association that occurs in urban places. Programs have been developed to reduce observable behavior to analytic numerical format. Numerical abstractions in "sets" are seized upon as a manageable and manipulatable analog to human associational webs. Whether such computerized analysis of urban life is possible and whether it can produce design and environmental gains are open questions. At the moment it appears highly questionable that man's behavior, desires, and experience can be reduced to numerical format in a meaningful and economically viable way.

Nicholas Negroponte, working at the Massachusetts Institute of Technology, sees the computer in perhaps a more realistic way. He recognizes that urban plan-

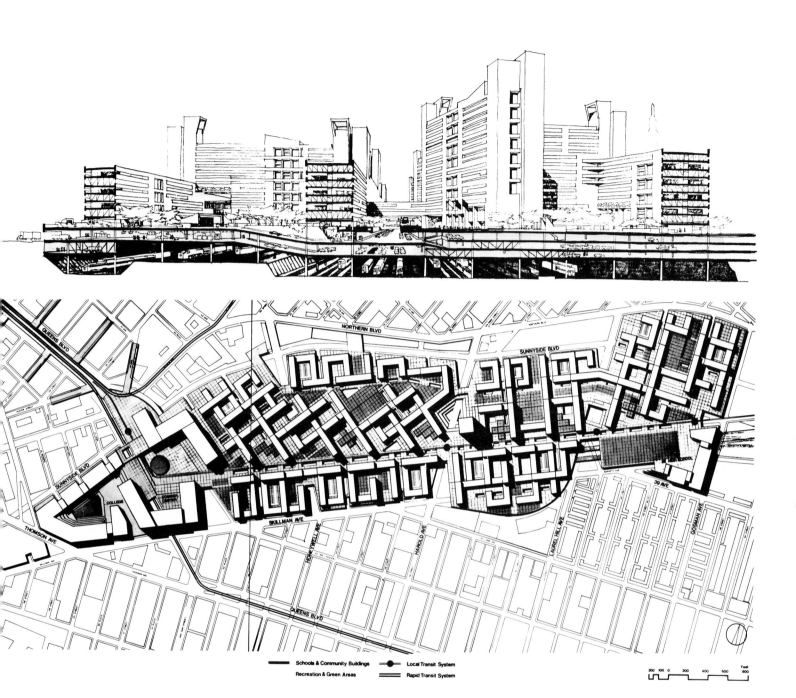

133–135. Sunnyside Railroad Yards Project, 1970. Site, aerial view (left); Section (top); Plan (above). Gruzen & Partners

The Sunnyside rail yards in Queens, New York now pre-empt other utilization of 300 acres of land and create a formidable barrier to activity in the middle of Long Island City, an active manufacturing center. A long-term, staged development scheme sponsored by the New York State Urban Development Corporation was proposed in 1970 to deck over these rail yards with a multi-use, multi-level urban district. The five-phase project contemplates high-rise housing and offices superimposed over retail and commercial uses, which in turn are placed over industry, loft space, and parking. At the principal deck level, a pedestrian promenade and mall are planned; at the level of the yards (which continue to function), transportation facilities of all sorts

for people and goods link to all parts of the city and region. A large measure of industrial space provides needed jobs in manufacturing, a type of space in increasingly short supply in the city. If this long-term program were ever realized, a divisive rail yard would become the foundation of a vital new urban subcenter.

Mixed use, multi-level decks, and complex integration of space and functions in a planned evolutionary building program are all hallmarks of planning and architectural development which emerged strongly in the 1960's. The qualitative achievements in phasing analysis, integration of space uses, and potential solution of a very wide spanning problem are unfortunately not paralleled by physical massing and open space planning of similar richness. Apparent accept-

ance of the typical superblock with central court throughout most of the project reveals a reliance on older patterns based on pre-existing grid street arrangements, although in reality, these need not constrain the planning for such a large new area on created land.

Since this plan was proposed, the scheme has been set aside due to a depressed market in New York for office space. In its place, a project has been proposed recently composed of two race tracks, a sports stadium, and a 1,000-room resort and convention hotel complex. Finding an economically defensible way to bridge this massive, complex but well-located site may elude developers and planners alike for some time to come.

136-137. Boston Government Service Center, 1962. Model (above)
Perspective drawing of section through the Gateway at the Northern Corner (right)
Paul Rudolph (Coordinating Architect)
Shepley, Bulfinch, Richardson & Abbott
(Architects, Division of Employment Security Building)
Desmond & Lord (Architects, Mental Health Building)
H. A. Dyer and Pedersen & Tilney
(Architects, Health, Welfare & Education Building)

A complex of linked building elements is used to provide a convenient service center for public health and welfare administration. Construction began in 1967 and was completed recently. Linear megastructures such as this are structural and planning devices which became increasingly evident in urban centers during the 1960's. They permit redevelopment at the meaningful "intermediate" scale while providing convenience to users and economies to builders. Here, the angular, linear megastructure tied to a tower is conceived to form a space-enclosing wall which creates a large-scale inner court shielded from street sounds, wind, and traffic exhaust. The Mental Health Building is to the left of the high-rise tower which contains the Department of Health, Education and Welfare. The long block in the foreground houses the Social Security Department. The various functional units are differentiated by scale modulations, but the entire complex is unified through similarity of material and continuity of mass. The necessity of working simultaneously to suit the demands of a number of functioning departments and federal, state, and city programs obstructed full realization of the Service Center complex.

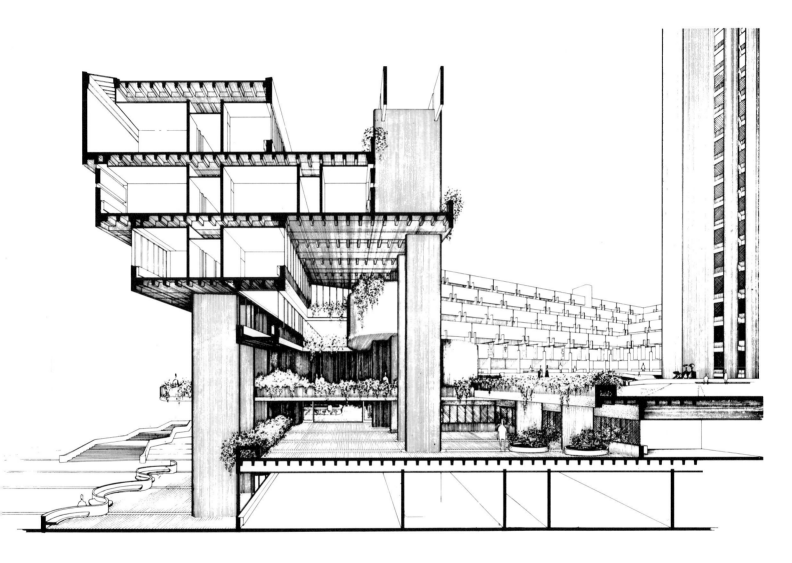

ning issues and data in great concentrations often exceed man's comfortable capability to discover, absorb, and retain. At the very small scale he recognizes, as does Alexander in his pattern language discussed later, that architects are likely to ignore or overlook details and problems that are crucial to a particular situation. Because of these limitations at each end of man's conceptual capability, Negroponte feels there is a creative role for the use of the computer. As he wrote recently:

"An environmental humanism might only be attainable in cooperation with machines that have been thought to be inhuman devices but in fact are devices that can re-spond intelligently to the tiny, individual, constantly changing bits of information that reflect the identity of each urbanite as well as the coherence of the city."[40]

This assertion, provocative as it is, ignores the ever-present reality that someone still has to prepare the computer with a core capability to adjust to new information; it must be continually advised through new programs. If this is done properly, it is just possible that the massive accretion of data could be creatively applied in all areas of urban concern.

Negroponte argues that the computer is likely to be useful in just that way. He anticipates a symbiosis between the de-signer and the machine, in which the computer is able to "*exhibit* alternatives, discern incompatibilities, make suggestions, oversee urban rights of individuals."[41] Negroponte suggests that the computer could free the architect or planner to act more as an *interpreter* between physical form and human needs. It could liberate him from many of the requirements of detail and memory. It could permit a greater degree of comprehensiveness than has been the case heretofore. In this way the architect or planner might be able to concentrate more effectively on determining the best solution to a physical design issue rather than remain preoccupied with discovering and remembering

1. THE IDEA OF UNIVERSITY:
THE NEED FOR AND EXCHANGE OF
GENERAL AND SPECIAL INFORMATION.

IDEA OF UNIVERSITY

2. THE UNIVERSITY IS COMPOSED OF
INDIVIDUALS AND GROUPS, WORKING
ALONE OR TOGETHER, IN DIFFERENT
DISCIPLINES. WHEN INDIVIDUALS
WORK TOGETHER THEY TAKE ON
NEW CHARACTERISTICS AND DEVELOP
NEW NEEDS.

INDIVIDUALS   GROUPS

3. THE UNIVERSITY AS IT SEEMS TO BE:
BUILDINGS CONTRIBUTE TO THE
ISOLATION OF SPECIFIC DISCIPLINES.

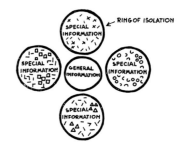

ATOMIZATION OF THE IDEA OF
UNIVERSITY

4. BUT THE REMOVAL OF BUILT BARRIERS
AND THE MIXING OF DISCIPLINES
IS NOT ENOUGH.
THE GROUP IS MEANINGLESS WHEN
THERE IS NO PLACE FOR THE
INDIVIDUAL.

GROUP IS EVERYWHERE

5. THE RELATIONSHIP OF GROUP AND
INDIVIDUAL MUST ALSO BE CONSIDERED.
AREAS OF ACTIVITY AND AREAS OF
TRANQUILITY MUST BE PROVIDED.
IF THE GROUP IS EVERYWHERE, THERE IS
NO GROUP BECAUSE THERE IS NO
INDIVIDUAL.

PLACES FOR INDIVIDUAL · PLACES FOR GROUP
TRANQUILITY AND ACTIVITY
ISOLATION AND EXCHANGE

6. THE EXTERNAL EXPRESSION OF
DIFFERENCES IN FUNCTION (ARE
THESE AS IMPORTANT AS THE
SIMILARITIES?) AND NOSTALGIA
FOR REPRESENTATIVE FORM ALSO
TEND TO SEGREGATE THE UNIVERSITY
INTO SPECIALIZED DISCIPLINES ONLY.

DISSOCIATION

7. WE SEEK RATHER A SYSTEM GIVING
THE MINIMUM ORGANIZATION
NECESSARY TO AN ASSOCIATION OF
DISCIPLINES. THE SPECIFIC
NATURES OF DIFFERENT FUNCTIONS
ARE ACCOMODATED WITHIN A
GENERAL FRAMEWORK WHICH
EXPRESSES UNIVERSITY.

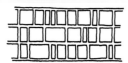

ASSOCIATION

8. IN SKYSCRAPER TYPE BUILDINGS
DISCIPLINES TEND TO BE SEGREGATED.
THE RELATIONSHIP FROM ONE FLOOR
TO ANOTHER IS TENUOUS, ALMOST
FORTUITOUS, PASSING THROUGH
THE SPACE · MACHINE · LIFT.

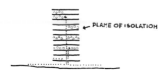

← PLANE OF ISOLATION

9. IN A GROUNDSCRAPER ORGANIZATION
GREATER POSSIBILITIES OF COMMUNITY
AND EXCHANGE ARE PRESENT WITHOUT
NECESSARILY SACRIFICING ANY
TRANQUILITY.

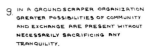

10. TENTATIVE USE OF A MINIMUM
STUCTURING SYSTEM WHERE INDIVIDUAL
AND GROUP MAY DETERMINE
DESIRABLE RELATIONSHIPS.

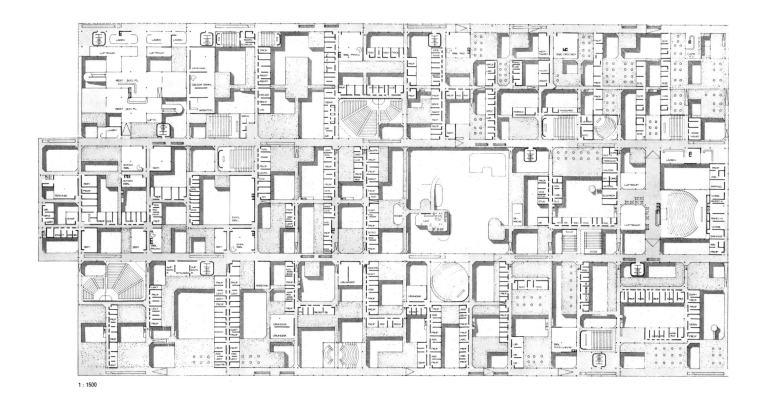

1 : 1500

**138-140. Free University of
Berlin Extension, Berlin, 1963**
Ten Planning Elements (left)
Plan and section (above)
Open Space System (right)
Built Circulation System (bottom right)
Shadrach Woods, George Candilis
and Alexis Josic with Manfred Schiedhelm
and Jonathan Grieg

The carefully studied arrangement of pedestrian ways, open areas, gathering places, and classrooms is the basis of this competition-winning plan which seeks to provide an association of spaces meant to promote interchange of ideas, privacy where needed, and economies in building and land use development, instead of the traditional isolation of academic disciplines within separate buildings each burdened with its own access, delivery, and community space problems. All university functions are incorporated into a carefully conceived matrix of levels, courts, and open spaces. Four parallel internal streets interconnected by perpendicular crosswalks provide the major organizing circulation system. Above ground, the university is kept at a two- or three-story scale, eliminating the need for elevators, elaborate roadway systems, and extensive land required by the conventional separation of university faculties and functions into different buildings. Below-ground service, storage, and delivery are provided so that pedestrian activity does not conflict with auto and truck traffic. A somewhat irregular grid plan with wider longitudal "avenues" and shorter, narrower perpendicular "streets" serves as a pedestrian circulation system. Multi-level linkage between enclosed spaces based on functional relationships, open areas, and desirable scale modulations is implied along and above the grid of streets which becomes, rather than a determinant of urban form, simply an element to serve the superstructure. In addition, this approach permits flexible, phased development in the future.

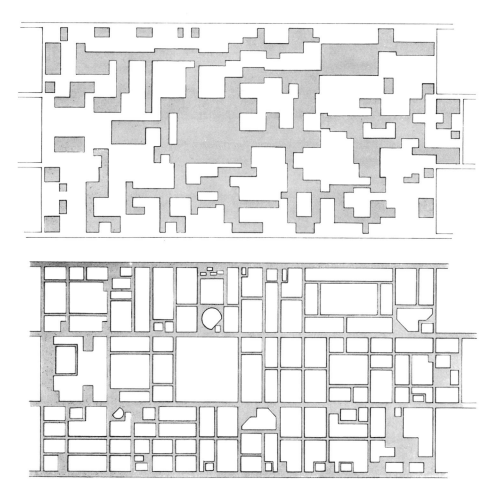

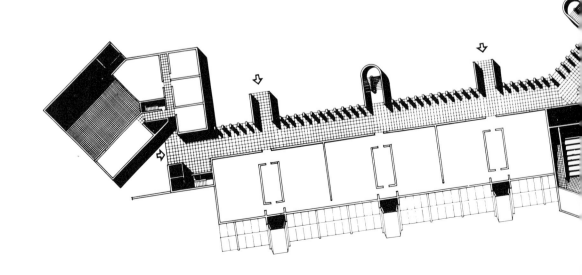

141–142. Scarborough College of the University of Toronto, Scarborough, 1964-66
Plan (below); Interior Pedestrian Spine (left). John Anderws and Page & Steele

This new campus for about 6000 people links all activities along a form-giving, space-organizing pedestrian spine (Figure 142, left). A system of enclosed, skylit pedestrian streets links administration, humanities, science, and other functional wings (Figure 141, below).

Whether government center, urban center, or university center, it is clear that major emphasis on internal pedestrian circulation within low-rise, mixed-use "megastructures" has gained prominence in Europe, America, and Canada during the last decade. The notion provides a degree of physical comfort, diversity, and potential human contact not easily available in an environment of scattered structures separated by traffic arteries or in dense skyscrapers. There is also a measure of structural economy in reduction of road, land use, utility service, and materials that offer a compelling impetus to continued exploration of the well-planned, multi-purpose megastructure.

However, in this project the superimposed levels of continuous pedestrian streets are likely to limit opportunities for desirable diversity, privacy, and quiet at the university. In addition, the continuous linear system necessitates long walks to get from here to there, somewhat like an ordinary airport concourse plan. And the imposing formal contours of the building suggest an embrace of the conventional architectural quest for monumentality as a quality disassociated from programmatic needs and the personal comfort of the building's inhabitants.

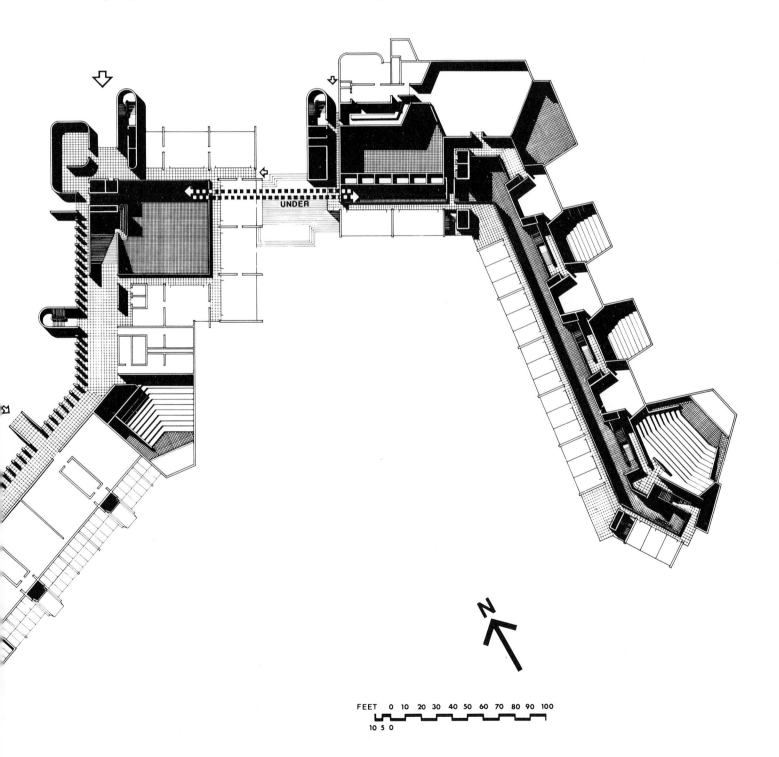

FEET 0 10 20 30 40 50 60 70 80 90 100
10 5 0

the various components of the potential solution itself.

Computers are also becoming popular devices by which a present planning decision can be assessed in terms of its future impact. Much as a businessman might try to use a computer to project the impact of a new product (about which certain assumptions are made in terms of cost, sales, profit, etc.), urbanists are trying to anticipate the future impact of planning and building. Present alternatives can be tested against future variables such as building form, settlement patterns, population, environmental quality, and hundreds of others, as Carl Steinitz and Peter Rogers have attempted in recent years in their work at Harvard. The exercise could theoretically yield valuable information that would make a correct present intervention more likely. Such games are popular because they gratify the age-old quest of man to predict the future. However, they must inevitably deal in such massive generalities, in such simplistic attitudes toward causality, in such static hierarchies and priorities over long time spans that their real utility and practical validity in assisting incremental change are questionable. They also omit the crucial ingredients of imagination, force of personality, and unanticipated circumstances (such as war, revolution, and economic turmoil) that accompany fundamental redirections in urbanism. The most promising use of the computer (as opposed to data research) as an urban planning device may very well be in capturing public interest through computerized games, as part of public education and the plan approval process, as discussed later.

Other Research. In research centers around the country, an expanding inquiry into the nature of cities and the nature of urban evolution, which only began with any intensity in the 1960's, has led broadening views within more theoretical segments of the planning profession on how the urbanist might best proceed, on what in fact is a reasonable basis for a working methodology. This inquiry is still generally centered in academic circles and planning departments such as the Center for Environmental Structure at Berkeley, where Christopher Alexander's work is primarily carried out, the Laboratory for Computer Graphics and Spatial Analysis, and the Center for Population Studies at Harvard, where Carl Steinitz and Peter Rogers undertake research, and in projects investigated by Nicholas Negroponte and others of the Architecture Machine Group at the Massachusetts Institute of Technology. These and other such centers are producing a body of theory and research, some of which may very well influence the day-by-day working procedures and planning approaches taken in the future. What are some of the principal concepts being considered at the research level across the country, other than those related specifically to the computer, that reveal potential new directions in urban planning methodology?

At the Center for Environmental Studies, for instance, mathematician-architect Christopher Alexander and his associates seek a method to "modernize" design methods and bring scientific rigor into the process of design itself. To do so they have developed a universal design vocabulary and grammar which they call "pattern language." Each pattern symbolizes a set of elements or components that need to be incorporated time and again into a physical plan, such as a certain type of office, a playroom or reception center. With each "pattern" comes the rules for its use. Each pattern is also capable of being combined with other patterns, so that eventually buildings, and theoretically even urban districts, might be symbolically represented by a linking and association of these symbol-pattern fragments.

Each of Alexander's "patterns" is composed of three parts: an "if statement," which defines precisely the situation to which the pattern applies; a "then statement," which describes a physical response, an appropriate space or building configuration; and a "problem statement," which opens the pattern to criticism and modification. Each pattern is placed in a glossary. Each is itself symbolized by a small, medallion-like drawing. These medallions may then be manipulated, interrelated, and connected to short circuit some parts of the conventional design process.

Alexander's pattern language is obviously a helpful means of prearranging and prepackaging clusters of thoughts that must be connected time and again during the design of buildings. It also provides a helpful checklist of component elements needed to properly satisfy certain design programs. It is then a valid design tool, one especially useful in assembling components of a complex building like a multipurpose service center, such as the one Alexander has developed from his pattern language. But it is limited as an urban planning device because pattern language is best used when restricted to a single building. The language itself ignores, as any relatively rigid symbolic system must, the large-scale external impacts of social, economic, and physical circumstances. And it is incapable of stretching to the vast number of complex issues that must be confronted when working at an urban scale. The pattern approach emphasizes user needs, but in doing so, it often excludes the wider issues with which urbanists must deal, such as finance, timing, and transit linkage.

Recently, Alexander has tried to extend the concept and procedure of pattern language to increase its potential application in urban planning methodology. He does this by concluding that "each situation specifies a certain physical pattern —and each pattern recurs many times in a given city."[42] Alexander proposes that these patterns, once understood, may then be put together to design a new city or improve an old one.

Such a conclusion, of course, associates physical form with specific behavior. This link may very well serve as a way to design a specific urban project if the language is developed to conform to the criteria which the project must satisfy. But it is not likely to be useful as a generic tool, for no pattern can hope to encompass all the needs imposed by the great variety of people nor the desire to adapt and modify places in very different ways for different purposes. At the same time Alexander recognizes that city planning is not just the organizing and building of places and spaces, but is rather, as he puts it, a matter of the "design of culture." This makes it all the more disappointing that he proposes such specific formal attributes to something as dynamic, as various, as complex as culture itself.

The theoretical work of Carl Steinitz at Harvard probes the issues of pattern and culture from the opposite direction. Where Alexander seeks a verbal basis to produce patterns which, when associated, would be capable of properly containing the situations that together compose a culture, Steinitz is anxious to determine whether the existing environment conveys a *meaning* which in turn defines or explains the culture. The purpose of his research is to "discover which patterns of urban growth and succession can be most meaningful initially and over longer time periods, and to test specific staged development patterns for their long-term values."[43]

Such a quest, of course, contains an interesting theoretical thesis, but one with an inherent non-urban bias. Form in the city is initiated by forces of land assembly, zoning, and finance, which are both dynamic and specific. It is within the often quite similar building types created by these easily understood aspects of our culture that man individuates urban spaces. The thesis also ignores the very great extent to which meaning and place are linked, not through physical patterns in urban places, but through signs, signals, words and accumulated personal experience. A city reveals itself, its meaning, to the *experienced* urban dweller in many ways, and many of them have little to do with physical form or formal patterns.

Research is just beginning into the nature of cities, which, together with associated social, mathematical, linguistic, and philosophical strains, such as the work of Alexander, Steinitz and others, signals expanded efforts to make the city both more comprehensible and more liveable. Such efforts, growing out of a concern for the urban environment, are expanding into national centers of research and development. It cannot be said that this research has led as yet to a markedly improved methodology in urban planning. But it is to be hoped that, as in other fields, the research will pay off in time to make urban planning and urban places more successful.

What Is a Plan

What is an "urban plan," anyway? The term is used to describe pictures, words, concepts, laws, regulations, ordinances, and people's dreams. Not long ago the term caused little confusion. It referred at the very least to a diagram of a city or a part of a city which illustrated physical development and redevelopment projects and proposals. Emphasis was on specific buildings and specific spaces in the city as physical entities. And almost always the plan was literally drawn up by an architect or someone who served more or less the functions now performed in our contemporary society by most architects.

But a lot has changed in a very short time. For one thing, as recently as the mid-1960's, architects began to lose their prominence in preparing urban plans. In their place, a Design Concept Team was often put together, especially if the project was on the intermediate scale or larger. Today, more often than not, in place of a single master planner or well-known design architect, large-scale work is approached at the outset by a "team" generally composed of experts in transportation, legal, economic, engineering, social science, and design aspects of urban planning. As a result, the former software of planning, the process, has become a product. In addition, new directions in a search for future flexibility in the development process, new concepts for mixed-use districts, an expanded scale of intervention from a single building to the intermediate scale, and other recent changes in planning concepts and methodology discussed pre- viously have redefined what makes up an urban plan. At the same time, new tendencies related to the plan approval process discussed later in this chapter have had a profound influence on redefining the nature of the contemporary plan.

As a consequence of the multidisciplinary approach to planning, other new tendencies, specific building appearance, and space design—the traditional colored maps and diagrammatic products of the planning process—are often considered beyond the domain of reasonable planning effort. Instead, a contemporary plan may very well be a series of codes, ordinances, and restrictions, mere descriptions of proscriptive regulations which must be adhered to in the preparation of a final physical design.

This definition of an urban plan has only emerged since the mid-1960's. For example, in 1966 the City Council, City Planning Commission, and various consultants developed a downtown plan for Cincinnati composed exclusively of 250 ordinances. As Jonathan Barnett commented at the time:

"It gives each block a strongly delineated functional relationship with the rest of the core, laying down sidewalk widths and access points, and suggesting arcade sections and second level circulation; but there is virtually nothing to indicate the architectural relationships of the actual buildings."[44]

In the same year, 1966, Robert Geddes, working as an architect-consultant to the Town of Rockville, Maryland, arrived independently at a rather similar approach. His proposed plan for a 46-acre mini-core area contained the older conventional elements—the public square, a shopping arcade, a conventional office center, and a residential block. But in addition it contained a proposed and prescribed multi-level framework of mechanical systems, utility ways, public walks, and open spaces which he recognized as the essential controlling elements of the scheme.

This direction was extended quite recently by the long-promised comprehensive "Plan for New York City" issued in 1969–70 after a decade of preparation as a "proposal." Introducing its five volumes and countless diagrams and charts illustrating the *present* situation, and thousands of words is the comment:

"This plan is not a conventional master plan. It is not, for one thing, primarily a physical plan . . . our purpose is not to present an overall design for physical development. Put on colored maps, such plans do present a nice sense of order, but one which does not have too much to do with reality. Our primary concern is with the *processes* (italics theirs) for the City's growth."[45]

By and large, the experience of the last decade in America proves decisively that the master plan, as a rigid guidance document to establish the physical "end state" of a large development program, is at best a flawed and inappropriate device. The end state, often five to 20 years in the making after the plan itself, cannot accurately be anticipated no matter how far-sighted its progenitor planners. Too much changes too fast. The accelerated pace of new needs and new demands, even new life styles of our future-shock filled new existence preclude the prudent use of a conventional master plan for large-scale projects that must extend over many years.

What kinds of projects can be planned in advance, then? How can professionals seek to guide large-scale development in a meaningful way? One supporting device in public and private development planning is a well-conceived *economic model.* This is a long-term analysis of supportable costs and potential land uses under a wide variety of rates of inflation, financing costs, time-lag determinants, land value increments achieved, rental and sales rates, and the like. Because it is based on *numbers* which interrelate, it can be easily modified through the simplest manipulations. It is also, as a set of numbers always is, decisively meaningful within its own frame of reference. As a skeletal reference point for social, physical, and politically oriented decisions it is crucial for long-term administration and

potential flexibility of any large-scale project. Without a well-conceived economic model, the developer or development agency is all the more locked into a preconceived and precalculated physical development since it is on that precise scheme alone that the financial analysis depends. Only uncharacteristic courage, unconcerned financial backing, or unenlightened management could be expected to deviate from a master plan without a flexible financial model to guide management decisions.

On the physical side, what can be prepared as a meaningful guide to large-scale planning? Rather, than the end-state physical plan showing exact location of all structures, all services, all transportation, all public facilities, it is increasingly evident that a more flexible, dynamic concept of land-use guidance systems and criteria can be established. An adaptive planning process can be established to evolve as the community changes. New development can be phased according to specific parcel sites or clusters of interrelated buildings. One such cluster has even been identified and recommended recently by the American Institute of Architects. It is composed of 500 to 3,000 dwelling units called "growth units." The growth unit is sufficiently large to sustain an elementary school, community center with recreational facilities, and convenience shopping and to define open space needs and uses. In large-scale projects, "growth units" could be incrementally added as, when, and where needed, but they would remain subject beforehand to analysis and redesign from any preliminary master plan, based on pre-established and continually evolving performance criteria. Thus the large-scale master plan, while partially a physical diagram, should contain in addition at the very least a meaningful, flexible economic model and a framework for integrating probabilities and contingencies and unanticipated development.

By 1972, the notion of urban *plan* for large-scale work had become so confused and so depreciated that the word itself is more and more often omitted in sophisti-

cated proposals. In its place one hears increasingly of concept *models* and process *models,* terms derived from computer vocabulary. Indeed, the dynamic concept of *process* has completely replaced the static concept of *plan* in advanced work. The redevelopment scheme for Hartford, Connecticut, prepared by the American City Corporation, the sophisticated planning arm of the Rouse Company, and released in 1972, for instance, is in fact called The Greater Hartford Process. And, rather than focusing exclusively on redevelopment and new development schemes, although these do receive considerable attention, great effort is made as part of the proposal to "set in motion a new way of thinking and working by which the community may constantly renew itself—may engage in a continuing self-examination."[46]

Such language contains, of course, a measure of intelligent public relations and reveals a sophistication about new tendencies for public intervention in the redevelopment process. But it also reflects a very real and very new move toward the incorporation of heretofore all but ignored parts of the urban population into city development and redevelopment decision-making procedures.

Semi-Public Environment and Transactional Space. In the preparation of most large-scale urban plans, for all their variety of type and aspect, one crucial opportunity is still generally ignored. This is the opportunity to deal with a part of the city which we might call, for lack of a better term, the *semi-public environment.* This is the generally unorganized, unplanned, unrecognized collectivity of spaces which are not clearly part of the public domain, supervised by a public body. Just as clearly, they are not really private property from an operational standpoint. They are, however, generally private property from an ownership point of view. These include spaces such as office building lobbies, shop interiors, the private sidewalk perimeter of buildings, parking lots, service alleys, and myriad other interconnected, actively used, privately owned space in which the public is permitted, which the public uses actively, and which strongly affect a person's experience of the city.

These spaces are ignored in most private planning efforts because no recognized private benefit is derived from them. Planning ordinances rarely require much attention to them. In public planning efforts, these spaces are generally ignored because they are usually privately owned. Only very recently have these collective semi-public spaces been recognized as a crucial and ignored system at the physical center of urban organization.

Why are these areas so important? They represent the urban space that all people move through within the city. They are the seam between the municipally controlled public environment and the privately controlled private space of the city.

Only in the last several years have these spaces received long-needed attention to try to discover how they can be more effectively used as a linked network, as part of the private environment, as part of the public space of the city. Seminal work initiated by Stanford Anderson at the Institute for Architecture and Urban Studies and at the Massachusetts Institute of Technology seeks to map and diagram these spaces for the first time so that they may be better revealed, analyzed, and understood (Figures 143, 144).

Out of this initial analysis a new urban element called *transactional space* has been isolated. As a working definition, transactional space is:

"that range of qualities of the public space which defines the character of the actual physical space by its use or its perception. The transactional space qualities relate the form of the public space to the use or social activity of the public space."[47]

In continuing research and analysis of the role and potential of transactional space in urban planning, inventive legal, zoning, economic, and social studies were completed at the Institute for Architecture and Urban Studies as part of a wider HUD-supported investigation of the urban street.[48]

The concept of transactional space does after all represent a systematic alternative to the conventional public-private use boundary which today still governs conventional planning and fundamental urban organization. An erosion of this boundary, based on actual physical and social usage, with the assistance of financial, legal, and zoning rule changes offers a way to entirely redefine land parceling in urban development so that private spaces, the street public space, and the semi-private spaces could be susceptible to unified and coherent design (Figure 145).

With additional experience and refinement of the initial work on the public-private use boundary and transactional space, it is likely that promising administrative, economic, legal, zoning, and design rule systems for joint public-private benefit will emerge. These will hopefully permit new planning emphasis on the crucial transactional spaces and semi-public spaces of cities—spaces which, after all, are the center of the pedestrian urban network and the most intensively used areas at all times of the day.

Intensive new effort will be necessary to devise, for instance, economic tradeoffs which encourage private owners and public planners to work together in the process of redevelopment and new development of these spaces. But tax incentives, development rights bonuses, and many other economic and planning strategies are potentially available once the social, economic, and environmental promise of transactional and semi-public space are recognized by planners, administrators, and private groups concerned about the future of cities.

In a few notable and innovative instances recently, the promising potential of working within the semi-public space of the city has been somewhat realized. The most visible examples are in scattered parts of midtown and downtown Manhattan, where concessions gained from developers by the city's planners, especially by the Office of Midtown Planning and Development under the direction of Jaquelin T. Robertson have produced a network of intricate circulation passages above and

below ground level, well-scaled small commercial plazas, midblock passageways, malls, galleries, and arcades. These include a prizewinning, handsomely designed, and heavily used through-block pedestrian passage from 42nd to 43rd Street west of Fifth Avenue through the Graduate Center of the City University of New York (Figure 146), a landscaped commercial midblock plaza surrounded by shops, an outdoor cafe between 45th and 46th Streets, and an uninterrupted midblock passage of shops and malls from 46th to 50th Street west of Sixth Avenue. Robertson calls these improvements, somewhat in jest, "notational architecture," since they began as city-inspired notations in the margins of the developers' plans, and were built finally in exchange for development bonuses, variances, zoning changes, and relaxation of other city controls. These people-oriented and people-serving spaces are predominantly on private land, built by private developers as public amenities.

In midtown New York, each improvement had to be invented, negotiated. The legal and economic tradeoffs could be considered because of the experience of the developers involved, the then-booming real estate market, and the good judgment and persistence brought by Robertson to his office. But in most cities throughout the country, and indeed at most times in New York, this happy combination of circumstances and talent does not exist. Thus a more highly codified and more thoroughly explored set of possibilities, criteria, goals, and objectives for urban transactional space is desirable. The ordinary town should be able to get the ordinary developer to work with the semi-public space.

The interlinked transactional space sub-segment of urban networks just being recognized and analyzed must now enter the mainstream of economic, legal, social, administrative, and physical planning if the link between the clearly public environment of the street and the clearly private environment of the office or apartment is to be dramatically improved as the city evolves. In years to come, whatever

143-44. Transactional Space Types, 1972

Graphic key (left); Street diagram (overleaf)
The Institute for Architecture and Urban Studies
and the Massachusetts Institute of Technology

The term "transactional space" was first used by
Stanford Anderson in urban space analysis
research. The term refers collectively to semi-
private and contiguous public spaces, a previously undefined and inadequately understood
network within the city. These can be mapped
with a special coding key developed to analyze
the transactional space configuration of the city
(Figure 143, left). Transactional space consists
of all so-called public spaces plus the many different types of publicly accessible private space
such as building lobbies, store interiors, and
parking lots. The latter, indeed, in terms of use
and control are far from private, being open to
the public and meant to be accessible to the
public. Thus the term "semi-private" is really
more appropriate than "private." These semi-
private spaces connect directly to the intensively
used public spaces of the city such as sidewalks,
parks, and transportation corridors. Transactional space is where the greatest density of
people are most of the time in all cities. And yet,
until very recently, this combined semi-private
and public space was not considered to be
susceptible to integrated planning because of
the separation of control—some private and
some public—by which the space is ultimately
owned and administered. The notion of transactional space, for the first time, seeks to relate
physical parts of the city under disparate ownership and control through the experienced reality
of social activity and public use.

The research now under way seeks to discover joint public-private planning techniques in
terms of development and maintenance economics, zoning devices, joint development
benefits, and long-term, flexible planning controls which would make it possible to plan for and
create a manageable entity of urban transactional space. This significant work, of which dia-
gramming and mapping such as shown here is
an initial stage, will hopefully make it possible to
develop legal, economic, and administrative
tools to allow the complex and ignored transactional space (which exceeds 40 per cent of
land in most cities) to be manipulated in the
public interest. More than mapping and analysis
of this new space network is necessary,
however. It must also be determined how people
would like to use this space in different parts of
cities, in different parts of the country, even
at different times of the year. This will require
considerable local effort on the part of urbanists,
researchers, planning boards, and planning
commissions once new generic and seminal
principles are developed for planning, modification, and use of transactional space.

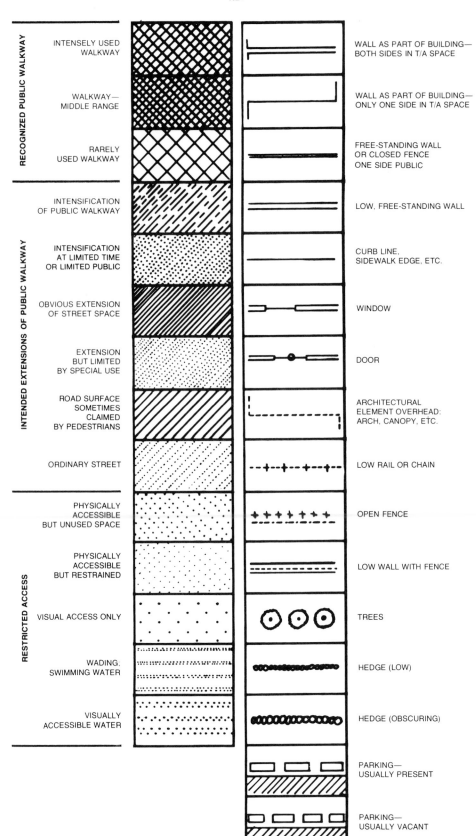

KEY

RECOGNIZED PUBLIC WALKWAY
- INTENSELY USED WALKWAY
- WALKWAY— MIDDLE RANGE
- RARELY USED WALKWAY

INTENDED EXTENSIONS OF PUBLIC WALKWAY
- INTENSIFICATION OF PUBLIC WALKWAY
- INTENSIFICATION AT LIMITED TIME OR LIMITED PUBLIC
- OBVIOUS EXTENSION OF STREET SPACE
- EXTENSION BUT LIMITED BY SPECIAL USE
- ROAD SURFACE SOMETIMES CLAIMED BY PEDESTRIANS
- ORDINARY STREET

RESTRICTED ACCESS
- PHYSICALLY ACCESSIBLE BUT UNUSED SPACE
- PHYSICALLY ACCESSIBLE BUT RESTRAINED
- VISUAL ACCESS ONLY
- WADING; SWIMMING WATER
- VISUALLY ACCESSIBLE WATER

- WALL AS PART OF BUILDING— BOTH SIDES IN T/A SPACE
- WALL AS PART OF BUILDING— ONLY ONE SIDE IN T/A SPACE
- FREE-STANDING WALL OR CLOSED FENCE ONE SIDE PUBLIC
- LOW, FREE-STANDING WALL
- CURB LINE, SIDEWALK EDGE, ETC.
- WINDOW
- DOOR
- ARCHITECTURAL ELEMENT OVERHEAD: ARCH, CANOPY, ETC.
- LOW RAIL OR CHAIN
- OPEN FENCE
- LOW WALL WITH FENCE
- TREES
- HEDGE (LOW)
- HEDGE (OBSCURING)
- PARKING— USUALLY PRESENT
- PARKING— USUALLY VACANT

the format of the "plan," there should be emphasis on the semi-public space, the transactional space. It is a difficult area in which to work because few prescriptions exist. But it is the very point through which greater public-private collaboration can become possible. And the benefits to be derived are as much in the public interest as in the interest of the private owner of undeveloped or developed urban real estate.

Plan Implementation

The third recent change in the practice of urbanism has to do with the way plans are approved. When a plan is completed, what happens? More often than not, nothing happens. Implementation is stalled or entirely averted by social, legal, political, economic, engineering, or marketing problems—alone, all together, or in any combination. When this occurs the plan may be at fault; less often, it is due to completely unavoidable and unanticipatable contingencies. But more and more is being learned today by planners about the approval process, as discussed later.

In those few instances when a major plan is given the go-ahead, what other issues then arise? More often than not, whether the plan is for a large-scale project such as a New Town, or an intermediate-scale project such as an urban area, or even a small-scale project of several buildings, it is often turned over to an architect or squads of architects who had little or nothing to do with the formulation of the plan itself. They are expected to build something, presumably in accordance with the concepts contained in the plan. The architect, a responsible professional, may very well disagree with some implications of the proposed plan and endeavor to modify these. The planner may very well feel the architect does not see the whole social, legal, and economic picture in adequate perspective and disagree with the architect's suggestions. There is enormous space and opportunity for a schism to develop between planner and architect; these in turn concern and often upset funding sources, clients, de-

velopment agencies. Should this all-too-often-experienced scenario be played out, the project is again in trouble. Finally, planners, architects, and the plan itself must encounter and successfully deal with a whole new set of constraints imposed by the developer if he is a separate entity, who must in turn satisfy the pragmatic requirements of a financing source and a profit requirement. The entire long and costly procedure from planning to obtaining a certificate of occupancy is still subject to these often very disjointed stages, often without good reason.

From the beginning, it would seem, all concerned, including planners, architects, builders, and financial institutions or program officers should work together. The result in most cases would be a very much better final product, one in which the realistic technical and financial constraints were dealt with initially, and one in which the overall planning concept and design ideas were agreed upon by all concerned at the outset. Any increase in services, costs, and fees sustained as a result of this integrated approach to the planning and implementation process would more likely than not be more than offset by economies gained in the consequent smooth procedure of the construction phase itself.

The final "plan," under this integrated services approach, could very well be a set of principles, a set of criteria, some overall design standards, and one new element, an *agreement* among all concerned public and private parties including planner, architect, developer, sponsor, public agencies, investors, and others. This agreement would make implementation smoother and long-term fulfillment of the initial planning objectives possible so long as these remained valid.

Other requirements for acceptance of a "plan" by the community at large or community to be affected, are also very much related to the implementation process these days. Indeed, a partial explanation for the shift from images and specific architectural suggestions to words, from physical form to networks, associations, and processes in presenting the "plan" is

related to the community approval process. Basic to the change is the long-delayed recognition that the final client is people—not a public authority or private developer. From this realization a variety of new procedures of exposure and discussion at the neighborhood or community level has emerged in the last few years. Until recently, any project approved simply by a sponsoring agency or private developer was built if funds were available and economic feasibility was established.

Today, in most cities, community review and approval is also a prerequisite to implementation. More and more often, community ideas are solicited as part of the initial plan development process. "Community" generally means a network of local planning boards and special-interest groups in the vicinity of the project who in one way or another represent or profess to represent local residents.

With the flattening out of the social pyramid and the expansion of the political base of most cities and towns since the early 1960's, economic and political realists involved in planning have come to recognize that community approval is necessary for major projects. People, in turn, have come to realize that what happens in their town or city is their business. These changes, often first revealed to the startled power structure as protests, strikes, and riots, have produced legislation requiring most types of development projects to be reviewed and accepted by affected communities.

Partially because of these new requirements of neighborhood or community review, an attempt has been made by nearly all planners to modify controversial qualities, such as the appearance of buildings, upon which everyone is likely to have a view and about which no objective standards can be cited. Another unforeseen consequence of local review is that neighborhood attitudes, desires, and needs, once thought to be relatively homogeneous and perceptible, are revealed in their actual diversity and complexity. In turn, proliferation of groups at the neighborhood level based on leadership splinters and inherent social, economic,

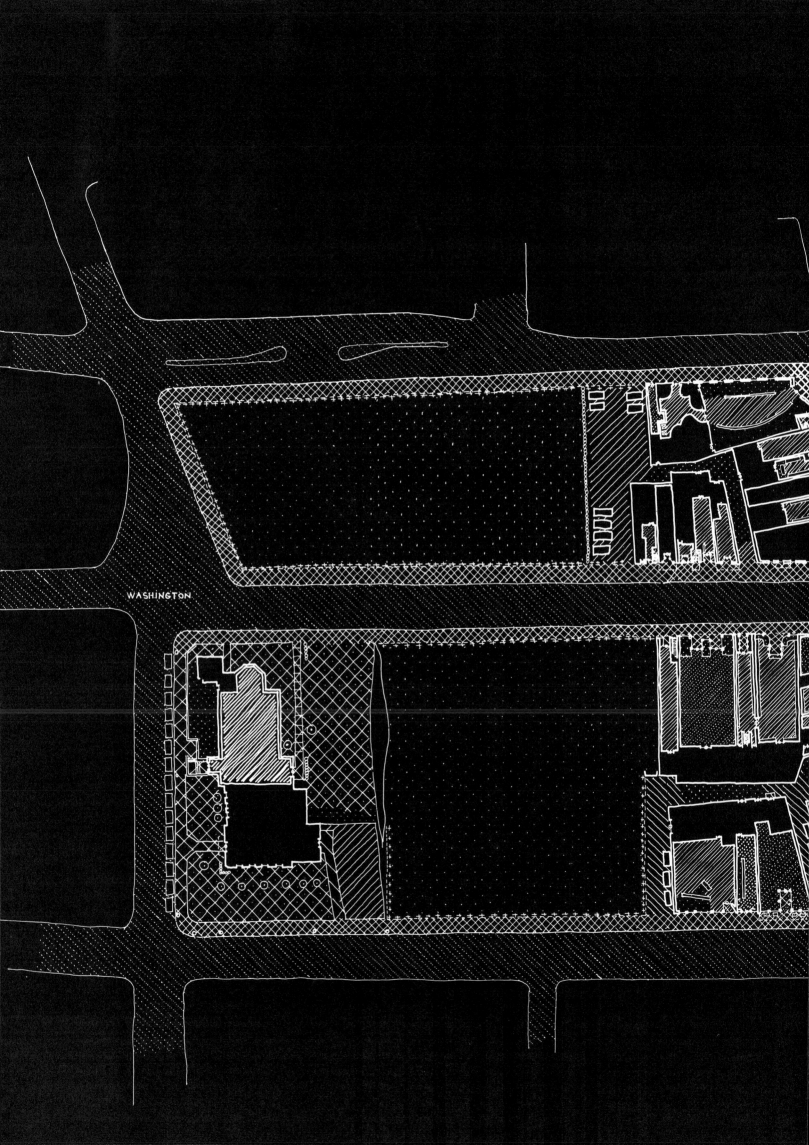

WASHINGTON

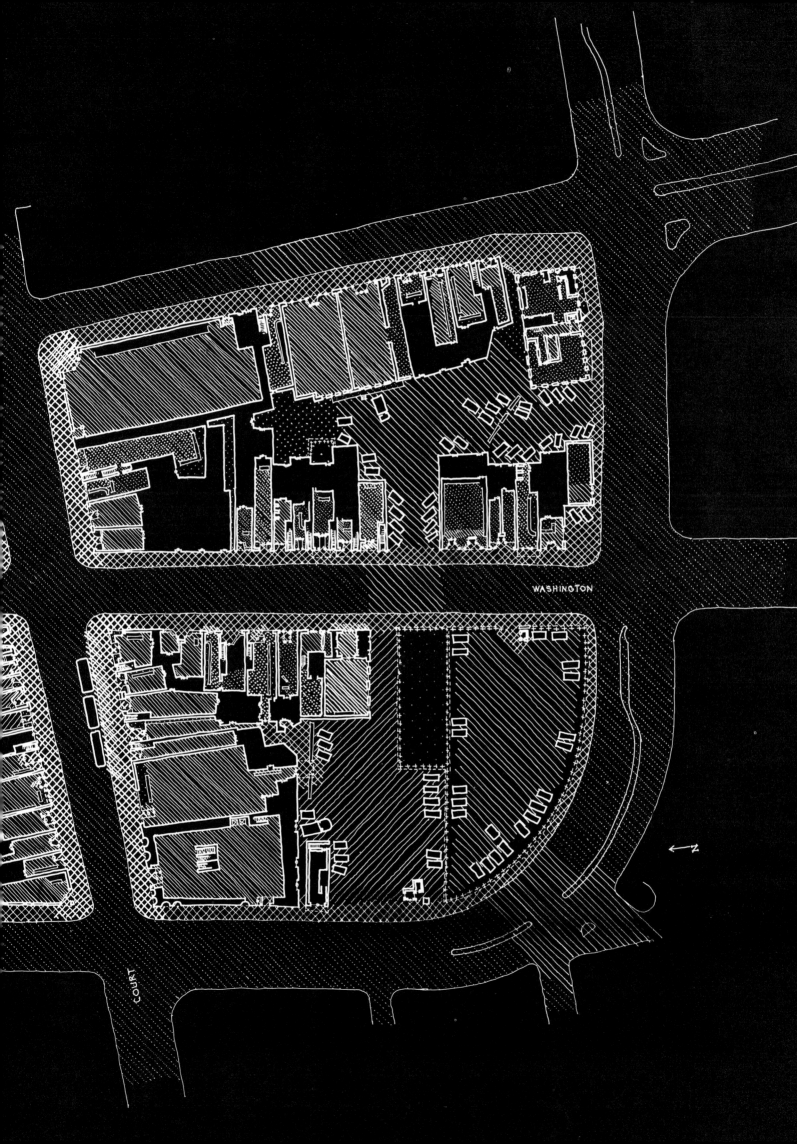

WASHINGTON

COURT

←→z

Traditional Parcelling
Parcels do not specifically
concern the street.

Traditional Development
Development limits and rule systems are
determined by parcel limits. Street relationships
are, at best, tenuously considered.

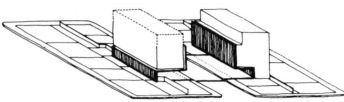

Public/Private Boundary
Public use of open space is not determined
systematically and is without consistency.
Breaks in the space and accessible interior continuity
of use of open space are common.

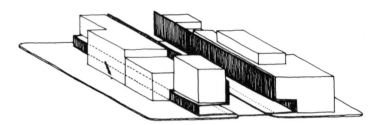

IAUS Proposed Parcelling Concept
New parcels include the street and extend
back to the public/private boundary to promote street
related development and continuity of use.

IAUS Proposed Public/Private Boundary
A new boundary is defined to include space
defining elements of the street space. This helps
to insure a correlation of continuity of use with physical
continuity within the public domain. New implementation
devices accompany the new boundary definition.

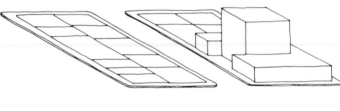

IAUS Proposed Development System
Outside of the new public/private boundary,
private development retains control of development
subject to other zoning and program controls.

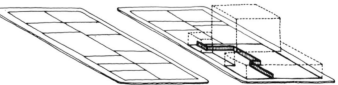

IAUS Proposed Development System Extended
Further street use/form consistency is provided
when development includes additional parcels.

145. Urban Land Parcelling and Public/Private Boundary Control Diagrams, 1972
The Institute for Architecture and Urban Studies

Traditional private parcelling of urban land on a plot-by-plot basis is compared to possibilities for new parcelling concepts which emerge when the public-private use boundary is carefully analyzed. The goal is to discover a way to promote increased vitality on and along the urban street. Then the parcel for development or redevelopment is seen to include the street itself as a central element in urban transactional space. A suburban mall shopping center contains this planning approach implicitly. A means is described in the diagram to integrate the street and land parcels on either side of the street in older urban areas. Insistence on activity or social usage rather than on ownership base as fundamental to meaningful and coherent planning is stressed. This approach to planning made possible by a new awareness of the semi-private and transactional space characteristics of the city provides a basis on which innovative legal and economic rule systems may be developed to permit a renewed consideration of man's social and physical experience as a fundamental component of new planning suggestions.

and racial diversity makes determination of acceptable planning programs at best a complex, and often an impossible, task. For example, community approval of a single publicly sponsored housing scheme for a three-block area of upper Manhattan recently required the participation and agreement of eight separate recognized community groups, including the Morningside Urban Renewal Council, Harlem Model Cities, Model Cities Harlem Community Organization, West Harlem Community Organization, Architects' Urban Renewal Council of Harlem, and Community Planning Boards 1, 6, and 7. Several of these groups represent a number of subordinate member organizations. Indeed, one of these umbrella groups, the Morningside Urban Renewal Council, is itself composed of about 60 different organizations.

The result of such extensive and often divisive community involvement, if leadership does not emerge, is extensive delay in plan implementation. In years to come, leadership in neighborhoods must become more unified and organized. Then, initial planning and design work can be coordinated with community aspirations. In addition, a mechanism for refinement and acceptance of proposed plans in a reasonable time period must be developed. The community responsive implementation process today, which is very new and very unorganized, can consume so much time and so much energy that final costs become high and energies dissipate. The result is often a diminished program, if one survives at all.

In addition, the role of Community Planning Boards or other local nonprofessional groups with the right to exercise some political power in the plan approval process in cities across the country, must be clarified. In most places there was no such thing as a Community Planning Board five years ago. Planning *for* the community was executed and approved "downtown," at the municipal government level. In response to ethnic and economic diversity in the cities and growing public demand for local control, a network of Community Planning Boards or other

powerful community groups with perhaps less official status now exists for the first time in many cities in the United States.

Lately, as their power and budgets have increased, these groups in cities and towns across the country have often obtained the explicit or at least implicit right to approve or disapprove major planning, building, and redevelopment proposals which would affect their districts. In many cases, if a local board disapproves a plan, it cannot gain full municipal support and thus does not go forward.

But how are these boards and groups organized? What is their mandate? What can they do? What should they be and what should they do? Currently, board members in most areas outside of central business districts are residents of the district over which the board has jurisdiction. But few other qualifications prevail. They may or may not represent a specific constituency or viewpoint that prevails in the community. They may or may not have any personal or professional skills or knowledge that would be useful. In most parts of the country they tend to be a collection of appointed, politically connected, or otherwise well-known citizens interested in the development of their district. In some places they are leaders of clubs or organizations.

The effectiveness of Community Planning Boards and other groups that influence the planning process could be very much improved if the board or group were constituted to fulfill a balanced representation of community views and interests. They would be even further improved if board members were elected from within the district itself to represent the different and often competing interests of, for instance, tenants, residential property owners, businesses, and city agencies.

In addition, most community planning groups operate without sufficient professional advice. The implications of many of the proposals they must consider are often inadequately understood. Impacts are often left unexplored. Also, these groups often do not have the competence or in most cases the budgets to initiate projects in their own communities, so

they are able only to react. The few that have been wise enough to use their resources to initiate projects and to see them through the maze of town or city administrative agencies with the help of their consultants include Manhattan Community Board 5, which recently instigated a redevelopment plan for Union Square Park in lower midtown Manhattan. The park, once a major center of recreation and political meeting activity—really the Hyde Park of New York—has become in recent decades an underutilized wasteland in a sea of motorized traffic. This unusually energetic and progressive planning board seeks to expand the present park and to return one of the few public spaces in its district to rich, varied uses for residents, shoppers, and workers.

The future of Community Planning Boards and other powerful groups which represent local citizen interests in large cities is certain. Their power is likely to grow as a result of continuous pressure for decentralization of authority in the cities and continuing increase in social, economic, and ethnic complexity in urban centers, along with considerable distrust of the authorities "downtown" and the growing inability of central city administrations to govern effectively. In towns, the role and power of the local planning board is also expected to grow.

The casualty of these trends may very well be—in the larger cities—the older centralized City Planning Commission. If not eliminated altogether, the conventional City Planning Commission is likely to be accorded a diminished role in actual urban planning in the years to come for most local, intermediate-scale development.

At the same time, it is clearly necessary that competing and often conflicting neighborhood groups of many kinds interested in planning and building become represented by and function within a rule system maintained by the local Community Planning Board or a similar organization. The alternative, which should be unacceptable to serious community groups as well as to public administrators, is a continuation of the present chaos at the level of community organizations involved in the planning and plan approval process.

Emerging recognition in this country by architects, planners, and public officials that the real client is people—not programs and agencies—is a fundamental and highly significant breakthrough accomplished in the later 1960's. If this new and still fragile recognition can be firmly established—as it will be if representative and authoritative local community planning boards evolve—it offers the potential for a new and promising basis for public architecture and urban design. The architect planner, or urban designer as interpreter of expressed wishes and translator of specific requirements could begin to design, to create optimum and appropriate places for people to live and work. He might even eventually be liberated through concerted public pressure from many of the stale strictures of outdated regulations promulgated by public agencies which are generally not in touch with the people they are supposed to serve. All of this will come in the 1970's as public pressure forces public agencies to recognize their real role—that of administrators of funds, not arbiters of design or local planning decisions.

Arbitration, Not Advocacy

Indeed, as implementation requirements and procedures have changed in recent years, a growing number of architects and planners have begun to represent residents rather than private clients or centralized government agencies. Clustered primarily in ghetto areas where they can give the poor a professional voice, these "advocate" planners reveal a social conscience and a transition of power to the neighborhood level that has emerged in the last decade. Professional groups such as Community Design Associates in Pittsburgh, People's Architecture in Berkeley, and the Architects' Technical Assistance Center in midtown Manhattan were organized to initiate, articulate, and advocate community and tenant needs and requirements, primarily to the political and financial power structure of the city, composed of government officials, real estate developers, property owners, and businessmen.

But the role of advocate, so enthusiastically assumed by generally younger, socially oriented urban architects in the latter 1960's and early 1970's, has distinct and generally unmentioned limitations. As in any dynamic situation, the insertion of an avowed professional advocate stimulates a response—it creates the opening for another role—that of the adversary. Thus advocacy of special rights, even special interests of a particular sub-group in the complex social and physical fabric of a city has not created optimal results. In addition, it necessarily removes the focus from the issue or problem itself to the desires of another special interest group.

A more constructive approach, and one that will hopefully be recognized and exploited in coming years, is for the professional planner and architect to become an *arbiter,* rather than an advocate. How would this work?

As arbiter the professional focuses on the needs of a given *situation* rather than the specialized needs of one group within a situation. The planner works to describe what is possible, what alternative possibilities are, and what the implication of each is likely to be. He functions as a knowledgeable and impartial professional. In addition, through various techniques which are now commonly used and will be discussed below, he allows each interest group to understand the goals and objectives of the other groups. In this way, conflicts which might otherwise surface in a picketline or in front of the bulldozer or much too late at a review meeting can be dealt with successfully around a table by the interested parties at the outset of a planning effort. Though the possibility of working this way may sound naive and even simplistic, we are learning every day in more and more instances that open discussion, explicit focus on points of agreement and of conflict, and open communication between the competing interests that cluster around any major planning problem produce good results and improve the potential for implementation of a plan or program that is in the interest of the affected community. Through a process of arbitration competently managed by a trained planner, the basis for agreement and implementation can be achieved that might otherwise be impossible—especially if each group were served by independent spokesmen.

This is an inclusive planning approach, one which anticipates conflict and insists on disclosure; one which recognizes the competing interests of, for instance, older, long-time central city residents, expanding downtown commercial enterprises, and federal public agencies with local jurisdiction, such as the former Model Cities or Urban Renewal Agencies.

Many new planning techniques are being developed which can assist in arbitrative planning and are helpful in making the planning possibilities, opportunities, and problems more understandable to people. For instance, urban planning encounter groups or workshops have been organized for the first time in recent years; some last a day, others extend over several days. Planners such as Lawrence Halprin have tried to bring opposing interests to some resolution through these intensive, information-filled encounters at which leaders of various groups are invited to participate. But the method remains unproven in spite of the workshops because, at least to date, the methodology used has been generally too limited. Rarely are there followups to determine whether or not participants have indeed achieved the same resolutions within their own constituencies as those brought forward in the encounter sessions. But this method for gathering information and revealing conflict seems a promising one for the planning profession.

Some professionals, such as the inventive Philadelphia architect-planner-educator Richard Saul Wurman, have seized on the clear, interesting, and accurate display of information through maps, designs, graphic standards, and all sorts of other relevant visual documentation as a helpful means to inform, educate, and make it possible for people to understand

146. Pedestrian Way. Carl J. Petrilli and Samuel J. DeSanto

The transactional space of the city is recognized in this exemplary project between 42nd and 43rd Streets west of Fifth Avenue through the Graduate Center of the City University of New York. The public space of the sidewalk is linked through the ground-level semi-private space of a building. Only the conventional semi-private lobby is removed and redefined for use as a continuous part of the urban transactional space. Access to private interior space above is from elevator banks inside a lobby within the through-block pedestrian way; access to other private space below is from a handsome, wide stairway within the arcade. The people of the city gain a handsome, weather-protected space at mid-block for meeting, for talking, for walking without pervasive traffic sound and smell, in short for enjoying. The further elaboration of such spaces for exhibitions, concerts, even restaurants, cafés and open-stall shopping will occur as the promise of transactional space is recognized by both the public and private sectors.

options available to them. Indeed, he has induced many people into the planning process by making it more understandable.

Another new approach more and more frequently tested these days is the computerized "game" session, in which roles are played and results, short and long term impacts, are calculated and displayed by the preprogrammed computer. For instance during 1972–73, the Cooper Hewitt Museum and Dr. Richard Duke, with some financial assistance from the New York State Council on the Arts, staged four different computer-related urban planning games, including Metropolis, Housing Plan, Metro Apex, and Community Land Use Game. This sequence culminated in a full-day exercise in city building of the future with conflicting political, social, and economic interests identified and represented. The Community Land Use Game (CLUG), developed at Cornell University in 1968, for instance, helps people to learn about the economic, land development, and transportation implications of a decision in advance of making the decision itself. And considerable other evidence indicates that interest in urban gaming devices and processes is an idea whose time has clearly arrived. The New School for Social Research in New York even gave a course in it last year. Urban games, especially those played out with set computer programs, may very well be helpful as *learning* tools for citizens and planners. Their limitation, as discussed earlier, and one which remains a limitation of the computer-programmed approach to planning, is as a *design* device.

In recent years, much simpler board games have also been invented by planners to assist in arbitrative planning exercises. The town, neighborhood, or street in question may be used as the game board. In a game session, actual moves are made on the board by representatives of each interest group using symbolic "chips" to reveal goals and objectives. A professional planner explains, to the extent possible, the micro- and macro-scale impact of each move. With a simple board game approach, conflicts, errors, and points of agreement come quickly and very vividly to the surface in all sorts of potential interventions—street use, traffic patterns, open-space planning, building form and location, public facility and institutional placement, etc. One such game, known as the Urban Streets Game, was developed recently by the Institute for Architecture and Urban Studies. It was subsequently tested, refined, and used to good advantage for all interest groups in a street redevelopment study in Binghamton, New York.

In general, the inclusionist or arbitrative approach to planning is sympathetic to reality, but calculated to overcome the inertia that reality generally causes. It should become increasingly well-known and perfected. Urban planners in coming years must adopt a more inclusive, more sensitive arbitrative role, rather than the exclusionist advocate role, if a more acceptable and more meaningful record in project implementation is to be achieved.

Expanded Roles

Architects and planners, in greater number, may also discover in the next several years the inherent potential for increased success with implementation by expanding their own professional role in another way, especially when they engage in private-sector planning and building. Traditionally, planner and architect serve the client; it is the client who generally remains a controlling external force. Traditionally, this service role has been acclaimed by professionals as the only really possible professional stance to take. But expanding the role from architect to architect *and* principal in a development project is certainly possible for an individual and/or a firm with suitable skills. Expanding from a planner into a planner *and* principal in a development project is equally possible. Certain independent architects and planners such as Charles Luckman in San Francisco, John Portman in Atlanta, and Jaquelin Robertson in New York have already successfully realized this expanded professional role.

The advantages to the professional, to the project, even to the society can be substantial if this expanded role is realized. The professional gains a measure of control generally relinquished in the traditional client relationship. The professional obtains an opportunity to exercise and test his best professional judgment without the necessity of elaborate and costly exercises generally needed to persuade a client. The professional becomes exposed to the realities of cost, risk, and reward in an utterly fundamental way rather than the superficial and ultimately trivial way that he normally is. This exposure can force the exercise of enhanced imagination. It can produce an economically viable scheme at the outset rather than one which exceeds cost limits or economic feasibility and thus remains unbuilt. In this way implementation is served in planning and building.

The horizontal extension of skills through the enterprise of planning and building the environment—the vehicle for our culture—need not be feared by individuals and firms with the curiosity, capability, or compulsion to expand roles. There is scant evidence in our society to prove that architects and planners in the conventional stance of servants to the society have done very much to produce a better one. Why should trained people deeply concerned with the issues of urbanism and skilled to be of profound assistance in making the built world a better place to live continue generally to refrain from the most intensive involvement possible in producing that world?

New Directions

The urban plan will be increasingly concerned with process and flexibility and less with form, place, space, and state.

The urban plan must focus on both horizontal and vertical channels of movement and service.

The *public-private use boundary* should become a focus for improved legal, financial, administrative, and urban design approaches.

The *semi-public environment* and *transactional space* must be better understood and should become fundamental considerations in progressive urbanism.

Meaningful redevelopment must occur at the intermediate scale, particularly in mixed-use buildings and districts.

Computerized games and simple board games which reveal the impact of planning interventions should be used more frequently to assist in the plan approval process.

An economic model should be the core of a long term new development plan if the plan is to be both flexible and implementable.

Land use systems for new development should be guided by an adaptive planning process established at the outset.

New types of innovative zoning will emerge as the negotiating tool by which public authorities gain amenities and fulfill public planning goals as concessions from private developers.

To be effective in the planning process, neighborhood and community leadership must become more unified and more representative of all concerned.

An arbitrative, or an inclusive approach, not advocacy, holds most promise for effective planning and implementation.

Conclusion

It is all too often assumed that the cities have had it, that their purpose and promise are not of our time. I doubt this assumption. The city remains one of man's few inventions which respects the increasingly evident and very new reality to Americans of finite physical human and natural resources that must be shared and managed in a reasonable way. In focusing on where change is beginning to appear, where new trends are beginning to be in evidence, and the quality of new planning concepts only recently evolved, it becomes evident that the future of the city is indeed promising.

This promise is exposed, I hope, in the various chapters of this book which consider trends and new directions affecting downtown, the street, the urban highway, public transportation, housing, the urban environment, historic preservation, urban conservation, land use regulation, and the practice of urbanism. Each of these offers a window into present-day integrated and multi-faceted new directions in urbanism.

Today there is not a rising, swelling movement of residents into the cities such as occurred during the industrial revolution. But the exodus is slowing; in some instances it has stopped. Urban employment is not expanding; indeed, it may continue to contract for some time. The jobs that are appropriately carried out in the city remain and continue to grow in number. Inappropriate activities for the city are finding their way to more suitable places now that established alternatives exist. There is not a strong building spree and physical expansion of the city in most places such as occurred after World War I, nor is one likely in coming years. Rather, I anticipate in the cities a consolidation of people and places into a qualitatively better environment in the years to come.

The first visible signs of new directions are already evident. New priorities in programs, funds, and public attitudes which will benefit urban areas, such as support for transit and pedestrian space rather than highways, has appeared since the mid-1960's. There is a focus, for the first time, in new planning concepts, to establish a well organized sequence of convenient multi-use neighborhoods and centers linked closely to one another. There is renewed awareness of the potential for the urban street, for older city districts, for waterways, and for downtowns. There are new trends with strong public support in land use regulation and environmental controls that will guide resources and even some people back into the city.

These new tendencies in urbanism are matched by a concurrent redirection on many levels in the way urbanism is practiced. New directions in how urbanists function, what they produce, who they are, what they are thinking about, and how the society functions in relation to them each in different ways holds promise, I suggest, for an improved planning and implementation record in coming years.

New concepts are scarcely needed. If nothing else, this book should make it clear that many available and promising concepts, plans, and proposals already exist. Intense focus on public, private, and most of all joint public-private procedures, mechanisms, and processes must now occur to assure a better place to live in cities and towns.

It is just conceivable that most cities grew too far and too fast the first time around. The adjustment has been difficult and painful. And the adjustment is not over. But American cities of the later 1970's and beyond may well be more contained, more humane, and far more desirable.

Actual planning studies and projects which I have completed in recent years contributed to the evolution of concepts and testing of ideas contained in this book. These projects were undertaken both alone and in concert with others. They were prepared for both public and private clients. Several of these projects, their objectives, and a very brief description of the work are presented. These studies, all completed since 1968, are not presented in chronological order. Rather, the first group was undertaken for public, institutional, and corporate clients and centers on land management, land use, public open space, preservation, transportation, and pedestrian-oriented problems. The second group was commissioned by private clients. These are principally investment management and feasibility investigations of large-scale land holdings.

Recent Projects

Project

Land Management Study, Proposed Watervliet Shaker Historic and Recreation District, for the Town of Colonie, New York

Objective

To develop a strategy to preserve and use over 700 acres of undeveloped land and about 25 original Shaker buildings in the original Shaker settlement in America, after listing in the National Register. Over half the land and the most important buildings are privately owned in this district, which is only 7 miles from Albany.

Work

Innovative but feasible economic, legal, and planning proposals were developed to create a combined historic, recreation, and conservation district. Federal programs were combined with potential public land donation options and private programs made possible by land ownership patterns in the district. A strategy was developed to: preserve crucial wetlands, provide a national center for Shaker culture, establish needed public institutional and recreational facilities, and preserve most of the land in question as open space. Open space uses include a nature sanctuary and model farm. Alternatives to municipal "taking" of land through use of development rights, easements, leases, and expanded potentials for town, county, state, and federal collaboration are emphasized. The multi-use, publicly controlled district could be established, as a result of study findings and recommendations, through sound public land management practices at nominal local cost.

Project

Union Square Park Redevelopment Project for Manhattan Community Board 5, in Conjunction with the Institute for Architecture and Urban Studies

Objective

Initially to survey and determine for a community planning board major opportunities and needs for intervention in its own district. Subsequently, following approval of recommendations, to initiate a redevelopment plan for the principal public open space in lower midtown Manhattan, and to prepare a financial, legal, and political strategy to assist implementation of the proposed plan.

Work

An analytic survey of all aspects of this complex segment of New York City was completed to determine problems and potentials. A project was developed to gain optimal leverage from the limited funds available to a community planning board and to initiate a redevelopment project that could become the focus of areawide incremental redevelopment by city agencies and in the private sector. Strategies to attract major financial support from federal programs were prepared, as were political and legal steps to gain optimum support for the project through the New York City Capital Budget process. Relevant areawide institutions, community groups, planning boards, tenant organizations, and private interests were made part of the planning and implementation process. Finally, political, legal, and planning objectives were pursued throughout the Capital Budget process.

Project

Economic Analysis and Transportation Research to Determine New Forms of the Urban Street, a Research and Demonstration Study for the United States Department of Housing and Urban Development, as Consultant to the Institute for Architecture and Urban Studies

Objective

To develop generic economic concepts and transportation recommendations for the redevelopment of urban streets.

Work

Economic concepts to extend the potential for public and private collaboration were developed for towns, cities, states, and federal-level opportunities. In addition, the economic basis of conventional zoning was examined and changes were recommended. The opportunity for reactivating the urban street by redefinition of the development parcel to include public and private space with special emphasis on the semi-private "transactional space" of the city was revealed.

In urban transportation all conventional and most relevant experimental modes for high-density urban centers were evaluated in terms of their impact on the street. Cost feasibility comparisons were developed for multi-level redevelopment opportunities as compared to on-grade solutions in conjunction with social and environmental impact considerations to create an evaluative framework for all modes considered.

Project

Streets Redevelopment Study, Binghamton, New York, for the United States Department of Housing and Urban Development, in Conjunction with the Institute for Architecture and Urban Studies

Objective

To determine the applicability of techniques and concepts developed in the "New Forms of the Urban Street" study at a test site and to refine innovative devices to facilitate implementation.

Work

All community interests, including commercial, residential, political, and administrative factions, were brought together in the evolution of an arbitrative rather than advocate professional planning role. In addition, the Urban Streets Game was invented to instantly and graphically reveal the impact of street-related redevelopment suggestions. Through these innovative devices, substantial agreement was obtained for a planned, evolutionary redevelopment of the residential core of the city center with emphasis on new types of development parceling, on the semi-private transactional space of the city, and on public open space.

The substance of this study, together with basic findings in the "New Forms of the Urban Street" research and demonstration work, is scheduled to be published in 1974 for the United States Department of Housing and Urban Development by the M.I.T. Press as a book entitled *On Streets*.

Project

Transportation Center Feasibility and Planning, Tarrytown, New York, for the New York Metropolitan Transportation Authority, in Conjunction with Wilbur Smith and Associates, New York and Harrison & Abramovitz, New York

Objective

To determine the scale, type, organization, and feasibility of an intermodal transportation center at the Tarrytown railroad station.

Work

Attributes of transportation issues within a suburban railroad station impact area interlinking rail, automobile, bus, and pedestrian ways were analyzed and projected considering evolving patterns of suburban land settlement, shifting balances in regionwide job location, and likely modifications of the regional transportation network. Site and market analyses were conducted to determine the potential for various multi-use and multipurpose facilities, including office space, hotel accomodations, shopping facilities, and housing, in order to establish a feasible building program. Development costs and return on investment in a range of possible building programs and financial structures were analyzed. An innovative partnership between an independent public authority, community interests, and private-sector financial resources was developed to assist implementation.

Project

Land Planning in Conjunction with Transportation Planning for the Baltimore Urban Design Team, Baltimore, and The Interstate 84 Corridor in Hartford, Connecticut, in Conjunction with Wilbur Smith and Associates, New York

Objective

To determine new land planning and transportation planning requirements and opportunities occasioned by the intervention of a highway into an established urban area.

Work

The topographical, social, physical, environmental, and demographic implications of a new urban highway were considered in relation to physical development constraints, opportunities, and requirements to assess parcel-by-parcel and section-by-section an appropriate stance as regards new highway construction and ancillary potential development in an urban area.

Project

Transportation and Pedestrian Planning for: Niagara Falls Central Business District; Roosevelt Raceway, New York; Morningside Heights, Manhattan; Douglas Circle, Manhattan; University of Pittsburgh; United Nations Development Corporation, in Conjunction with Wilbur Smith and Associates, New York

Objective

To develop optimal pedestrian and transportation planning potentials within the constraints of an intense redevelopment of urban land, including requirements for linkage to transit and automobile.

Work

Following analysis and projection of demand based on alternative building programs, occupancy rate estimates, personal visit considerations, and rhythm of facilities' use over the 24-hour day cycle, emphasis was placed on sizing and locating open and enclosed corridors of intense pedestrian usage.

Alternative programs and phased implementation schemes were analyzed to determine generation of all potential activity including residential, commercial, visitors', entertainment, retail, and others. Model splits were developed incorporating projections of area-wide planning, as well as anticipated changes in habits and usage. Transportation, pedestrian, and parking requirements were projected by phase and incorporated into schematic design to assure proper scale, location, environmental quality, and linkage between structures and accessways.

Project

Low-Rise High-Density Housing, Development of a Prototype and Schemes for Brooklyn and Staten Island, New York, for the New York State Urban Development Corporation, in Conjunction with the New York State Urban Development Corporation and the Institute for Architecture and Urban Studies

Objective

To determine how innovative low-rise subsidized housing can be planned, designed, and built in urban areas to satisfy present economic restrictions and density requirements of urban areas.

Work

Initially, fundamental organizing principles and basic criteria were established in a research and analysis program. From these a generic housing prototype susceptible to use in a wide variety of urban and suburban circumstances for subsidized or free-market housing was designed.

The prototype was then applied as a high-density but low-rise housing solution to parts of ten contiguous blocks in the Brownsville section of Brooklyn, New York, and studied further for alternative innovative cluster planning and design solutions as a suburban application of the prototype in Staten Island, New York.

Prototypes, work under construction, and projects were displayed at the Museum of Modern Art, New York, in the summer of 1973, as "Another Chance for Housing: Low-Rise Alternatives."

Project

Land Use and Housing Feasibility Analysis for the Albany Medical Center, Albany, New York, as Consultant to Donald J. Stephens Associates, Albany, New York

Objective

To determine if land in an older residential neighborhood adjacent to a major urban institution could be used more effectively for institutional staff housing through selective rehabilitation, redevelopment of marginal properties, and utilization of open lots.

Work

The specific range of housing characteristics and requirements of the institutional staff was determined through a detailed questionnaire and interviews, with the data refined through analysis and computer program. The site was subject to analysis for acceptability, safety, access, environmental quality, physical texture, and economic feasibility. Low- and medium-rise housing concepts were tested in conjunction with selective rehabilitation to determine with and without an array of potential subsidy programs the marketability and suitability of the alternatives.

Project

Impact Study of Metroflight and Metroport Centers throughout the Northeast Corridor for Pan American World Airways, Inc.

Objective

To determine the impact of center-city-to-center-city air travel between well-positioned urban transportation centers.

Work

The impact of such travel was evaluated in terms of induced travel characteristics, urban and regional development consequences, land conservation potentials, community service facilities opportunities, environmental planning objectives and criteria, regional distribution networks, and community compatibility.

Project

Land Investment Management Study of 7,300 Acres for a Private Client, Houston, Texas

Objective

To determine the alternative uses and projected financial characteristics during the next five, 10, and 20 years of underutilized agricultural land on the urbanizing fringe of a major city in order for the owners to make appropriate land investment decisions.

Work

Regional and local area planning and development assumptions and trends were analyzed thoroughly. Redefinition of these trends based on new tendencies and anticipated tendencies in land use patterns, settlement patterns, land absorption rates, ecological and environmental considerations, and transportation patterns was determined. Other land ownership characteristics in the affected sector were reviewed and analyzed to determine the scale of potentially competing property. Costs to hold and carry land under a variety of yield expectations, rates of inflation, cost of funds, and tax schedules were computed. Overall planning and development strategies which considered anticipated trends in the sector as well as local need and land character were projected to estimate in a variety of ways, including a present and future worth analysis, various investment management alternatives.

Project

Preliminary Planning, Investment Analysis, and Economic Feasibility of a New Community, Houston, Texas, in Conjunction with Investment Research Corporation, Dallas, Texas

Objective

To determine the implications and advisability of initiating land use and detailed economic planning for a new community on a particular piece of property and simultaneously to determine the approximate current market value of the property itself.

Work

Long-term alternative sector-by-sector land use potentials were determined; cost of holding, financing, and development was computed against likely market parameters. Social, political, and environmental considerations were built into analysis and projection stages. A long-term optimal multi-use, comprehensive development program was established and used as a basis for residual land value determinations and land use recommendations.

Project

Golf-Centered, 1,200-Acre Community Development Feasibility Study for a Private Client Group, Bucks County, Pennsylvania, in Conjunction with Wilbur Smith and Associates, New York

Objective

To decide whether or not a golf-centered recreation community should be developed on a particular site of about 1,200 acres.

Work

Market characteristics of the site, accessibility of the site, competing and proposed recreation resources, and suitability of the land were evaluated. Development costs of recreation, community, and housing facilities were compared to anticipated value during the period of development, marketing, and sales. Marginal feasibility was exposed due to especially relevant economic and transportation deficiencies.

Project

Land Investment Management Study of about 1,500 Acres for a Private Client, Aspen, Colorado

Objective

To determine the potential impact of proposed innovative environmental land use legislation on the value, planning opportunities, and investment characteristics of well-positioned, generally undeveloped land near a growing winter and summer resort.

Work

Progressive national tendencies in public land use control as well as their political and legal bases were reviewed with emphasis on special circumstances in Colorado and in Pitkin County to anticipate likely legal and planning conditions in the future. Positive attributes and potential flaws in proposed draft regulations were isolated. Some suggested restructuring of basic concepts for discussion with public authorities was proposed to achieve optimal environmental and planning goals. The economic feasibility of carrying undeveloped land under alternate regulatory conditions and with various evolutionary development possibilities was considered.

Notes

1. Mayor Wes Uhlman of Seattle, *New York Times*, 21 June, 1970.

2. *Ibid.*

3. Melvin Webber, "Urban Place and Non-Place Urban Realm," *Explorations into Urban Structure* (Philadelphia: University of Pennsylvania Press, 1964), p. 83.

4. Françoise Choay, *The Modern City: Planning in the 19th Century* (New York: Braziller, 1969), p. 103.

5. Thomas Adams, *The Building of the City* (New York: Regional Plan Association, 1931), p. 299.

6. A history of redevelopment proposals for Philadelphia is documented by Edmund Bacon in *Design of Cities,* rev. ed. (New York: Viking, 1973). Included is important work from the 1940's to the present by Edmund Bacon himself; by architects Vincent Kling, Roy Larson, and Oskar Stonorow in 1957; by Preston Andrade and Willo von Moltke in 1958; by Ieoh Ming Pei, working for William Zeckendorf; by Louis I. Kahn in the 1950's and later; by Robert Geddes for the development of the Delaware Waterfront; and by Skidmore, Owings and Merrill for the Philadelphia Redevelopment Authority on Market Street East. Work is continuing in Philadelphia at an even larger scale. The high-speed transportation line planned between Boston and Washington, D.C. is being considered for its possible urban design implications.

7. CIAM (*Congrès Internationaux d'Architecture Moderne*) was formed in 1928 by progressive Europeans such as Le Corbusier, Gerrit Rietveld, José Sert, Walter Gropius, Ludwig Hilberseimer, and others, as well as some representatives from the United States and other countries. After meetings held in 1930, problems in urbanism became the dominant concern of this group. In 1933, the group adopted the Athens Charter, which contained basic urban planning precepts approved by CIAM. *See La Charte d'Athènes, l'Urbanisme des CIAM,* Le Corbusier, (Paris: 1943). *The Athens Charter,* new ed. (New York: Grossman, 1973).

8. Team 10 had its first meeting at Aix-en-Provence during the 1953 Congress of CIAM. Its initial members were J.B. Bakema and Aldo van Eyck (Holland); G. Candilis and S. Woods (France); A. and P. Smithson, William Howell, and John Volcker (England). Team 10 "came together in the first place certainly because of mutual realization of the inadequacies of the processes of architectural thought which had been inherited from the modern movement . . ." Alison Smithson, ed., *Team Ten Primer* (Cambridge, Mass: M.I.T. Press, 1968), p. 1.

9. Complete descriptive text and illustrations of this proposal are to be contained in a duograph by Peter Wolf entitled *Street*; a film of the proposal with the same title was completed in 1973 by Francis Thompson.

10. Original members of the Urban Design Group which formed in 1967 were Jonathan Barnett, Jaquelin Robertson, Richard Weinstein, and Myles Weintraub. Later, Robertson became Director of the Office of Midtown Planning and Development.

11. Urban Advisors to the Federal Highway Administration (Michael Rapuano, Lawrence Halprin, Thomas C. Kavanagh, Harry R. Powell, Kevin Roche, Matthew L. Rockwell, John O. Simonds, Marvin R. Springer), *The Freeway in the City: Principles of Planning and Design,* a report to the Secretary, Department of Transportation, Washington, D.C., 1968.

12. *Ibid.,* p. 8.

13. *Ibid.,* p. 18.

14. *Ibid.,* p. 19.

15. U.S. Department of Transportation, Federal Highway Administration, Instructional Memoranda 34–50, 1969.

16. Rudolph's study is to be completely illustrated and described in a duograph by Peter Wolf and a film of the proposed scheme is to be made by Francis Thompson. Both the film and the publication are to be issued in 1974.

17. *See* U.S. Department of Housing and Urban Development, *Tomorrow's Transportation—New Systems for the Urban Future,* Washington, D.C., 1968.

18. *See* U.S. Department of Housing and Urban Development, *A Summary of Urban Mass Transportation Demonstration Projects,* Washington, D.C., 1968.

19. *See* note 4.

20. For a summary discussion of many housing issues including prefabrication, *see* Martin Pawley, *Architecture Versus Housing* (New York: Praeger, 1971).

21. Oscar Newman, *Defensible Space* (New York: Macmillan, 1972).

22. Pawley, *Architecture Versus Housing,* p. 112f.

23. *See,* for example, Richard O. Toftner, "A Balance Sheet for the Environment," *Planning* (22 July 1973), pp. 21–25.

24. Mayor's Task Force on Noise Control, *Toward a Quieter City,* New York, 1970, pp. 6–10.

25. Raymond F. Dasmann, *Environmental Conservation,* 2nd ed. (New York: Wiley, 1968), p. 37.

26. Antonio Sant' Elia, "Messagio," *Nuove Tendenze* catalogue (Milan, May 1914).

27. Aldo van Eyck, Otterlo Meeting of Team 10, 1959, *Team Ten Primer,* ed. Alison Smithson (Cambridge, Mass: M.I.T. Press, 1968).

28. *See* Peter Wolf, *Proposed Watervliet Shaker Historic and Recreation District,* a report to the Town of Colonie, New York (September, 1973).

29. Citizens' Advisory Committee on Environmental Quality, *Land Use and Urban Growth Summary,* Washington, D.C., 1973.

30. The so-called "takings clause" in the Fifth Amendment to the U.S. Constitution: "nor shall private property be taken for public use, without just compensation."

31. Citizens' Advisory Comm., *Land Use and Urban Growth.*

32. Fred Bosselman and David Callies, *The Quiet Revolution in Land Use Control,* prepared for the Council on Environmental Quality (Washington, D.C.: U.S. Government Printing Office, 1971), p. 1.

33. American Law Institute, *Model Land Development Code,* Washington, D.C. (March, 1973).

34. Fred P. Bosselman, "The Right to Move, the Need to Grow," *Planning* (September 1973), p. 9.

35. Kevin Lynch, *The Image of the City,* tenth printing (Cambridge, Mass: The M.I.T. Press, 1972), p. 9.

36. Alison and Peter Smithson, *Urban Structuring* (London: Van Nostrand Reinhold, 1967), p. 29. These concepts were derived from work by the Smithsons on the Golden Lane project, London, 1952, and elaborated into a general theory and presented to the CIAM meeting in 1953.

37. *Ibid.,* p. 29.

38. Shadrach Woods, *Candilis-Josic-Woods* (Stuttgart: Karl Krämer Verlag, 1968), p. 9.

39. *Ibid.,* p. 10.

40. Nicholas Negroponte, *The Architecture Machine* (Cambridge, Mass: The M.I.T. Press, 1970), p. 3.

41. *Ibid.,* p. 7.

42. Christopher Alexander, "Major Changes in Environmental Form Required by Social and Psychological Demands," *Ekistics* (August 1969), p. 79.

43. Carl Steinitz, "Meaning and the Congruence of Urban Form and Activity," *Journal of the American Institute of Planners* (July 1968), p. 246.

44. Jonathan Barnett, "A New Planning Process of Built-In Political Support," *Architectural Record* (May 1966), pp. 141–146.

45. Department of City Planning, City of New York, *A Plan for New York City, Introduction and Summary* (New York, 1969), p. 6.

46. *The Greater Hartford Process* (Hartford, Conn., 1972), p. 11.

47. The Institute for Architecture and Urban Studies, "Streets as Components of the Urban Structure, Phase III" (Unpublished draft report presented to the United States Department of Housing and Urban Development, 1972), p. 4.

48. This work is to be published by M.I.T. Press in 1974 as a book entitled *On Streets.* It is currently contained in a 3-volume unpublished report, "Streets as Components of the Urban Structure," prepared by the Institute for Architecture and Urban Studies following a HUD Research and Demonstration Grant Project, 1970–72.

Illustration Credits

107. Drawing by Ellen Cheng Koutsoftas. Courtesy of
the Institute for Architecture and Urban Studies

108. Photograph by Dick Frank. Courtesy of
the Institute for Architecture and Urban Studies

109. © William A. Garnett

110–111. Courtesy of Gerald D. Hines Interests

112. Photograph by Clyde May Photography, Inc.
Courtesy of John Portman & Associates

113. Courtesy of John Portman & Associates

114–115. Courtesy of Conklin & Rossant

116. © Buckminster Fuller. Courtesy of Buckminster Fuller

117. Courtesy of Conklin & Rossant

118. Reprinted from *Arcology: The City in the Image of Man*
by Paolo Soleri by permission of The M.I.T. Press,
Cambridge, Massachusetts

119. Courtesy of Lawrence Halprin & Associates

120. Photograph by Jeremiah O. Bragstad
Courtesy of Lawrence Halprin & Associates

122–123. Courtesy of the City of New York
Landmarks Preservation Commission

125. © William A. Garnett

126. Photograph by Blue Ridge Aerial Surveys
Courtesy of Gulf Reston, Inc.

127. Courtesy of the Bancroft Library,
University of California, Berkeley

128. Courtesy of Shadrach Woods

129. Courtesy of the Office of Midtown Planning
and Development, City of New York

130. Arcade rendering by Donald C. Mallow
Reprinted with permission of *New York* magazine

131. Courtesy of Skidmore, Owings & Merrill

132. Photograph by Ezra Stoller © ESTO
Courtesy of Skidmore, Owings & Merrill

133–135. Courtesy of the New York State
Urban Development Corporation

136–137. Courtesy of Paul Rudolph

138–140. Courtesy of Shadrach Woods

141. Courtesy of John Andrews

142. Photograph by John Reeves. Courtesy of John Andrews

143–145. Courtesy of the Institute
for Architecture and Urban Studies

146. Photograph by Frank English. Courtesy of
the Graduate Center, City University of New York

Acknowledgments

I am grateful to the American Federation of Arts for commissioning this publication and to The Ford Foundation for the financial support that made it possible.

I want to thank Ulrich Franzen, Paul Rudolph, and Constance Eiseman for suggesting that I get involved in this project, though at the outset, over four years ago, we had no idea that this kind of book would be the result.

A considerable number of people helped me arrive at the final scope and content of the manuscript through discussion and critical comment. Among them I must especially thank Robert A. M. Stern, Myles Weintraub, Alessandra Cantey Wolf, and the late Shadrach Woods for early critical readings of text. The death of Shadrach Woods at the age of 50 in 1973 is a loss to me personally and a loss to progressive urbanism in America.

Deeply appreciated good advice and continual assistance from Roy Moyer and Wilder Green, successive Directors of the American Federation of Arts, made organization, administration, and production of this book through all its many stages a reality. Without Wilder Green's continuing interest and involvement I doubt that this book would have been published in its present generous format.

I am also indebted to my colleagues at the Institute for Architecture and Urban Studies, with whom certain ideas, projects, and insights contained in this book were developed.

I am grateful to Otto E. Nelson for help with certain photographs. For much appreciated, crucial assistance with rights, permissions, and the manuscript itself, I thank Gwenn Burnham, Kathleen Madden, Georgianna Maxfield, and Lynn Anderson. Finally, for interest in the manuscript and assistance throughout the publishing, I am indebted to Don Holden.

Index

Designed by James Craig and Robert Fillie
Set in 10 point Times Roman by Gerard Associates / Graphic Arts, Inc.
Printed and bound by Halliday Lithograph Corporation